... ys is the re... ...
a... ...on to this major new work, she ... ...thor ... ...e key
groundbreaking text, *Anticlimax: A Feminist Perspective on
the Sexual Revolution* (The Women's Press, 1990) and of
*The Spinster and Her Enemies: Feminism and Sexuality
1880–1930* (1985).

Sheila Jeffreys was a founding member of London Women
Against Violence Against Women (WAVAW); and of the
London Lesbian Archive, and the London Lesbian History
Group. She contributed to *Not a Passing Phase: Reclaiming
Lesbians in History 1840–1985* edited by the Lesbian History
Group (The Women's Press, 1989) and edited *The Sexuality
Debates* (1987). She is currently a Senior Lecturer in the
Department of Political Science at the University of
Melbourne, Australia.

Sheila Jeffreys

The Lesbian HERESY

A feminist perspective
on the lesbian sexual revolution

Published in Great Britain by The Women's Press Ltd, 1994
A member of the Namara Group
34 Great Sutton Street, London EC1V 0DX

First published in Australia by Spinifex Press, 1993

British Library Cataloguing-in-Publication Data
A catalogue record for this book is available
from the British Library

ISBN 0 7043 4382 7

Typeset in Sabon by Intype, London

Printed and bound in Great Britain by
BPCC Paperbacks Ltd
Member of BPCC Ltd

CONTENTS

Dedication to Sandy Horn   vi
Introduction   viii
1   The Creation of Sexual Difference   1
2   The Lesbian Sexual Revolution   20
3   Lesbian Sex Therapy   58
4   The Essential Lesbian   73
5   Return to Gender: Postmodernism and Lesbian and
    Gay Theory   97
6   The Lesbian Outlaw   121
7   A Pale Version of the Male: Lesbians and
    Gay Male Culture   142
8   A Deeper Separation   183
Appendix: Sadomasochism: The Erotic Cult of Fascism   210
References   235
Index   248

DEDICATION TO SANDY HORN

This book is dedicated to my friend Sandy Horn. For me Sandy represents the humour, the creativity and the sheer guts that the lesbian community has needed for its survival. Sandy learnt about the necessity of community in San Francisco in the late fifties when she survived the sexual McCarthyism of the time through the support of other lesbian and gay friends who were in the same boat. They coped with a hostile society by sending it up with a bitter laughter which Sandy still employs to great effect. Sandy left San Francisco before it became a city in which lesbians and gays could begin to relax and came to London in 1965. In the US and in Britain she was involved in the lesbian political organisations of the sixties such as the Daughters of Bilitis and in London, the Minorities Research Group.

In 1974 Sandy produced the first edition of *Gaia's Guide*, the very first travel guide for women and lesbian travellers with information on safe places to stay and socialise. From the first she included a host of feminist resources such as women's centres, clinics, bookstores, rape crisis centres. She produced *Gaia's Guide* for 18 years, selling 8,500 at its peak in 1986, accomplishing a remarkable feat in international lesbian networking. Sandy is an extraordinarily talented builder of lesbian networks. She is a fount of information and busily introduces lesbians to each other, taking the responsibility of *Gaia's Guide* as far as personally introducing travelling dykes to places they should go and lesbians they should know in London. Sandy has always been one of those at the hub of the lesbian community, one who has helped to keep it going and she still does.

I met Sandy in 1985 but didn't get to know her until 1986 when she got involved in the London Lesbian History Group and also in Women Against Violence Against Women. She is a mainstay of the Lesbian History Group striking awe into new and younger members with her breadth of knowledge and experience of lesbian history and culture. In 1988 she organised the publicity for the Lesbian Archive Summer School and since the Archive fell on hard times and lost its grant in April 1991 she has thrown her energies into helping to keep the Archive going and open to lesbians through sheer determination. Sandy combines a dedication to the welfare of lesbians, and to the building of lesbian culture with an acute feminist consciousness, particularly around violence against women and the sexual abuse of girls.

There is much in *The Lesbian Heresy* which might make lesbians despair for the future of our community. For this reason it is important to be aware of the work of lesbians such as Sandy who have helped to keep the lesbian community going in the bad times as well as the good, and who can see through and beyond the exigencies of the moment such as the lesbian sexual revolution.

Sandy has a gift for friendship. Here in Australia I meet and hear of lesbians who have benefited from the gift even twenty or twenty five years ago. I am delighted to be a friend of Sandy's and our friendship means to me the uniting of two traditions of how it is to be a lesbian. We come from very different directions, San Francisco in the fifties and the political lesbianism of Britain in the seventies, to find ourselves bound together by affection and in considerable, though rarely complete, agreement over what is needed for lesbian liberation in the nineties.

In warmest lesbian friendship.

Sheila Jeffreys, Melbourne, March 1993.

INTRODUCTION

The political theory of lesbian feminism transformed lesbianism from a stigmatised sexual practice into an idea and a political practice that posed a challenge to male supremacy and its basic institution of heterosexuality. Lesbian feminists articulated this challenge in the 1970s. They were heretics. Fundamental to lesbian feminist practice was the rejection of the sexological construction of lesbianism. The ideas of the medical establishment – that lesbianism was a congenital anomaly, that lesbianism was psychologically determined, a result of penis envy, that lesbianism was a sexual deviation which deserved to reside in sexological textbooks alongside child molestation and underwear fetishism – were thrown out of the window.

We were constructing a new feminist universe. Starting with consciousness-raising, in an atmosphere of great optimism, we re-labelled lesbianism as a healthy choice for women based upon self-love, the love of other women and the rejection of male oppression. Any woman could be a lesbian. It was a revolutionary political choice which, if adopted by millions of women, would lead to the destabilisation of male supremacy as men lost the foundation of their power in women's selfless and unpaid, domestic, sexual, reproductive, economic and emotional servicing. It was to be the base from which we could reach out to dismantle men's power. It was to be an alternative universe in which we would construct a new sexuality, a new ethics, a new culture in opposition to malestream culture. It was to be a powerhouse from which new feminist and lesbian positive values would reach to transform the world for women and bring the sado-society to an end.

Lesbian feminists were instrumental in creating most of the building blocks of the lesbian community which are now taken for granted by young women coming out. We set up lesbian presses and archives, dances, community centres, support and coming out groups and poured out an ocean of ideas in newsletters, journals, books. Some of those instrumental in the construction of lesbian culture in these years are now deeply critical of lesbian feminism and are disassociating themselves from it but I would still contend that most, whether old lesbian or new political lesbians held to some common lesbian feminist values in those days only a few years ago, and that it was the energy created by a revolutionary movement that fuelled these developments. Working class lesbians, black lesbians, ethnic minority lesbians and indigenous lesbians were all involved from the beginning in lesbian feminism in all the countries of the western world, though they may not have been in large numbers and their voices may not have been those most usually heard before the late seventies.

This book has been written in order to help myself and other lesbian feminists understand the backlash against these politics which has taken place in the 1980s and nineties. The backlash against feminism in general has been documented powerfully by Naomi Wolf and Susan Faludi and the backlash against feminist analyses of sexuality and pornography has been well covered in the excellent collection *The Sexual Liberals and the Attack on Feminism*.[1] The backlash against feminism is probably mostly understood as an attack by the forces of male supremacist reaction outside the women's liberation movement itself. Such an attack has certainly been happening as the result of the triumph of conservative politics in the western world in the last decade. But it needs to be acknowledged that as forces outside the feminist movement increase their pressures, there will be a breaking of ranks within the movement itself. As the *Sexual Liberals* volume showed, many of those defending pornography in the eighties were experienced feminists, even teachers of women's studies, not just the mainstream pornography industry.

Within the lesbian community there has been a parallel backlash. The conservatism of the eighties in the malestream world had a particularly damaging effect on the lives of lesbians and gay men. Conservative groups and governments sought to scapegoat lesbians and gay men to divert attention from the widening social divisions that their economic policies were creating. In Britain an amendment to the *Local Government Act* in 1988 forbade the 'promotion of homosexuality' and there were unsuccessful attempts to pass similar legislation in the US and Queensland, Australia. The wording of these attempts was the same and international organisations funded and masterminded the onslaught on lesbian and gay rights. The attacks were aided by AIDS hysteria which targeted gay men and lesbians though lesbians were very unlikely to contract the virus through sexual practice. Anti-gay feeling led to an upsurge in physical attacks. This was a difficult time in which to be a lesbian. These pressures led to changes in the lesbian community, more acceptance of gay male politics and priorities, and, interestingly, a return to the sexological model by some lesbian theorists. There was a new politics of outlawry, of sexual deviance which depended upon the constructions of sexology, a politics which was already well developed by some gay men and which was in direct contradiction to lesbian feminist philosophy.

This book is about the splintering of the lesbian community as feminist politics have come under attack. Whereas in the seventies lesbian feminist ideas seemed to be dominant in lesbian politics, in the eighties this situation was clearly reversed. As the sexological model that lesbian feminists had been so determined to uproot made a comeback, we were attacked as anti-sex, politically correct, essentialist, idealist. Many lesbian feminists who had seen the lesbian community as home found they now had to accept that they were often regarded by other lesbians as an extremist and very unpopular minority. In the early seventies it was precisely lesbian feminists who organised the sort of events that enabled lesbians to build community. It was the work of lesbian feminists that was crucial in western countries to the creation of a lesbian community that is now marginalising lesbian feminism.

I suspect that some lesbian readers will react indignantly to my suggestions in this book that pornography, sadomasochism and roleplaying are hostile to the lesbian feminist project. Not all of those involved in or positive towards these practices reject feminism. Some will say that they are feminists and be understandably angry that anyone should be suggesting otherwise. For this reason I think it is useful to make a distinction between lesbian feminists and lesbians who are also feminists. In lesbian feminist philosophy the words 'lesbian' and 'feminist' are integral to each other, the lesbianism is feminist and the feminism is lesbian. There are many lesbians who are active in an equal rights lesbian politics which are not specifically feminist, they may indeed be almost indistinguishable from those of gay men, and who are also feminists in regard to issues such as equal pay, abortion, sexual harassment. But the lesbianism and the feminism are separate. They exist in compartments which are hermetically sealed.

In lesbian feminist philosophy the theory and practice of lesbianism is constructed through feminism. Thus the feminist understanding that the personal is political means that all aspects of lesbian life will be examined to see how they fit with the feminist project. A fundamental insight of feminism is the importance of holism and connectedness. Everything affects everything else. No one lives in a vacuum and no part of our lives is really quite separate from any other. In the seventies there was a thoroughgoing determination to make over our lives anew to fit into our vision of the feminist future. For many this is still the case though the exigencies of life in the eighties, the necessity to get jobs, the impact of conservative governments have led many of us to be less rigorous.

The seriousness of lesbian feminism in the 70s can be illustrated by the discussions that took place over such aspects of personal politics as attraction based simply on physical appearance, 'fancying'. Fancying was, and is, seen by many as objectifying, as based on rules about physical perfection which were deeply discriminatory, even sometimes racist and ableist, and as reflecting a construction of sexuality which was hostile to women's interests. It was felt that a simple and learned physical urge towards a stranger was not a good way to begin relationships. Not all lesbians felt that they had overcome, or wanted to overcome, the learned sexual practice of 'fancying' but there was great good will and commitment to discussing these ideas. Though they might seem bizarre today they were actually quite generally understood ideas amongst gay men involved in a gay liberation movement deeply infused with feminist principles. Some men were casting an equally critical eye onto the politics of everyday life.[2] This is hard to credit in contemporary gay male culture where media and entertainments are funded by the sex industry and based precisely on the principal of 'fancying'.

Monogamy and non-monogamy were debated with some heat. The ethics of personal relationships, which were understood to be a microcosm of the political relationships of male supremacy and not unimportant, were in the political spotlight. This is not to say that there was general agreement, that would be very unlikely amongst any group of lesbians, but everyone was arguing from the basis that the way we treated each other should reflect our feminist vision and purpose. There were no areas of personal life which were considered politically off limits. Property ownership was subjected to criticism, communal living and income sharing were embarked upon. There was and still is in lesbian feminist organising a concern to offer a range of prices for events and to work out ways of sharing access to resources. This can seem rather quaint now too when new lesbian and gay entrepreneurs are seeking to survive by operating within the rules of the market. The business of everyday life was conducted, as far as possible, in accordance with a feminist perspective which was also socialist and anti-racist.

The feminism of lesbian feminism is different from what some lesbian feminist theorists have described as 'heterofeminism'. Heterofeminism assumes that lesbians are and always will be a minority and that heterosexuality is, by some mystery, the majority sexual preference. Lesbian feminism transforms feminism by calling the naturalness of heterosexuality into doubt, by pointing out that it is a political institution and seeking to bring that institution to an end in the interests of women's freedom and sexual self-determination. Most importantly lesbian feminism sees the creation of a world fit for lesbians as a world in which all women will be free.

There are some lesbian feminists who, feeling exhausted and disillusioned by the struggle to persuade heterosexual feminists to take lesbians seriously into account, have chosen to drop the title feminist. They call themselves radical lesbians or just separatists. I do not see how the interests of lesbians can be separated out from the interests of women as a class and I do not think that these latter groups of lesbians really think they can be either. Monique Wittig's famous statement that 'Lesbians are not women' because woman can exist only in relation to man and 'women' constitute a political class, has inspired some to drop the word feminist and to question whether there can be 'women's liberation' since we should all really be pursuing liberation from being in the political class of women.[3] Wittig sees lesbians as refugees from their class. But even as refugees we are likely to be treated as members of the class 'women' on the bus, at work. Though lesbians might have made a break for freedom from some fundamental aspects of women's oppression, such as unpaid domestic, sexual, emotional work for a man and the appalling working conditions which can sometimes prevail in the form of violence, or unwanted childbearing, there are some we cannot so easily avoid.

Chapter by chapter *The Lesbian Heresy* will examine some of the developments within the lesbian community which have undermined any lesbian feminist consensus, developments which have made lesbian feminism a heresy not just against the hetero-patriarchy but apparently within lesbian culture too. Chapter 1 on 'The creation of sexual difference' will look at the controversy that has developed between lesbian historians about the impact of sexology on the construction of lesbian identity in the early twentieth century. Some historians such as Caroll Smith-Rosenberg and Lillian Faderman have seen the impact of sexology as damaging because it stigmatised women's passionate friendships and undermined feminism. Others, such as Esther Newton and some male gay historians, have seen the sexological construction of homosexuality as useful in providing a lesbian role and identity and allowing lesbians to be sexual in a way that the passionate friendships of the nineteenth century did not. I argue, in agreement with Caroll Smith-Rosenberg, that in adopting sexological definitions, lesbians of the twenties lost contact with a previous generation of feminist sisters and experienced an unbridgeable gap in communication. I will suggest that a similar process has taken place in the 1980s when a new generation of lesbians has re-adopted the language of sexology, of deviance and congenitality, of butch and femme in a way which has created a similarly destructive gap in communication with the lesbian feminists of the seventies. In subsequent chapters I examine the ways in which lesbianism has been reconstructed by some lesbian theorists, by lesbian sex industrialists and sex therapists, by lesbian pornographers, in the eighties to fit the sexological prescription.

Chapter 2 'The Lesbian Sexual Revolution' looks at the importance of approaching sexual practice politically and the way that the concepts and language of liberalism have made this difficult. It will challenge the idea that any area of sexual life is entirely politically neutral, private and individual, and consider why it is so difficult to politicise sexual practice without being accused of moralism and judgementalism by other lesbians. It then traces the development of a lesbian sex industry in the US, Britain and Australia. It will look at the politics of lesbian erotica, lesbian sex toys and prostitution. It will suggest the dangers of accepting that lesbianism is simply about sex and that the way to lesbian liberation is to expand the sex industry.

Chapter 3 looks at where the theory of the new lesbian sexual politics is coming from, a vital component of the lesbian sex industry, sex therapy. I will suggest that the new lesbian sex therapists are teaching a sexuality modelled on heteropatriarchal principles of dominance and submission, objectification, woman-hating. They are explicitly opposing lesbian feminist efforts to reconstruct sexuality along egalitarian, woman-loving lines which can empower lesbians and contribute to women's and lesbian liberation.

Lesbian feminists have tended to take an extreme social constructionist approach to lesbian identity summed up in the slogan on badges in the seventies that 'Any woman can be a lesbian'. This certainty amongst lesbian theorists has unravelled in the eighties and nineties. It is from some of the lesbian sex therapists that a new essentialism is being propagated. The lesbian sex therapist JoAnn Loulan avers in her 1990 book, *The Lesbian Erotic Dance*, that 'Some of us are just born that way.'[4] Chapter 4 will look at the rebirth of essentialism in lesbian theory. This new essentialism has been employed in particular to defend the reintroduction into lesbian culture of eroticised power imbalance in the form of butch and femme roleplaying. The concept of butch and femme is being used now to define not just lesbian eroticism but all aspects of lesbian culture and the lesbian 'aesthetic'. I will argue for the continued political importance of a radical social constructionist approach to lesbian identity and of challenging the orchestrated intrusion of eroticised polarity, division and hierarchy into lesbian culture and community.

Chapter 5 'Return to Gender' looks at the 'high' theory which is being used to justify practices like roleplaying. It looks at the impact of postmodernist ideas on a particular brand of lesbian and gay theory. It will argue that these ideas, which usually derive from the works of French male intellectuals who did not consider women let alone lesbians in the construction of their theories, are, not surprisingly, hostile to the politics of lesbian feminism. It will concentrate on the way in which some lesbian theorists who follow postmodern masters are arguing that gender can be played with in a revolutionary way so as to destabilise the heteropatriarchy. These theorists argue that gender cannot be pushed aside or rejected and that feminist attempts to do this are essentialist or doomed to failure. Some of these lesbian theorists see not lesbian feminism, but roleplaying, drag and transsexualism as the only way forward politically for lesbians and gays.

Poststructuralism, the theory of postmodernism, has been very influential in the academy in the eighties and nineties because it is a philosophy suited to conservative times, one which is committed to fatalism and non-action, yet one which manages to look fashionable because many of its avatars were gay or sadomasochists or paid lip service to the politics of minorities. Because of its hegemony within those portals from which much of the intellectual life of the lesbian and gay community flows it has had a considerable impact. Lesbian feminism and radical feminism generally have been consistently derided in postmodernist theory. Such theory in its lesbian guise has provided a power base for the assault on lesbian feminism and a vital theoretical justification, in the name of playing with gender, or 'difference', for those developments which have been most influential in undermining the lesbian feminist project.

Chapter 6 'The Lesbian Outlaw' examines the romantic attraction felt by lesbians of many persuasions, including myself, towards outlawry and decadence, a lesbian version of what the Oscar Wilde circle in the 1890s called *nostalgie de la boue*. This decadence involved an identification with the underclass of hetero-relational culture as in the use of opium dens or simply bars frequented by pimps. As symbolised in the titles of novels like A. T. Fitzroy's *Despised and Rejected* there was a romanticising of oppression itself and the outsiderhood that resulted.[5] In lesbian feminism the courage and rebelliousness of the lesbian outlaw are expressed politically in the destabilising of male supremacy. Presently more traditional forms of gay decadence are exerting their attractions and being legitimated by postmodern gay male theorists as transgressive reinscription. The politics of transgression will be criticised here and I will suggest that an understanding of the romance of lesbian outlawry might help us to understand lesbian roleplaying and sadomasochism. It could form the basis for a redirection of lesbian rebellion into challenging male supremacy instead of romanticising our oppression itself.

Chapter 7 'A Pale Version of the Male' looks at the influence of gay male culture on lesbian culture and politics. It is clear from the writings of many contemporary lesbians, some sex therapists, novelists and pornographers, that they admire and seek to emulate gay male culture and practice. Such writers see lesbians as boring and repressed and inferior to their gay brothers. The gay male standard becomes the measure of all things in some areas of the lesbian community. This total identification with gay men is necessarily accompanied by an attack on lesbian feminism which has sought to distinguish lesbian culture and politics from that of gay men. I will reassert the contradiction which exists between the traditional agenda of gay men and the political agenda of lesbian feminism. I ask why some lesbians are so enthralled by gay men that they publicly state their longing to be gay men or even undertake transsexual operations to become gay men. I suggest that this could be partly the result of male money and power which might appear to offer lesbians vicarious or even real glamour and influence, and of the deep-seated self-loathing of 1990s lesbians who feel defeated by the failure of feminist dreams and try to rejoin the malestream. I ask whether it is inevitable that lesbian feminism must be extinguished beneath the shadow of that powerful part of gay male culture which is financed by the sex industry, impervious to lesbian feminism and in direct contradiction to our interests.

The final chapter 8 'A Deeper Separation' will look at how the building of lesbian friendship, community, ethics, and theory, based on feminist values, can help us sustain the vision and practice of lesbian feminism for the future. It will celebrate lesbian separatism whilst asking how separatists can best survive in the new situation of lesbianism in the nineties. How can any notion of community survive the development of lesbian sadomasochism which attacks a fundamental value of lesbian feminism, the importance of equality and the fight against hierarchies of power in any form? I will suggest that lesbian communities have been badly damaged as their basic lesbian feminist values have been challenged and ask whether the creation of a deeper separation, particularly an intellectual and ethical separation from heteropatriarchal values can help sustain the lesbian heresy and the lesbian feminist challenge to male supremacy.

The Appendix 'Sadomasochism: the Erotic Cult of Fascism' was originally written in 1984 and published in *Lesbian Ethics* in the US in 1986. It criticises the S/M movement for eroticising dominance and submission and fascism itself. It compares the situation in London with that of Berlin in the early thirties when gay men eroticised the costumes and violence of the fascism which was to destroy them. It is of historical interest today as it was written from a position of active involvement in a political campaign, Lesbians Against Sadomasochism, LASM for short, which was formed to challenge the development of what was seen as a serious threat to the ethics and general politics of lesbian feminism. It shows that there was serious opposition to these new politics not just from LASM but other lesbian feminists in the US and Australia from the very beginning and the degree of shock that we experienced in those early days of the lesbian sexual revolution as we saw many lesbians determinedly abandon the egalitarian philosophy that is feminism.

1. Faludi, Susan (1991). *Backlash. The Undeclared War Against Women*. London: Chatto and Windus. Wolf, Naomi (1990). *The Beauty Myth*. London: Vintage. Leidholdt, Dorchen and Raymond, Janice G. (Eds.) (1990). *The Sexual Liberals and the Attack on Feminism*. Oxford and New York: Pergamon Press (now TCP).
2. See Walters, Aubrey (1980). *Come Together: Collected writings from Gay Liberation in the UK*. London: Gay Men's Press.
3. Wittig, Monique (1992). *The Straight Mind and Other Essays*. Boston: Beacon Press.
4. Loulan, JoAnn (1990). *The Lesbian Erotic Dance*. San Francisco: Spinsters. p. 193.
5. Fitzroy, A. T. (1988). *Despised and Rejected*. London: Gay Men's Press. First Published 1918.

Chapter 1

THE CREATION OF SEXUAL DIFFERENCE

In the 1980s a serious battle was joined over the meaning of lesbianism. In this ideological conflict the opposing definitions are those of lesbian feminism and sexology. Some lesbians, particularly the proponents of lesbian roleplaying, are opposing the lesbian feminist political definition with one based upon sexual difference. Lesbians who see themselves as sexually different are accepting the framework for categorising sexual behaviour that the 'scientists' of sex, Richard von Krafft-Ebing and Henry Havelock Ellis and their kind, set up in the late nineteenth century. The sexologists and their modern followers see lesbianism as one of a range of strange sexual behaviours which differ from the sexual norm or missionary-position heterosexual intercourse. Other groups of the sexually different include gay men, but also pedophiles, transsexuals, various varieties of fetishists. Apart from lesbianism these are mainly categories of male sexual behaviour and women appear only as the victims of the sexually different behaviour.

The politics of sexual difference throw lesbians into the company of gay men and the other groups of the sexually different. The politics of sexual difference are manifesting themselves presently in much of the writing of the new 'queer' literature. The politics of lesbian feminism throw lesbians into the company of the political class of women or onto their own resources as lesbians. Lesbian feminists have tended to see themselves as the norm for free women rather than as sexually different. It is a different vision. To understand the roots of this conflict of defi-

nitions it is useful to look back at the creation of sexual difference in sexology and how lesbian and gay scholars have viewed
this.

Lesbian and gay theorists such as Mary McIntosh and Jeffrey
Weeks have argued persuasively that the idea of the homosexual
as a particular kind of person, of a 'homosexual role' was a
relatively recent invention of the eighteenth or nineteenth
century.[1] Prior to this development sexual activity between men,
though stigmatised, was seen as something that any man might
do. The concept of the 'homosexual', a man whose behaviour
had a particular causation, who had a recognisable homosexual
career, whose sexual interests were directed exclusively to those
of the same sex and who had recognisable characteristics, was
not yet developed.

Lesbian and feminist historians such as Lillian Faderman and
Caroll Smith-Rosenberg have also argued that a specific lesbian
identity based upon the categorisations of sexology was created
in the late nineteenth century.[2] They have shown that before
that time middle-class British and American women, married
and single, would routinely engage in passionate, romantic,
often very long-term friendships with each other which included
constant expressions of fulsome love and sleeping in each other's
arms and on the same pillow even for a lifetime without seeing
this as something unusual or suspicious. There were some
women though, throughout the nineteenth century, who might
have matched the later sexological model, some who even
dressed in men's clothes and loved women, despite the absence
of a sexological model. One woman, for instance, from early
nineteenth-century Yorkshire, Ann Lister, did engage in enthusiastic sexual relationships with neighbour women even to the
extent of contracting venereal disease as she outlines in her
diaries, and did have a concept of herself as 'different'.[3] But the
existence of such women does not seem to have influenced
the innocence with which passionate friends approached their
relationships with other women or the social acceptability of
women's same sex love. It was the rise of sexology that publi-
cised and stigmatised a category of 'sexual difference'.

Lesbian and gay historians have disagreed over whether sexological constructions of homosexuality had positive or negative

results for the development of lesbian and gay identities. Lesbian and feminist historians such as Lillian Faderman, Caroll Smith-Rosenberg and myself have seen sexology as a hostile force which undermined feminism, stigmatised women's passionate friendships, and created a damaging stereotype of the masculine female invert. Male gay historians such as Jeffrey Weeks, have tended to be more positive and have argued that sexological categorisation helped the development of a homosexual rights movement by providing male homosexuals with a definite identity around which they could come together and organise.[4]

It is important to be aware of the components of the sexological construction not just because it has become the source of controversy, but because it is making a reappearance in contemporary lesbian politics and it is useful to be able to recognise it. One generally accepted component of the sexological model was the attribution of congenitality. Havelock Ellis, the sexologist whose *Sexual Inversion* of 1897 was most influential in constructing the stereotype of the lesbian in Britain, argued that 'any theory of the etiology of homosexuality which leaves out of account the hereditary factor in inversion cannot be admitted' and adduces as evidence the 'frequency of inversion among the near relatives of the inverted'.[5] This idea led to some amusing material in his case studies. It looks as if when his subjects were asked to produce evidence of a hereditary factor they were sometimes most imaginative in their replies. One man offered the following:

My grandfather might be said to be of abnormal temperament, for, though of very humble origin, he organised and carried out an extremely arduous mission work and became an accomplished linguist, translating the Bible into an Eastern tongue and compiling the first dictionary of that language.[6]

Admittedly this may sound suspicious to some, but not necessarily connected with homosexuality. But the congenital idea inspired some homosexual rights campaigners in the nineties in Britain and Germany. It offered the possibility of asking for public sympathy and the repeal of hostile legislation on the grounds that homosexuals were just a part of nature's creation rather than sinners, and therefore had to be accepted. Radclyffe Hall, when she took up sexological arguments in the twenties, employed this strategy in *The Well of Loneliness* and had Ellis write a preface to the book so that her argument could be seen to be backed by science. The sexological model became more sophisticated with an admixture of psychoanalysis which posited a similarly determinist causation but psychological rather than biological. Because psychoanalysis appeared to offer possibilities of cure it was less popular with inverts and became more popular with sexologists in the fifties who were committed to the elimination of homosexuality through psycho-engineering. Both versions of sexology are having something of a rebirth. The new popularity of biological explanations will be examined in detail in my chapter on 'The Essential Lesbian'.

The current controversy on the impact of sexology hinges on the way in which it was picked up and employed by the inverts themselves. The work of Edward Carpenter, the British homosexual rights campaigner, is a good example of what some historians would see as the positive use of these ideas.[7] He based much of his argument for the social acceptability of homosexuality on the work of a formidable array of sexologists. He took up the idea of congenitality to build his theory of the 'intermediate sex'. In his work he reproduced the understanding of some sexologists that the third or intermediate sex was possessed of the biologically ordained characteristics of masculinity and femininity in unusual combinations. This is clearest in his description of the 'extreme specimens'. The extreme male intermediate was 'a distinctly effeminate type, sentimental, lackadaisical, mincing in gait and manners.' The extreme version of the 'homogenic' female was similarly possessed of inappropriate gender characteristics.

> ... a rather markedly aggressive person, of strong passions, masculine manners and movements, practical in the conduct of life, sensuous rather than sentimental in love, often untidy and outre in attire; her figure muscular, her voice rather low in pitch; her dwelling-room decorated with sporting-scenes, pistols, etc., and not without a suspicion of the fragrant weed in the atmosphere; while her love (generally to rather soft and

feminine specimens of her own sex) is often a sort of furor, similar to the ordinary masculine love, and at times almost uncontrollable.[8]

The fragrant weed was probably, rather disappointingly, tobacco. Such extreme specimens, Carpenter tells us, are rare. The majority do not look unusual in outward appearance. The body of the 'more normal' homogenic woman was 'thoroughly feminine' but the 'inner nature is to a great extent masculine.'

... a temperament active, brave, originative, somewhat decisive, not too emotional; fond of out-door life, of games and sports, of science, politics, or even business; good at organisation, and well-pleased with positions of responsibility, sometimes indeed making an excellent and generous leader.[9]

Today's reader might not easily be able to see what was 'masculine' about this description. In fact it demonstrates another characteristic of the sexological approach to the female invert. Homosexual rights campaigners like Carpenter and the men of science like Ellis all tended to associate self-assertion in women, independence and a feminist turn of mind with lesbianism. Such qualities were sufficient to draw accusations of inversion in the 1890s as they are today. Strong women could be classified as unnatural.

Another characteristic of the sexological approach to the lesbian was to prescribe roleplaying for lesbian relationships. Carpenter follows the tradition by saying that the very masculine, sporting pistols type would 'generally' love 'rather soft and feminine specimens of her own sex'.[10] The sexologists explained this phenomenon by asserting that there were two types of female homosexuals. There were 'congenital' inverts who would be masculine in orientation and 'pseudolesbians' who might otherwise have been heterosexual had they not fallen victim to the wiles of the true invert. The latter would look and behave like the effeminate heterosexual woman of her time. In this way the foundations were laid for the idea that butch/femme roleplaying was the essential lesbian relationship.

Interestingly, the sexological model of lesbianism was not

5

necessarily based on genital contact. The sexologists threw their nets wide and included women in the case studies of inversion who would have fitted into the most innocent image of passionate friends. For this reason feminist historians have found the work of the sexologists particularly damaging. It is seen as having created a suspicion which limited the possibilities of women's friendships for any who did not wish to join a stigmatised, roleplaying minority. The sexologists' work stimulated a campaign, as Faderman details in her book, to warn women and girls against lesbianism in schools and colleges until by the twenties passionate female friendship had acquired quite generally the aura of perversion.[11] Lillian Faderman indicts sexology for having made lesbianism into something perverse, outcast and doomed. The effects were:

> . . . many women fled into heterosexual marriage or developed great self-loathing or self-pity if they accepted the label of 'invert'. By the early twentieth century, European popular literature, influenced largely by the sexologists, was referring to 'thousands of unhappy beings' who 'experience the tragedy of inversion in their lives,' and to passions which 'end in madness or suicide'. In the popular imagination, love between women was becoming identified with disease, insanity, and tragedy.[12]

Lesbian feminist historians see the sexological categorisation of lesbians as constituting a mechanism of social control of both women's love for women and of feminism, phenomena which were particularly powerful in combination.

Carroll Smith-Rosenberg, who wrote the germinal article on passionate friendships *The Female World of Love and Ritual*, sees the sexological takeover from feminist discourse in the twenties as damaging.[13] She talks about the importance in feminist and lesbian history of the 'new woman' in the late nineteenth century. The 'new women' formed passionate friendships to support each other through college, worked at settlement houses and in the developing careers of social work and teaching. They 'wove their mothers' intensely loving, often passionate friendships into the fabric of their brave new world.'[14] They were social reformers who networked and created a machine for change, often strongly feminist. They were of course the backbone of many feminist campaigns, notably in the UK the Women's Social and Political Union (WSPU). Smith-Rosenberg explains that late Victorian medical men characterised the 'new women' as masculine and then as 'mannish lesbians'. She sees the sexual definition of lesbianism offered by the sexologists as subordinating lesbians rather than empowering them. 'By constituting her a sexual subject, they made her subject to the political regulation of the state.'[15]

Passionate or romantic friendships have generated controversy amongst lesbian scholars. Celebrated by Smith-Rosenberg and Faderman they have been derided as middle class or anti-sex by others. Disagreement over passionate friendships arises from different views about what constitutes lesbian identity. When she wrote *Surpassing the Love of Men* Faderman saw the women involved in such friendships as resembling the lesbian feminists of the 1970s. Faderman saw lesbian-feminism as an 'analogue' of romantic friendships which she saw as those in which 'two women were everything to each other and had little connection with men who were so alienatingly and totally different.'[16] She suggests that 'had the romantic friends of other eras lived today, many of them would have been lesbian-feminists; and had the lesbian-feminists of our day lived in other eras, most of them would have been romantic friends.' Faderman's definition of lesbianism did not depend on genital contact. She says 'love between women has been primarily a sexual phenomenon only in male fantasy literature.'[17] She founds her definition on emotions and says 'Sexual contact may be a part of the relationship to a greater or lesser degree, or it may be entirely absent.' She tells us that contemporary lesbian feminists are not innocent about sex but 'the sexual aspects of their relationships generally have less significance than the emotional sustenance and the freedom they have to define themselves.'[18] She suggests that many lesbian-feminist relationships continue long after 'the sexual component has worn off.'

Faderman's critics have accused her of an act of betrayal, of 'desexualising' lesbianism by including women who did not have genital contact in the past or infrequent genital contact in the present, in her definition of lesbianism.[19] To those who see lesbianism as sexual difference romantic friends would clearly not qualify. But for feminists for whom choosing and loving women is the basis of a lesbian identity they do. Genital connection is hard to prove. Lesbians in history might prove to be rather scarce and lesbian history to start only in the nineteenth century if a sexual difference model based upon genital connection is adopted. The history of heterosexuality has never been limited by the need to prove genital connection. Heterosexuality is a political institution which did not begin with sexology in 1890. It is not just a variety of sexual difference. As I and other members of the London Lesbian History Group have suggested, the task of the lesbian historian is to analyse the history of women's resistance to heterosexuality as an institution rather than simply searching for women who fitted a twentieth century stereotype based upon sexology.[20]

The new characterisation was not simply roundly rejected by women who loved women. Some chose to adopt it as their self-definition in the twenties. There was pressure on women generally to be sexual. As I have detailed elsewhere, the 'sexual revolution' of the twenties aimed to cure feminism, manhating, lesbianism and spinsterhood, the great bugbears of the men of science, by gaining heterosexual women's, preferably all women's, enthusiastic participation in sexual intercourse.[21] Woman's sexual pleasure in that practice was expected to subordinate her to her husband in marriage and in other areas of life. There was considerable pressure exerted to conscript woman into the missionary position in heterosexuality so that her pleasures could be orchestrated towards her subordination. Young heterosexual women accepted this diversion, Smith-Rosenberg argues.

> Divorcing women's rights from their political and economic context, they made the daughter's quest for heterosexual pleasures, not the mother's demand for political power, personify female freedom.[22]

The stigmatising of lesbianism was one powerful weapon which could be used to pressure women into heterosexuality. The outcast lesbian was a necessary complement to the enthusiastic heterosexual housewife.

Women who loved women, and were aware of the sexological discourse, had to make a choice about how to relate to the new prescription. There were three possibilities open to them. They could abandon passionate friendships in an attempt to avoid the stigma of deviance. They could continue with their passionate friendships but reject the sexological model as having nothing to do with them. Many undoubtedly took this course but it must have been fraught with difficulties. Or they could embrace the new identity they were being offered. Smith-Rosenberg and Newton both argue that many did and that their decisions had results for feminism and future lesbian history. They felt anger towards the older generation who had not offered a specifically sexual definition for women's love, at a time when sex was becoming de rigeur, and had therefore failed to provide the next generation with a 'sexual vocabulary'. The most famous example, of course, is Radclyffe Hall, who chose to adopt a sexological model in *The Well of Loneliness* because she believed it would lead to great social sympathy for despised lesbians if they were seen as being congenitally flawed rather than deliberate perverts.

Smith-Rosenberg argues that the adoption of the 'mannish lesbian' stereotype had negative implications for feminism. The new lesbians were cut off from the older generation of feminists so that they were helpless when men reasserted their power in a backlash against the feminist victories. The adoption of the symbols of masculinity was not liberating despite the efforts of the twenties and subsequent lesbians to invest them with new and lesbian positive meanings. In the latter task she states 'They failed'. Faderman explains that the adoption of an outlaw stigmatised status led to the preoccupation of lesbian literature with doom and punishment until the 1960s.

The lesbian historian Esther Newton takes a very different approach. She derides the way she sees lesbian feminist historians as having written about the world of passionate friendships, 'the nineteenth century becomes a kind of lesbian Golden Age, replete with loving, innocent feminist couples.'[23] She sees the 'mannish lesbian' identity as having been embraced by those who wanted to 'break out of the asexual model of romantic friendship'. Radclyffe Hall, she explains, wanted to make the woman-loving woman a sexual being and could only do so by adopting the masculine stereotype and becoming sexual on male terms 'To become avowedly sexual, the New Woman had to enter the male world, either as a heterosexual on male terms . . . or as a lesbian in male body drag.'[24] She sees this as a radical and progressive act which challenges gender stereotypes. By making a woman play the masculine part so Hall 'questions the inevitability of traditional gender categories' but she also 'assents to it'. She accepts that men have been able to use the butch image to 'condemn lesbians and intimidate straight women' and recognises that Hall's vision of lesbian identity, which she characterises as 'sexual difference and as masculinity is inimical to lesbian feminist ideology.'[25]

The very different interpretations of the impact of sexology that are rife today were similarly marked when the novel was first published. Feminists were often very unhappy with Hall's creation. Vera Brittain is one of the feminists who edited *Time and Tide*. She was well aware of the potential of loving women since she had been involved in a passionate friendship with Winifred Holtby.[26] In her review she accepts that there is a category of lesbians that is inherently abnormal and one that is not, identified later in the book as inverts versus perverts.

> . . . women of the type of Stephen Gordon, in so far as their abnormality is inherent and not merely the unnecessary cult of exotic erotics, deserve the fullest consideration and compassion from all who are fortunate enough to have escaped one of Nature's cruellest dispensations.[27]

Brittain clearly does not see herself as having any connection with such abnormals as inverts and perverts despite her love for women. This shows that one impact of sexology is to separate lesbians off from the class of women. The 'cult of exotic erotics' sounds most tempting, almost a clarion call for 'queer' politics. But when considering the exaggerated manifestations of masculinity and femininity of Stephen and her lover Mary Llewellyn, Brittain rejects the message that these stem from biology. She indicts instead the imposition of such exaggerated gender distinction in the late nineteenth century.

> It certainly seems likely that a problem of this type must be intensified by the exaggeration of sex differences which has been peculiarly marked in certain ages of the world, and to which the English middle classes of the eighteenth and nineteenth centuries were particularly prone. Miss Hall appears to take for granted that this over-emphasis of sex characteristics is part of the correct education of the normal human being; she therefore makes her 'normal' woman clinging and 'feminine' to exasperation and even describes the attitudes towards love as 'an end in itself' as being a necessary attribute of womanhood.[28]

Brittain was writing in 1928 long before the term 'gender' was in use but she is able to analyse what would now be called gender critically and see its social and political construction. Brittain was not about to accept the idea of lesbian roleplaying since she clearly believed women did not have to behave in masculine or feminine ways, 'This confusion between what is "male" or "female" and what is merely human in our complex make-up, persists throughout the book.' She doesn't accept that Stephen's childhood behaviour is a clue to her abnormality. She says the 'supposedly sinister predilections of the child' seem to her to be 'the quite usual preferences of any vigorous young female who happens to possess more vitality and intelligence than her fellows.'[29] Brittain's commonsense feminism is in stark contrast with the views of Esther Newton and other protagonists of roleplaying today. It is encouraging to note that feminists in the twenties could be as determinedly resistant to the sexological model of masculine inverts and feminine pseudo-homosexuals as any contemporary lesbian feminists.

Brittain saw that women's desire for freedom had been captured within a masculine lesbian stereotype, that the sexological category was about control not liberation.

> If one of the results of women's education in the eighteen-nineties really was to attach the ugly label 'pervert' to a human

being whose chief desire was for a wider expression of her humanity than contemporary convention permitted, then that education was an evil thing indeed.[30]

It is somewhat puzzling that this discussion is being replicated in the eighties and nineties as some lesbians seek again to resume sexological stereotypes, even rather old-fashioned ones, because the times are so different now. A feminist critique of those stereotypes was part of a massive lesbian movement. The reassertion of roles is an explicit rejection of lesbian feminist insights. Why would 1920s ideas which were adopted in self-defence by a group of lesbians who felt there was no alternative be picked up with enthusiasm by lesbians today who have far more choices?

Newton explains her interest in the argument about sexology and Radclyffe Hall at the end of her article. She identifies directly with the 'mannish lesbian'. She states that like Hall she sees lesbianism as 'sexual difference'. Newton is one of those eighties lesbians who chose the sexological model of lesbianism in opposition to what she sees as the invidious influence of lesbian feminism. She embraces sexology with zeal. All her language and concepts about lesbianism come from that source. One example is her quest for an explanation for lesbianism. Lesbian feminists do not tend to seek an explanation because they do not see lesbianism as a minority condition but as a positive choice for all women. Newton seeks answers in traditional psychology. She says she sees 'mother/daughter eroticism' as a 'central component of lesbian orientation'.[31] This is a concept which derives from psychoanalysis. She goes on to wish that 'feminist psychology' will solve the 'riddle of sexual orientation.'

Though she seems earlier to see adoption of the masculine stereotype as a choice made in order to acquire a sexual identity by 1920s lesbians she demonstrates in her conclusion a commitment to a kind of psychological determinism. She says that Hall and the sexologists were 'describing something real' when describing mannish lesbians. This was the phenomenon of 'gender dysphoria' or 'a strong feeling that one's assigned gender as a man or a woman does not agree with one's sense of self.'[32]

This idea comes from sexology. Apparently 'gender dysphoria' is unchangeable and not subject to choice because:

> Masculinity and femininity are like two dialects of the same language. Though we all understand both, most of us 'speak' only one. Many lesbians, like Stephen Gordon, are biological females who grow up thinking in and 'speaking' the 'wrong' gender dialect.[33]

It is not subject to change in adulthood because 'gender identity is determined in early childhood.' Thus, Newton argues, we should support 'masculine women and feminine men' because 'Many lesbians *are* masculine; most have composite styles; many are emphatically feminine.' It is difficult to guess exactly why Newton emphasised the 'are' in the previous sentence unless it were to establish the essential and inevitable quality of lesbian 'masculinity'. This is clearly not a feminist approach. Lesbian feminists believe, not just from an ideological commitment to social constructionism, but because of their own experience, that human behaviour can be changed. Feminists, after all, are demanding that men change their masculine behaviour, a behaviour seen as asserting membership of a male ruling class which depends for its very existence on the subordination of women. Many profeminist men are demanding the very same thing. But Newton, a teacher of women's studies at State University, New York, tells us that masculinity in butch lesbians should be supported at the same time as so much feminist effort is going into the task of getting rid of it in men.

Newton chose to 'come out' in 1984 as a butch lesbian. This was, I suggest, a political decision, though Newton would not like to see it that way. She sees herself as somehow essentially butch. She says that she was unable to come out as a butch before 1984 because as a middle class and educated lesbian she associated butchness with the working classness of the bars she came out in in 1959. Apparently she needed to find a 'middle-class way of being butch.'[34] She found that in a butch support group in New York. She says it was a 'very difficult identity to come to terms with for many of us.'[35] As a women's studies teacher she must have been aware of a mountain of feminist and men's studies literature seeking to deconstruct and eliminate masculinity. Probably it is because she was aware of it that she needed support against what she calls 'dominant lesbian-feminist ideology'. It seems that the 'butches' in the group were determined to do masculinity properly and found themselves bedevilled by the limitations of the male role. Group proceedings sound like an unintentional parody of the consciousness raising of men against sexism groups in the seventies.

> We found we had a lack of social skills, we didn't have anyone there to kind of mediate and make small talk. Most of us had difficulties talking about our feelings, talking personally.[36]

They worried about things such as 'I'm not tall enough. You're butcher than I am... Are there internal problems to being butch? Over-control? Do you wish you could cry more?' But unlike men against sexism, these women did not want to lose the masculinity which was their prized possession, just to ameliorate some of the problems that masculine behaviour gave them. The 'butches' imitated woman-hating male behaviour as is to be expected if masculinity really is founded upon the disparagement of and the importance of not being women. Another topic, she says, was 'femmes' and 'indulging in some bitching about femmes and feminism.' This sounds like the malebonding behaviour of stereotypical males in bars who are trying to persuade themselves that they cannot be anything like women.

Newton seems to have some real ambivalence about being a woman. Once this could have been resolved in a feminist CR group where women might discuss in safety their self-hatred as members of the despised and lowly political class of women, and develop pride. Instead she has chosen to adopt a caricatured masculinity and pretend that she has no choice. As an intelligent, educated, academic woman, she is able to turn her self-justification into 'theory' about the positive effects of sexology which created the butch stereotype she seeks to perfect. In the eighties the feminist habit of rigorous self-questioning and political analysis, allied to a belief in the possibility of personal change in the interests of personal and lesbian liberation was overthrown in some lesbian circles by a belief in inviolable and inevitable identity or destiny based on unquestioned feelings of 'who you really were'. The idea of social construction and certainly the idea that it was good to subject your 'feelings' to analysis in a feminist context came to be seen as insulting to other lesbians' self-concepts. Feminism interrupted the search for truth.

The idea of gay male historians, and of Newton, that sexological constructions had a positive effect, finds its theoretical basis in the work of Michel Foucault. Foucault argued that though sexology provided the possibility of greater social control through its creation of perversity it also provided the possibility of a 'reverse discourse'. According to this idea the objects of sexological categorising could use those very categories to fight back against the forces of power.

> ... homosexuality began to speak in its own behalf, to demand that its legitimacy or 'naturality' be acknowledged, often in the same vocabulary, using the same categories by which it was medically disqualified.[37]

Radclyffe Hall's *The Well of Loneliness* has been seen by some lesbian and gay scholars as creating the possibility of a 'reverse discourse' for lesbians. Jonathan Dollimore explains that *The Well*:

> ... helped initiate a reverse discourse in Foucault's sense: lesbians were able to identify themselves, often for the first time, albeit in the very language of their oppression.[38]

Hall did more than simply accept a damned and outcast status for lesbians. By joining in Stephen 'the (religious) martyr and the (romantic) outsider' a powerful image was created of 'a superior sensibility and integrity being persecuted by the ordinary and the normal.'[39] Dollimore accepts, as many other gay scholars do, that the 'reverse discourse' thus created led to a positive sexual politics.

> Bizarre as it may now seem, many subsequent developments in sexual liberation and radical sexual politics can be traced

back to the kind of appropriations made by Hall, even those developments which would have appalled her, for example the idea of sexual deviance as potentially revolutionary, subverting the corrupt and oppressive centre from the deviant margins.[40]

The question then much debated by gay theorists is the extent to which a homosexual rights movement which used such categories was imprisoned by them and undermined and how much it was really able to subvert the categories for use in an effective resistance.

The sexual liberation movement that Dollimore has in mind is surely that suited to the interests of gay men. It does not follow that such politics for lesbians who are in the sex class women could appear so positive. The adoption of sexological categories by lesbians, I suggest – however useful it might have appeared in the short term in arguing for heterosexual sympathy, and offering a definite identity around which to organise – meant that twentieth century lesbians accepted the language and ideas of sexology to describe themselves. Lesbianism became a deviant minority based upon genital sexual activity which accepted either biological or psychological causation and frequently also accepted the terrible constraints of roleplaying. Lesbians were required to split themselves and their communities into two groups according to quite arbitrary criteria, to seek their friends in one and their lovers in another, and model their behaviour on the inappropriate and male invented behaviours of masculinity and femininity. Lesbians were also effectively split off from other women and feminists; as a separate and deviant minority they were under control.

It is understandable that male gay historians might be more positive about the impact of sexology because the historical situation of homosexual men was rather different from that of women. The sexologists linked sexual inversion in women with feminism and engaged in damaging attacks on the women's movement. The sexologists did not see homosexual men as being representative of a social freedom movement of which they were afraid. Passionate friendship is another way in which the history of homosexual men is different. Little history of men's passionate friendship has been written. If men's potential for such friendship was damaged by the sexological construction, and it might well have been, this has not been a concern of gay history. Gay men can be satisfied with deviant status since they are members of the ruling class and do not need to fight against their sex class status. The Foucauldian orthodoxy does not necessarily fit lesbians. Foucault did not after all give lesbians any consideration and gave women extremely little. It is a measure of the power of gay male culture and theory to define sexual politics particularly in the academy, that such an unsuitable model should be seen as applicable to women as well as men.

It is precisely the sexological model of lesbianism which is being adopted even in the eighties and nineties by those lesbians most opposed to feminism. Such lesbians are striving to fit themselves into the medical textbooks and believe that they are speaking the 'truth', that sexology is the 'truth', about themselves. It is difficult to understand why the medical model should suddenly have a new currency at this time. Gay students have suggested to me that this relates to the way that the medical profession is reasserting its command of male homosexuality because of its importance during the AIDS epidemic. But this can't explain why lesbians such as Esther Newton chose this model in the early eighties. Understanding the appeal of the medical model is one of the projects of *The Lesbian Heresy*.

The impact of sexological ideas and the decade of the twenties in particular can now be seen as pivotal, if not in the construction of lesbian identity, then at least in the contemporary lesbian sexuality debates. Lesbian feminists and 'sexual difference' lesbians see this historical period very differently. The decade of the twenties may have more direct relevance for the present. There may be some clues in what happened in the twenties to the rending of the lesbian community in the eighties. As some lesbians adopted sexological categories then to make sense of their experience and found this to be in conflict with feminist understandings of sexuality, so sexual libertarian lesbians more recently have used sexology again to explain their lesbianism in terms of biology, sexual difference, butch and femme with a similar rejection of feminist theory and practice.

1. For detail on the construction of the homosexual role see McIntosh, Mary (1968). 'The Homosexual Role.' *Sexual Problems* 16, pp. 182–191. (Reprinted in Plummer, Kenneth (Ed.) (1981). London: Hutchinson; and Weeks, Jeffrey (1977), *Coming Out*. London: Quartet.

2. See Faderman, Lillian (1985). *Surpassing the Love of Men*. London: The Women's Press; (1981). New York: Quill, and Smith-Rosenberg, Caroll (1991), 'Discourses of Sexuality and Subjectivity: The New Woman', 1870–1936. In Duberman, Martin *et al* (Eds.) (1991). *Hidden From History*. London: Penguin; (1990), New York: Plume.

3. Two volumes of Ann Lister's diaries have now been published, edited by Helena Whitbread. See Whitbread (1988) and Whitbread (1992).

4. See Weeks, Jeffrey (1985). *Sexuality and Its Discontents. Meanings, Myths and Modern Sexualities*. London: Routledge and Kegan Paul.

5. Ellis, Henry Havelock (1913). *Studies in the Psychology of Sex Vol. 2. Sexual Inversion*. Philadelphia: F. A. Davies. First published 1903. p. 308.

6. Ibid. p. 108.

7. See Carpenter, Edward (1921). *The Intermediate Sex. A Study of Some Transitional Types of Men and Women*. London: George Allen and Unwin Ltd. First Published 1908.

8. Ibid. pp. 30–31.

9. Ibid. p. 36.

10. Ibid. p. 31.

11. See also: Sahli, Nancy (1979). 'Smashing. Women's Relationships Before the Fall.' *Chrysalis*. No. 8.
Auchmuty, Rosemary (1989). 'You're a Dyke, Angela! Elsie J. Oxenham and the Rise and Fall of the Schoolgirl Story.' In Lesbian History Group (Eds.). *Not A Passing Phase. Reclaiming Lesbians in History 1840–1985*. London: The Women's Press.

12. Faderman (1985) p. 252.

13. Smith-Rosenberg, Carroll (1979). 'The Female World of Love and Ritual: Relations between women in nineteenth-century America.' In Cott N. F. and Pleck E. H. (Eds.) (1979). *A Heritage of Her Own*. New York: Touchstone Books, Simon and Schuster.

14. Smith-Rosenberg (1991). op. cit. 1979 p. 266.

15. Ibid. p. 269.

16. Faderman (1985). p. 20.

17. Ibid. p. 17.

18. Ibid. p. 414.

19. See Ruehl, Sonja (1983). 'Sexual Theory and Practice: Another Double

Standard.' In Cartledge, Sue and Ryan, Joanna (Eds.) (1983). *Sex and Love*. London: The Women's Press.

20. See the introduction to Lesbian History Group (Eds.) (1989).

21. See my (1985). *The Spinster and Her Enemies. Feminism and Sexuality 1880–1930*.

22. Smith-Rosenberg (1991). p. 272.

23. Newton, Esther (1991). 'The Mythic Mannish Lesbian: Radclyffe Hall and the New Woman.' In Duberman, Martin *et al* (Eds.). *Hidden from History: Reclaiming the Gay and Lesbian Past*. p. 283.

24. Ibid. p. 291.

25. Ibid.

26. For details of this friendship see Brittain, Vera (1980). *Testament of Friendship*. London: Virago. First published 1940.

27. Brittain, Vera (1968). *Radclyffe Hall. A Case of Obscenity?* London: Femina Books. pp. 49–50.

28. Ibid.

29. Ibid. p. 51.

30. Ibid.

31. Newton (1991). p. 290.

32. Ibid. p. 292.

33. Ibid.

34. Esther Newton quoted in Loulan, JoAnn (1990). *The Lesbian Erotic Dance*. San Francisco: Spinsters. p. 46.

35. Ibid. p. 120.

36. Ibid. p. 121.

37. Foucault, Michel (1978). *The History of Sexuality Volume 1: An Introduction*. London: Allen Lane. p. 101.

38. Dollimore, Jonathan (1991). *Sexual Dissidence. Augustine to Wilde, Freud to Foucault*. Oxford: Clarendon Press. p. 48.

39. Ibid. p. 49.

40. Ibid. p. 50.

Chapter 2

THE LESBIAN SEXUAL REVOLUTION

In the 1980s a lesbian sexual revolution took place. Traditional malestream historians of sexuality represent the two heterosexual revolutions that are supposed to have taken place in the 1920s and sixties as very positive developments that brought liberation and pleasure to women. My two previous books have set out to show that these revolutions actually represent adjustments in the forces of male supremacy.[1] Male power was bolstered by conscripting women into sexual intercourse and orchestrating their sexual response so that they would eroticise their own subordination. The revolutions, or adjustments in male supremacist techniques of control, were conducted in the name of science and health but using the rhetoric of liberalism.

Through the revolutions a massively expanding pornography industry was legitimated, an industry of sex therapy and sex advice books constructed, and sex shops and sex tupperware parties set up to provide sex hardware such as dildos and leather, rubber and vinyl costumes. Through all this period lesbians somehow managed to love each other and make love without paraphernalia, whilst in the heterosexual world, sex without 'how to' books, pornography, and equipment was made to seem all but impossible. Lesbian sex was innovative, imaginative, self-taught, low-tech, did not cost any money or provide any sex industrialists with an income. In the eighties this changed and a lesbian sex industry developed. In order for a lesbian sex industry to be profitable it was necessary to transform lesbian sexuality so that it would take the objectifying form necessary to construct lesbian sex consumers, consumers not just of mechanical products but of other women in pornography and prostitution. At last lesbian sexuality began to attract the attention of entrepreneurs, sex therapists, pornographers.

The result of this dramatic onslaught designed to reconstruct lesbian sexuality has been the partial incorporation of lesbians into the political structures of control of the heteropatriarchy. Whilst lesbians invented their sexuality they were a loose wheel, providing a possible alternative vision of what sex could be when it was not centred on penises, goal orientation, objectification, dominance and submission. They were not subject to the powerful sexual control of male supremacy carried out through the shaping of sexual pleasure. They were not necessarily effectively eroticising their own subordination, and they were potentially threatening to the heteropatriarchal sexual system. The lesbian sexual revolution is capturing lesbians and casting us too into sexual subjection.

But this is not the way that the lesbian sexual revolution is seen in the mixed gay media, in academic lesbian and gay studies literature.[2] The new and glittering array of possibilities, dildos, pornography, sex clubs, prostitutes available, is represented as providing choice, fun, pleasure, individual freedom as the epitome of all lesbians have been striving for, the goal of lesbian revolution. Lesbian political struggle is being diverted into a false liberation which, I suggest, will prove as illusory for lesbians as the sexual freedom offered to heterosexual women in the sixties and seventies turned out to be. Women gained a great deal of sexual intercourse but did not get to be free. The success of the lesbian sexual revolution depends on the stifling of political discussion of the construction of sexual pleasure and the way that this fits into lesbian and feminist revolution. It depends on an acceptance of the public/private split when it comes to sexual pleasure, an acceptance that what turns us on has no relevance for political struggle. It depends on a language of sexual liberalism. When it comes to sex many lesbians who would see themselves as politically progressive, feminist, socialist, anti-racist take leave of their politics and adopt a deep-dyed liberalism.[3]

When seeking to analyse such topics as sex therapy or sadomasochism politically, I have found myself labelled moralistic or judgemental and such a political critique has been seen as politically off limits. I would like to look at what has become off limits, and why it has become so and seek to draw sexual pleasure and sexual practice back within the pale of political discussion. The accusation of moralism tends to be directed only at political analysis of sexual practice and is unlikely to be made about such analysis of other issues. In fact it would seem likely that political judgements aré most commonly based upon morality. It is likely to be a sense of what is right and wrong which fuels anger at what is seen to be oppression. It is not fashionable to discuss morals in capitalist society, particularly in the eighties and nineties when the market is ruling all such discussion irrelevant. But it is just such a sense of right and wrong rather than any more mysterious process which underlies political judgements. In some areas of life precisely the same people who would see it as moralistic to analyse sexual practice politically, do make moral judgements. Someone who protested at economic inequality, for instance, would not usually be called moralistic. It is sexuality that is singled out as an area that should be free of moral or political judgement. I'd like to look at the way that feminists have seen sex as political, starting with some of those areas which might seem uncontroversial and ending with the area which causes most difficulty, that of sexual practice.

An area in which most feminists would probably agree that sex is political is that of men's sexual violence towards women. Feminist theorists have written many volumes on the political role of sexual violence as a crucial, functional support to the whole political system of male supremacy.[4] The spectrum of sexual violence which includes sexual abuse in childhood, flashing and sexual harassment, having pornography used on us, marital rape and the murder of women functions to control and undermine women and keep us in subjection.

There have been good examples of the ways in which sexual violence can restrict women's lives and opportunities at the university where I teach. At one time there were notices in three areas simultaneously warning women students to be on their guard. There were notices in the women's toilets in the Students'

22

Union building warning women of attacks and telling them not to enter the toilets alone and to check behind cubicle doors. Similar notices adorned the women's changing rooms at the sports centre and various parts of the library. Thus women were seriously restricted in their 'equal' opportunities to engage in recreation, study or urination. It is likely that most universities have similar or worse problems of male sexual violence. All the precautions that women routinely take can begin to seem like second nature, but a feminist analysis tells us that women are experiencing a system of political control. There are disagreements amongst feminist theorists as to how to define marital rape or sexual harassment but most would agree that sexual violence is politically constructed and serves a political purpose under male supremacy.

Another area in which most feminist theorists would agree that sexuality is political is that of the construction of heterosexuality as the organising principle of the social relations of male supremacy.[5] Feminist theorists may disagree as to how important they consider heterosexuality as an institution to be to the maintenance of male power but would probably all agree that the pressuring of women into heterosexuality serves the purposes of male supremacy. Without heterosexuality it would be difficult for individual men to extract unpaid sexual, reproductive, economic, domestic and emotional servicing from women. Heterosexual orientation is not generally seen by feminists today as purely a private and individual matter unmediated by male power.

It is in the area of the construction of sexual pleasure and sexual practice that problems have arisen for seeing sexuality as political. It is sex that is seen as private, individual, consensual that is still seen as off limits for political analysis. Feminism is a philosophy that makes connections and the connections in this case might seem clear. Both heterosexuality as a political system and sexual violence as social control depend upon the construction of heterosexual desire. By heterosexual desire I mean the eroticised power difference which originates in heterorelations but can also exist in same sex unions. A feminist analysis would suggest that the reconstruction of sexuality is necessary to undermine the sexual system of male supremacy. This would require

23

the construction of what I call 'homosexual' desire or eroticised equality. In my book, *Anticlimax*, I suggest that there is no chance for women to be free while women's subordination remains sexy.

But when it comes to sexual pleasure some feminists and lesbians are not prepared to make the connections. To see sexual practice as political it is necessary to question the liberal notion of privacy. Feminists and lesbian and gay activists have been prepared to use the notion of privacy strategically to advance their aims because it is a notion understood by the liberal state. In the sixties in the UK for example, the idea of an individual's right to sexual privacy underlay the liberalising of the law on male homosexuality in 1967.[6] But this idea is very problematic for feminists.

The American feminist theorist Catherine MacKinnon explains very well the problem that the notion of privacy in law creates for women as it 'reaffirms and reinforces what the feminist critique of sexuality criticizes: the public/private split.'[7] To fight for the criminalisation of marital rape and sexual abuse generally it was necessary for feminists to stress that women's oppression takes place as much in the private realm of the home and the bedroom as in the public realm. Feminists fighting male violence as well as those protesting unpaid domestic labour found it necessary to expound the campaigning slogan that 'the personal is political'. As MacKinnon points out:

> It is probably not coincidence that the very things feminism regards as central to the subjection of women – the very place, the body; the very relations, heterosexual; the very activities, intercourse and reproduction; and the very feelings, intimate – form the core of what is covered by privacy doctrine. From this perspective, the legal concept of privacy can and has shielded the place of battery, marital rape, and women's exploited labour; has preserved the central institutions whereby women are deprived of identity, autonomy, control and self-definition; and has protected the primary activity through which male supremacy is expressed and enforced.[8]

The sacredly non-political nature of the 'personal' can be challenged in order to fight sexual abuse. There can be serious disagreements about what constitutes 'marital rape' but feminists would generally agree that such a phenomenon exists and needs to be stopped. It can seem more difficult to make the personal political when the sexual practice taking place is apparently consensual though the usefulness of the notion of consent has been much challenged itself by feminist work on marital rape and will be later in this chapter in relation to sadomasochism.[9] There is still an area of sex which is privatised for feminist sexual liberals. It seems important to sexual liberals to maintain an area of life which still somehow remains in a state of nature, a conservation zone to which the hard pressed individual can retreat for succour.

The difficulty in seeing 'consensual' sex as political arises not just from the liberal notion of privacy but from some other key ideas of the sexual revolution which have become the conventional wisdom about sex and bedevil even feminist discussion. One of these is the notion that sex is good, positive and necessary for human health in all its 'consensual' forms. A dualism about sex is built into the masculine frame of mind. Sex is seen either as 'good' or 'bad'. From the 1890s onwards sex reformers fought against puritanism and what they saw as sex negative values and promoted the idea that sex is an ultimate good. Sex became so wrapped around with an aura of sanctity and buoyed up by the notion that it was the elixir of life that it became hard to question. It was understood by those who considered themselves progressive that to criticise any form of sexual expression is to fall into the hands of the deep, dark forces of repression, the Catholic Church, the inquisition and Victorianism. The male supremacist forces that represent the 'sex is bad' side of the dualism still exist and need to be challenged but should not be used to prove that it is too dangerous to talk about sex politically.

Another key idea that inhibits the political discussion of sexual practice is that there must be a suspension of values when sexuality is approached. My favourite example of this is the supposedly very progressive sixties book *The ABZ of Love* which encouraged a morally neutral approach to various forms of male sexual behaviour which constituted abuse of power or violence such as necrophilia.

> Necrophilia, necromania, necrosadism: Are all the sexual things people can think of doing with dead persons' bodies. It is not exactly an unknown phenomenon for people whose sexual urges have not found outlet in the more normal fashion to allow themselves to be tempted by corpses.[11]

Presumably women are not supposed to feel distressed by the notion that their bodies might be raped by morgue attendants. Such arguments in favour of the suspension of values when values are clearly not suspended, in fact, are used by those who maintain that we are still fighting Victorianism, a legacy which is supposed to go on and on forever and to have new representatives in the current generation of feminist anti-violence campaigners. The main bearers of this ideology of sexual liberalism today are therapists who carry the language of therapy into feminism and bring with them a severe dose of moral relativism.[12]

In my books, *The Spinster and Her Enemies* and *Anticlimax* I demonstrated that sex has always been seen as having a political function by sexologists. An industry of sexology and sex therapy has been devoted for the last hundred years to orchestrating the submission of women to men and in marriage through getting them to accept sexual intercourse and experience the pleasure of 'surrender' in that act. For the sexologists, psychoanalysts, doctors, gynecologists, advice columnists, social workers involved in this campaign, women's 'pleasure' of a supposedly consensual, personal, private and individual variety was seen as crucially linked with the maintenance of male power and women's submission, as very political indeed. The sexologists of the early twentieth century were least self-conscious about expressing their political message. Sexologists such as Wilhelm Stekel were unabashedly fighting feminism and believed that women's pleasure in sexual intercourse would conquer feminism, man-hating, spinsterhood and lesbianism which were all said to be threats to 'civilisation' as they saw it. A statement by Stekel in his 1926 book, *Frigidity in Woman in Relation to Her*

Love Life, indicates that he clearly understood woman's pleasure in sexual intercourse to have political effects. He said 'To be roused by a man means acknowledging one's self as conquered.'[13]

Sexologists later in the century have been equally forthright about the political function of women's sexual pleasure. Eustace Chesser, the most popular of sexologists in fifties' Britain wrote that a girl may:

> ... find it impossible to surrender herself completely in the sex act. And complete surrender is the only way in which she can bring the highest pleasure to herself and her husband. Submission is not the same thing as surrender. Many a wife submits, but retains, deep within herself, an area which is not conquered, and, which, indeed, is in fierce opposition to submission.[14]

Considering that the science of sex promotes itself in the present as specifically value free it might seem surprising that the political importance of women's sexual pleasure would be so well understood by sexologists. The sexologists were often happy to explain that once a woman had surrendered in sexual intercourse she could be expected to surrender in other areas too such as decision making in the marriage.

The history and literature of sexology is a good illustration of the ways in which sexuality is politically constructed. Sexology has been devoted to the construction of sexual intercourse. Women were seen as not liking it enough and men as being unable to do it efficiently. Reading the sexologists on sexual intercourse would disabuse any reader of the idea that this practice was in any sense 'natural'. They promoted sexual intercourse as vital for women at a time when women were gaining more opportunities because of its role in maintaining male power. It was seen as making a man a 'man' and a woman 'submissive'. Still in the eighties and nineties women's magazines and sex education literature emphasise the importance of surrender for women in sexual intercourse.[15] It is a supposedly scientific and respectable version of what is often said by men about

27

stroppy women at work and on the street, 'What she needs is a good fuck.'

The sexologists were aided in their quest to subordinate women through sexual 'pleasure' by the fact that women have the capacity to eroticise their own subordination and take 'pleasure' in it. Women learn their emotions and sexual responses in a situation of inequality as they grow up and frequently in situations of actual abuse. The word 'pleasure' needs to be carefully analysed. Women can have orgasms during rape and sexual abuse. Such orgasms do not prove that the women 'wanted it' or that anything positive has happened. There are not words as yet to describe sexual feelings which are the opposite of positive. There are only words such as pleasure and enjoyment. It is important to call the whole concept of sexual pleasure into question and not assume that sexual feelings are necessarily positive. It will then be possible to develop a more sensitive and nuanced vocabulary which will enable women to express a wider range of sexual feelings including those which are experienced as unambiguously negative.

There are many who would argue, including some lesbians, that sexual response in the form of eroticised dominance and submission is either harmless, private, personal and individual or even useful for gaining enhanced sexual sensations and enabling sexual response to those whose sex life has been damaged by abuse. Those who support sadomasochism either in 'fantasy' or reality include the sexologists of course but also in recent years the publishers of the new women's erotica, many heterosexual as well as lesbian sex therapists, the members of heterosexual and lesbian and gay sadomasochist organisations.[16] But the sexological concern with women's sexual surrender is evidence for the political importance of sexual feelings. It is reasonable to credit the male sexologists with some astuteness. If they have acted for the past hundred years on the assumption that the voluntary embrace of masochistic sexual response would weaken women politically and personally then this should be good enough reason for feminist theorists to at least consider this possibility.

The first sign of a growing lesbian sex industry in the US was the appearance of lesbian pornography created by a new breed of lesbian entrepreneurs. In the first few years of feminist anti-pornography organising, speakers from Women Against Violence Against Women in Britain would be asked 'How can we create positive erotica for women and particularly for lesbians?' One result of the pornographic revolution of the sixties was to establish the idea that erotica was necessary to sex. This assumption was so widespread even amongst feminists that anti-pornography campaigners were pushed into the position of asserting a distinction between erotica and pornography in order to prove they were not killjoys or anti-sex. Gloria Steinem defines the erotic as 'a mutually pleasurable, sexual expression between people who have enough power to be there by positive choice.' She defines the pornographic thus: 'its message is violence, dominance, and conquest. It is sex being used to reinforce some inequality, or to create one . . .'[17]

Some anti-porn campaigners refused to travel this road and asserted from the very beginning that erotica and pornography were not qualitatively different. Andrea Dworkin explains the connection thus:

This book [*Pornography: Men Possessing Women*] is not about the difference between pornography and erotica. Feminists have made honourable efforts to define the difference, in general asserting that erotica involves mutuality and reciprocity, whereas pornography involves dominance and violence. But in the male sexual lexicon, which is the vocabulary of power, erotica is simply high-class pornography: better packaged, designed for a better class of consumer. As with the call girl and the streetwalker, one is turned out better but both perform the same service. Intellectuals, especially, call what they themselves produce or like 'erotica', which means simply that a very bright person made or likes whatever it is . . . In the male system, erotica is a sub-category of pornography.[18]

Some anti-pornography campaigners though they did not wish to devote their time and energy to the creation of a positive erotica waited expectantly for its arrival in order to see what such a phenomenon would look like. We were convinced that this new woman-produced erotica would be quite different from

29

male-produced pornography. It would have completely different values and represent the new sexuality that would presage the post-revolutionary future. Some feminists did indeed create what they called a new kind of erotica. Tee Corinne is an example. In the service of validating the vulva she has photographed female genitals in landscape, on trees and in beaches. The association of the female genitals with natural forms, shells, flowers, fruits, has quite a long history in lesbian art. Such photographs are clearly a break with the traditions of male pornography where the vulva appears in order to stimulate the male to erection with thoughts of penetration. Women, it seems, can create art with sexual content which does not replicate male pornography.

But the new industry of erotica which has developed in the eighties is not about celebrating the beauty of the vulva. It is aimed at arousal and the simplest way to achieve this seems to be the stimulation of women's ability to eroticise our oppression. Pat Califia, who writes sadomasochistic pornography, explains this point quite well.

> Sadly, a lot of the new lesbian porn (brave as it is) flunks what Dorothy Allison calls 'the wet test' . . . 'Feminist erotica' that presents a simplistic view of lesbian sex as two women in love in a bed who embody all the good things the patriarchy is trying to destroy isn't very sexy.[19]

The porn which apparently does fulfil the 'wet test' was a considerable shock to women who were expecting the representation of a new form of female sexuality. The overwhelming bulk of the material revolves around the eroticising of women's subordination. The producers of the erotica say it represents a new approach to female sexuality because it shows women as raunchy, hot, aggressive instead of passive and submissive. The new erotica provides women with two roles. It allows women to put themselves in the place of men and find the objectification, fetishisation and humiliation of women exciting or to adopt the old-fashioned submissive roles which are also plentifully available in this erotica, so women now have a choice whether to get turned on by taking either a dominant or submissive role towards another woman. Barbara Smith, a British writer of erotica, explains why lesbian porn in which women simply take both the roles available in heterosexual porn without any change to the values represented is perfectly acceptable:

> Pornography for lesbians is unique in that it presumes a *female* gaze, and a lesbian one at that. It presumes active female sexuality. It celebrates autonomous female sexual enjoyment. It still presents women as objects, but through the eyes, and to the eyes, of other women as *subjects*. It takes stereotyped images, and, with some humour at times, utterly subverts them in both intention and context. Pornography for lesbians at least portrays us in our true light as the spectrum of womanhood – strong, sexually demanding and fulfilled, active, passive, and always assertive.[20]

Feminist anti-pornography theorists have expressly fought the objectification involved in pornography. We have argued that such objectification subordinates the one objectified and constructs and reinforces a sexuality of dominance and submission, specifically women's submission. Objectification has been seen by feminist anti-pornography campaigners as the basic mechanism involved in men's sexual violence. Catharine MacKinnon expresses the dynamics of pornography well.

> Under male dominance, whatever sexually arouses a man is sex. In pornography, the violence *is* the sex. The inequality is sex. Pornography does not work, sexually, without hierarchy. If there is no inequality, no violation, no dominance, no force, there is no sexual arousal.[21]

If erotica means simply the representation of sex which is not directed at arousal but simply part of a plot, then it would not necessarily involve inequality. But the new erotica which is aimed at arousal goes for the lowest common denominator of sex under male supremacy, dominance and submission.

Some feminist presses which might once have been devoted to the publication of texts with new and feminist values have now started to publish erotica because it pays. One of these is

Sheba in Britain. Their first collection, *Serious Pleasure*, purported to contain alternative and feminist erotica. One of the attempts at 'feminist' erotica in the collection shows quite amusingly the attempt to represent alternative values in the new erotica. In this story a group of women are introduced who are clearly not the stereotypically beautiful models of pornography. As they prepare for a party we are introduced to their childcare problems. They are neither young nor rich.

> Amy was watching TV while she dried her long gray hair. On the table by the armchair was a mug of soup and a half-eaten piece of toast. Couldn't miss Coronation Street, not even for the Goddess herself.[22]

The six women have been meeting for 13 weeks of sexual abstinence to prepare for a mystical sexual happening, surrounded by candles, spirits and chants. The setting may be unusual but the language of sexuality used is that of traditional male porn. There is a slight nineteenth century tone as in 'exploring the pearly abundance that was Sally'. Meanwhile Sally has another woman urging her to 'fuck her harder'. It seems that even lesbians who are committed feminists and can be imaginative about so many things are reduced to patriarchal cliches when producing erotica. They are not constructing a new sexuality but putting new trimmings on the old.

The new American erotica magazines do not have such scruples. They do not seem anxious to portray lesbians as grey haired, fat, or poor. The most established is called *On Our Backs*. The title establishes the intention to subvert feminism. The most longstanding feminist newspaper in the US is called *Off Our Backs*. Such magazines have a very definite politics which is aimed at the depoliticising of lesbianism. A subs page in *On Our Backs* illustrates this very well. Where the Radicalesbians had stated in an early lesbian feminist manifesto that 'A lesbian is the rage of all women condensed to the point of explosion,' *On Our Backs* states 'A lesbian is the lust of all women condensed to the point of explosion.'[23] This statement appears over a picture of a woman's torso trussed in black leather with tightly tourniqueted breasts. This substitutes personal sexual satisfaction through S/M practice for political change.

The magazines sell the full gamut of products which the traditional heterosexual sex industry sells. The articles and ads promote sex toys, porn videos, sex phone lines and prostitution. Everything from which money is to be made in the commercialisation and commodification of sex is represented here. They are full of dildos. These dildos are clearly penis-shaped and they come with harnesses so that lesbians can imitate men fucking women. They should not be confused with vibrators which come in many shapes and are also advertised in the magazines. The dildos are commonly incorporated into sadomasochistic scenarios presumably because, like the penis, they symbolise male power and the ability to violate women. The following example is an extract from a story in *Bad Attitude* about sex at the hairdresser's.

> I snapped a small collar quickly around her neck and attached it to one of the faucets. Then I opened a drawer and removed two dildos, one large and one medium in size.
> 'Spread your legs,' I snapped. She obeyed immediately, moving her feet apart . . .'[24]

The aggression and cruelty, the forcible penetration central to traditional men's pornography is in clear evidence here.

One of the many services advertised in such magazines is sex toy parties. These function like tupperware parties in women's homes and like every supposed innovation of the lesbian sex industry they were pioneered by male sex industrialists. These parties sell dildos. Susie Bright who writes advice columns in *On Our Backs* runs such parties and explains that women often complain that the dildos they have been sold are too large. She says the answer is to use lubricant and 'tease the dildo in'.[25] An avalanche of sex advice literature this century has aimed to suit reluctant or inadequate women to being efficient holes for the penis with varying therapies suggested from lubricants to counselling and surgery. As lesbian feminists we had to counter the sexological lies that lesbians really wanted to be men and could not do anything with each other without an imitation penis. It is ironic that it is now lesbian sex industrialists who see it as necessary to cure lesbians of an inability to admit the dildo, a penis substitute.

The dildo allows for the slavish imitation of heterosexual sex in the new erotica in such unlikely activities as 'cocksucking'. Joan Nestle includes this bizarre phenomenon in an 'erotic' story in her book *A Restricted Country*. In the story a 'butch' straps on a dildo which is called a 'cock' throughout the story. One of the 'femmes' performs fellatio on the inanimate object and 'told the butch what a wonderful cock she had and how much she wanted it.'[26] This is a form of phallus worship, well suited to a D. H. Lawrence novel. The butch goes on to an imitation of heterosexual fucking with the dildo. This is all that takes place sexually. No other kind of contact redeems this from being simply a re-enactment between women of the most oppressive heterosexual scenario, though Nestle by some twist of logic seeks to explain this imitation of heterosexual roles as actually a subversion of heterosexuality simply because a woman is playing the male part.

This avalanche of dildos does seem to be a new lesbian sexuality. Though sexologists, who were unable to imagine how sex could take place without the presence of a penis, have argued for a hundred years that lesbians used dildos, there is no evidence to suggest that the use of penis substitutes was common. The use of dildos before the advent of the new lesbian sex industry did exist but seems to have been very much a minority practice. The Kinsey Institute study, published in 1978, does not mention dildos at all in the section on sexual techniques. It reports that cunnilingus was the most popular activity by far and the most common was masturbation.[27] None of the lesbians quoted in the *Hite Report* section on sexual techniques mention dildos either except for one who questions whether lesbians really use them at all.

Such a question can only look innocent today faced with the onslaught of dildos in lesbian sex magazines. The new lesbian sex industry is aimed at making money like any other capitalist enterprise. The manufacture and sale of sex toys is an important part of this industry. New needs have to be created in women which they may never before have imagined so that they will buy the goods. Meantime a new sexuality is being constructed for lesbians. It just happens to resemble precisely the prescriptions of male pornographers and the founding fathers of sexology. It resembles neither traditional lesbian sexual practice, nor a vision of some different and revolutionary possibility.

What is astonishing is the lack of a widespread lesbian revolt against the incursion of the dildo, a symbol of male power and the oppression of women, into lesbian culture. The lesbian pornographers and sex industrialists are telling us that lesbians are disadvantaged by the absence of a penis. They are repeating and promoting all the most oppressive sexological mythmaking. For the lesbians involved in this new industry sex and penises are clearly inextricably connected and they do not see this assumed connection as anti-lesbian. To feminists who oppose the implications of the dildo culture the lesbian sex industrialists can be ruthless. In the first issue of a British lesbian sex toy company's catalogue, a dildo was named after me, as a form of sexual harassment. It was called 'The Sheila – the Spinster's best friend' in reference to the fact that my first book was called *The Spinster and Her Enemies*.

In the new lesbian sex industry the real material oppression of women is used as a sex aid for the consumers. Lesbian strippers describe their incest experience to provide sexual stimulation for other lesbians. Lesbians use their painful experience not just for their own sexual gratification but for that of others. The industry demonstrates the extent of the damage which women's oppression and lesbian oppression has effected and illustrates the low self esteem and even hatred of our bodies and sexuality which can be the result. Some examples from stories in the magazines will show the extent of the self-hatred that lesbians can suffer. One story in *On Our Backs* is entitled 'Letter from a Mistress to her Pet'. The description of the Pet contains a concentrated fury of woman-hatred such as could only have been discovered previously in men's pornography.

Sometimes Fluffy's mistress forces her to wear a lubricated chain in the cleft of her cunt and her ass, attached to a belly chain. When she pulls it tight, Fluffy knows who her mistress is. Still, she continues her slutty ways. In fact, the little bitch is never satisfied until all her holes have been filled, sucked, bitten, eaten and thoroughly used.[28]

The new lesbian porn needs to be read with an understanding of the effects of oppression, and sexual abuse in particular, on the construction of women's sexuality. Some of the material can create a terrible sadness in the reader as it demonstrates the damage that has been done to women. One story about a top (sadist) who forces her bottom to be prepared to die by immolation should be read in the context of the real existence of self-mutilation and suicide in the lesbian community. After torturing the bottom (masochist) by tying her to a chair with a hole in the seat and placing a burning candle beneath it nearer and nearer to her genitals the top is described as pouring petrol all over the bottom's body and the chair. The top seeks to get the bottom to ignite a lighter in her hand so that she will become a human bonfire. She succeeds in achieving this:

> You hesitate again. The gasoline is dripping off the hand holding the lighter. You're shaking with fear, and barely breathing. When you do breathe, you can almost taste the gasoline in the air. 'Give it up,' I whisper. 'Give it to me. Burn for me.'
> Your thumb moves, but not enough to spark the flint. Then, you go over. You replace your thumb with determination on the top of the wheel, and firmly give it the spin needed to light it. The tiny flame grows into a bright orange burst, then races up your arm and towards your face. You scream and scream, and a huge stream of piss sprays the floor beneath the chair.[29]

In an afterword the writer explains that only the towel on the woman's head was soaked in petrol. Her body was really covered in water but the bottom did not know that she was not offering up her life. It may be that this is a safety tip lest enthusiastic lesbians try this scenario. It has to be remembered when proponents of sadomasochism justify their practice with the idea of consent that there are lesbians who are prepared to die as well as submit themselves to brutal mutilation. In a male supremacist culture which hates women and in which women are routinely violently abused, women can lose the capacity to protect their bodies and their lives. They can decide that they are not worth protecting.

The products of the new lesbian pornography industry provide us with an opportunity for analysing the construction of women's sexuality and its connection with our experience of abuse. Cindy Patton, an American AIDS activist and safe sex educator, says that child sexual abuse has become more of an issue in relation to adult lesbian sexuality through the medium of safe sex discussion. She also reports that research indicates a particular prevalence of sexual abuse experience among 'gay people' and says that in the US a large number of lesbian and gay S/M practitioners talked from the mid-eighties onwards of having been sexually abused.

> There has also been an interesting development in politically progressive SM culture more recently, particularly around these new studies which seem to indicate that gay people have been more sexually abused than other people. As a result, there's now a real 'claiming' of childhood sexual abuse by SM practitioners.[30]

The extent to which women and lesbians are now talking about their experience of abuse has caused some lesbians to downplay its seriousness. Sue O'Sullivan, for instance, a former editor at Sheba publishers, a press which has ventured into erotica, expresses a desire to take such abuse less seriously in her conversation with Cindy Patton. She says she feels 'itchy' about the issue and suggests that fantasy might play a part in women's apparent recall of sexual abuse.

> But I do wonder if there hasn't been a strange disowning of the complexity and importance of fantasy; a misunderstanding of how fantasy can work in the construction of present reality and, as importantly, in the reconstruction of the past. It has become a feminist heresy to suggest that there may be an element of fantasy that is being claimed as a physical reality, particularly in recollections of child sexual abuse.[31]

O'Sullivan has chosen to abandon the important feminist principle that women should be believed, a principle set up in opposition to the routine disbelief of women practised by psychoanalysis and the justice system. Patton, too, thinks women are too easily believed, particularly by psychoanalysts.

> ... so in cases of child sexual abuse, it's simply assumed that the stories the adult tells have to be really true. That denies the child, or the adult recalling the child, the power to interpret – which is ultimately very damaging because in this framework sexual abuse has to be claimed as a real event which was enormously formative.[32]

She is critical of feminists who 'encourage women to claim victimhood' because, apparently this makes women rewrite their child sexual experiences as 'narratives of victimization', instead of good clean fun perhaps. Sue O'Sullivan mused that if she had a different personality and history even she could read relatively harmless memories about her father into clues that she had been sexually abused. Patton goes on to say that sexual abuse has been seen as too important in influencing adult experience of sexuality relative to other childhood experiences. The example she gives of something that may be more significant than sexual abuse is a child not being able to have her room as she wants it.

> A child may be subjected to one instance of abuse but may experience twenty-five occasions when she can't have her room as she wants it – and that form of disciplinary control is just as much a part of what forms the child's sexuality as are more obviously 'sexual' events.[33]

Cindy Patton has worked on the American lesbian erotica magazine *Bad Attitude*. It does look as if being involved in the lesbian sexual revolution requires the de-emphasising of sexual violence. It is a common theme of the promoters of the new erotica that anti-pornography feminists tend to see women as victims and show far too much alarm about sexual violence. It could be that sexual abuse is just inconvenient for those who wish to 'play' with the toys of the new sex industry and concentrate on an unalloyed pleasure. It could be seen as rather vulgar for the new sex industry to use sexual abuse itself as its raw material if that abuse is taken seriously. Lesbians are, for instance, being encouraged to fantasise not only father rape but how they might like to use children sexually themselves in the Sydney S/M magazine, *Wicked Women*.[34]

Other forms of male violence have also been cited as justification for S/M as a practice which allows lesbians to experience an otherwise elusive sexual satisfaction. One contributor to the Samois anthology explains that S/M is particularly suited to her as a woman who has been battered.

> I am tired of being accused by hysterical dykes who beat up their lovers of being a rapist/brutalizer/male-identified oppressor of battered womyn. *I* was a battered womyn for years & claim the right to release & transform the pain & fear of those experiences any way I damn well please.[35]

Some abuse survivors would argue that women who have experienced abuse and enter S/M are not 'survivors' at all. They have not managed to heal from the effects of the abuse and free themselves from its thrall. Julia Penelope is a lesbian theorist who did seek such healing from her childhood sexual abuse through an incest survivors group. In her writings she explains how abuse and the entry into S/M could be linked.

> My capacity to trust was violated by adult perpetrators at an early age ... as a survivor, I can't predict that I'll ever be able to heal myself completely. I'll probably be dealing with my childhood experiences until I die ... I know the barrier or wall so often described in the literature of S/M, I know what it feels like, and I know how frustrating it is to try to breach that wall. But I also know the origins of that wall – I built it as a last defence to protect my autonomy and sense of self against the perpetual assaults of adult predators ... [36]

The literature of S/M says the wall can be breached through S/M practice and that lesbians who are not conscious of having experienced the same kind of abuse should not question or criticise them. But survivors who are healing from their abuse and reject S/M as any kind of panacea are in a position, like Julia Penelope, to help us understand the ways in which sex and violence can become linked and how we can begin to unlock the connections. Penelope explains:

In the mind of the beaten child, violence as an exercise of control equals love. In the mind of the raped daughter, sex as an exercise of power equals love ... Love, sex, and violence are intertwined in our minds ... We take that construction with us into our adult lives to enact and re-enact in intimate contexts.[37]

The healing that abuse survivors go through is not qualitatively different from the healing which all women need to do around sexuality. It would be unlikely that any woman has completely escaped the establishment of some nexus between sex and abusive power through her everyday experience of growing up as a woman.

The celebratory tone in which S/M tends to be discussed by its promoters can make it difficult to question the way in which it might be connected with the harm that abuse and oppression do to us as lesbians. Lesbians who have escaped from injurious S/M relationships are starting to arrive in battered women's shelters in the US. A correspondent in *Sojourner* describes the way in which S/M relationships can be abusive.

Sadomasochism was a part of the abuse I endured in a recent lesbian relationship ... Sadomasochism, in my experience, has nothing to do with love. It is the externalization of self-hatred poured on to another woman's body ... My experience shows me that sadomasochism's involvement of an imbalance of power leads to an inherent tendency towards abuse of another's vulnerability. The pretense of consent and free choice advocated among sadomasochists does not account for the intimidation that one person can exert in that type of relationship.[38]

This writer was in a battering relationship and did not consent

40

to S/M. Even where lesbians enter S/M with common agreement, it would be very surprising if the dynamics of the whole relationship were not affected in any way.

It is helpful to an understanding of sadomasochism to see it as a form of self-injury. This self-injury can be purely emotional or physical. In Britain the Bristol Crisis Service for Women was set up in 1986 to help self-injurers with a crisis line. Those involved on the line and as callers were mostly lesbian and had experienced sexual abuse. Self-injurers feel a compulsive urge towards cutting, of wrists, throat or other parts of the body, injury with lighted cigarettes, attempts at suicide. The compulsion can be kept at bay for months at a time but then tends to return. In S/M practice another person performs the injury but at the behest of the self-mutilator. Self-injury is a relatively new concern within the lesbian movement. American feminist media are beginning to carry news about groups for women self-injurers.[39]

While most people would consider self-injury in non-sexual forms to be undesirable and would find it unacceptable that panel discussions should take place as to whether such self-injury was positive or negative, sadomasochism is seen as being about sex and therefore beyond serious criticism. Thus we find that feminists are expected to take part in 'debates' on the merits of practices of psychological humiliation and physical mutilation which in any other context would be seen as clearly abusive.

The new lesbian sex industry already uses and will increasingly use women as sex workers in pornography and other forms of prostitution. Those who celebrate the right of individual lesbians to sexual pleasure tend to see such work as unobjectionable. The problematic forms of a male supremacist sexual system, such as sexual abuse and the use of women in prostitution, can either be ignored, or reclaimed. The libertarians who produce the theory and artifacts of the new lesbian sex industry are mostly the privileged products of the sixties revolution in women's education and opportunities in the US. They do not wish to accept that areas of their consciousness or life may be unliberated, particularly around sexuality. They criticise feminist work against male violence for portraying women as 'victims' and not understanding women's strengths. These women, successful academics and pornographers, do not see themselves as oppressed and certainly not as oppressors of other women. They want equal opportunities in sexuality as liberal feminists might demand such equal opportunities in equal pay or promotion. The sex industry, pornography and prostitution enslave women in sexual subjection. When women demand access to equal opportunities in sex they are demanding equal access to women.

The ultimate aim of these self-actualising, 'liberated' women is to have what they see as the privileges of men. This extends to the use of women in prostitution. Lesbians who consume pornography are using women in the sex industry. It should not be necessary to state this but the fact that real live women are the raw material of both erotica and pornography is often forgotten, even by anti-pornography feminists. Gloria Steinem, who wanted to establish a difference between pornography and erotica gave this definition of erotica,

> Look at any photo or film of people making love; really making love. The images may be diverse, but there is usually a sensuality and touch and warmth, an acceptance of bodies and nerve endings. There is always a spontaneous sense of people who are there because they want to be, out of shared pleasure.[40]

But both erotica and pornography require the use of women in the sex industry. They are unlikely to be 'really' making love – whatever that means – but earning a crust. They are certainly unlikely to be there out of 'shared pleasure'. The new pornbrokers argue that the new lesbian porn stars are there by 'choice' as if the choice to be a porn video star was one that any woman might make. But most lesbians would feel uncomfortable with the idea of starring in this way and should really ask themselves why they think it reasonable to expect other women to do it. Before using women in the new lesbian sex industry it is important to think about how such a woman got into the industry. Was it through poverty, homelessness, child sexual abuse, drug use, through learning at the hands of men that the only way to get praise or status was to be sexually used? Lesbians who want to use women in pornography must take responsibility for their abuse of women and for the way that they are profiting from the results of women's oppression.

The new erotica magazines carry ads for talklines which lesbians can phone to have erotic conversations with lesbian prostitutes. There are ads for striptease. Some of these ads are clearly from the male run sex industry. The magazines seem not the least fussy about their advertisers. *On Our Backs* has an article about the use of a lesbian prostitute, presumably with the purpose of overcoming women's inhibitions in this area. Marjan Sax, a journalist, visited a prostitute to report. The cost was $25 for a massage and $40 for 'extra'. Sax chose to have extra and was made uncomfortable when the prostitute undressed and felt 'confused, suddenly having a strange body all over me.'[41] Sax had expected to be serviced by a machine and was put off when the prostitute showed her humanity. Sax asks at the end of her article 'Do you kiss a prostitute when you leave?'

The creation of an objectifying lesbian sexuality will increasingly lead to the use by lesbians of other women in prostitution. Since sexuality is socially constructed it is possible to train women to objectify. It would not be possible for women to effectively objectify men since the attraction of men in heterosexuality is precisely their power and ruling class status. This is evidenced by the failure of attempts to create heterosexual women into a market for male beefcake magazines. The magazine *Playgirl* is an example. The photos of naked men standing or reclining, even in fairly dignified positions, strip the models of power along with their clothes and the magazine now resides on the gay men's shelves in sex shops. The dynamics of heterosexual desire by which both men and women eroticise women's subordination, not men's, are broken down by the objectification of men. A generalised objectification of men by women would not be possible unless women had power over men as a class. Objectification is a part of ruling class sexuality. In an egalitarian society objectification would not exist because no class or group would be seen as dispensable and inferior. It is possible for a small group of lesbians to have access to some of the male privilege that is expressed in the use of women as expendable sex toys without offering any threat to male power. Lesbians can identify with the male gaze and sexual position towards other lesbians. They become an honorary and co-opted part of the ruling class, but they will receive no privileges save a share in the degradation of other women. Their feeling of power inspired by their treatment of women is not real power in the world vis-a-vis men.

Though lesbian users may convince themselves they are more civilised and attractive as clients than men would be, a prostitution industry necessitates the abuse of women. The feminist theorist Carol Pateman describes prostitution as a temporary slavery. She explains that the client receives the woman's whole self for the period of the prostitution contract, not just the work of her hands or her mind.[42] Contemporary defenders of prostitution, including some prostitutes' collectives do argue that prostitution is a job like any other but there are ways in which it is very different. Prostitutes in Eileen McLeod's book on prostitution in Birmingham explain that they do not 'kiss' clients in order to keep something of themselves and their sexuality intact.[43] Prostitution is also not a job like any other because it depends quite specifically on the oppression of women. It can exist only because a ruling class is able to set aside a group of people as objects to service their needs. In the absence of such a ruling class sexuality and sexual privilege, poverty and exploitation, prostitution would not exist. The stigma attached to women who work in prostitution is connected with the real abuse that the use of women in prostitution entails. It is not a form of irrational prejudice that will wither away but a functional necessity. If a group of people are to be treated as less than fully human, then they must be singled out as inferior to justify their abuse.

The new lesbian sex industry has developed with considerable speed. This could be because so many prostitutes have always been lesbians and part of the lesbian community. Lesbians who wish to use other women in prostitution have a pool of women seasoned by men available to them. The notion of sexual liberation current in some areas of the lesbian community has come to mean simply the employment of sex industry practices and sex workers. It is a notion of liberation that suits the interests of male supremacy very well. The producer of the Sydney lesbian S/M magazine, *Wicked Women*, which promotes the lesbian sex industry, is a female-to-male transsexual. She has a high profile in the Sydney community and now runs a press as well. Her contribution to lesbian culture is to increase the confusion between lesbianism and prostitution. One contributor to the magazine defines what she sees as the difference between boring straightness and bentness. She describes a scene not uncommon in prostitution in which she 'was fucking the wife of a married couple whose husband watched a lesbian orgy between 6 women while he sat amused on the cistern.'[44] She proclaims trimphantly that 'those straight people were not straight.' Her client who 'gets off on the smell of plastic forced down his face by a beautiful woman' is not straight either she says. Thus both the male clients and the prostitutes become revolutionaries of the new sexuality.

Quite swiftly S/M clubs have developed in Melbourne which were ostensibly for lesbians. Heterosexual male punters were in evidence from the beginning, able to get access to the live sex acts much more cheaply than in the established sex industry. Now heterosexual S/M clubs are being set up on the same model with the same activities. Lesbianism is becoming a form of a cheap sex show for men. It is perhaps not surprising that the behaviour of the lesbian audiences at some nightspots has deteriorated to resemble that of male clients in a brothel. A columnist in the Melbourne gay paper *Brother/Sister* describes her shock at seeing this abusive behaviour.

> I went to a recent women's night . . . I noticed two very drunk women, leering at and jeering the podium dancers . . . They started grabbing at the dancers, one woman . . . actually shoved her face in one of the dancer's butts when she bent over.[45]

She goes on to describe more violent harassment happening on the dancefloor but this time from a jilted lover. She states 'We can no longer stand by and allow ourselves to do this to each other', speaks of using the police, and putting energy into 'our community, our ethics and our honour.' I would suggest that trying to sanitise a lesbian sex industry will not work. It is likely that the feminist analysis that it is an abuse of power to turn women into sex objects is right. Lesbian honour and pride will require a transformation of sexuality so that sexual practice fits into an ethical lesbian life. Whilst a sexuality of cruelty is seen as being revolutionary and having no effect on our lives, community and relationships, the abuse of other lesbians is to be expected.

The language of liberalism has been used to defend all the new developments of the lesbian sexual revolution. Consent and choice are the catch words. A model of sexuality based upon the idea of consent is a male supremacist one. In this model one person, generally male, uses the body of another who is not necessarily sexually interested and possibly generally reluctant or distressed, as a sex aid. It is a dominant/submissive and active/passive model. It is not mutual. It is not about the sexual involvement of both parties. It bespeaks not equality, but the absence of it. Consent is a tool for negotiating inequality in heterosexual relations. Women are expected to have their bodies used but the idea of consent manages to make this use and abuse seem fair and justified. In certain situations where this use might seem particularly and obviously unwelcome, such as street rape, women are given a limited right to object, but in general the idea of consent allows the sexual use and abuse of women to remain invisible as harm or a contravention of human rights. In this liberal approach to sex it is vulgar to ask political questions such as how the consent and choice are constructed. Women's consent, the kind that can cause them to undergo furiously resented sexual intercourse in marriage, or just to accept that they should be used as a masturbation aid, is constructed by the pressures exerted upon women throughout their lives. Such pressures include economic dependency, sexual abuse, battering, and a cultural barrage of propaganda about what women are good for. They can induce a profound lack of self-determination. Lesbians are women too. That any lesbian should think consent a useful concept when it emerges from the circumstances of women's oppression and relates to the material inequality of women is a surprise.

The main foundation of the argument that S/M is a legitimate sexual practice lies in the idea that it is consensual. Sadomasochists have picked up the idea of consent as an important one in liberal male supremacist understandings of sexuality. The proponents of sadomasochism adhere to a rigidly subject/object, active/passive mode of interaction which lends itself to a consent approach in a similar way to traditional male dominant hetero-sexual intercourse. Bet Power, director of SHELIX, the Western New England Woman-to-Woman S/M Support Group uses the language of choice and sexual preference in reply to a letter in the Boston feminist newspaper from anti-violence campaigners which called S/M a 'clear enactment of unequal power over one individual by another.'[46]

> Desire/sexual preference is not violence ... Some feminist women have for so long solely focused on the issue of violence against women that they can now only see the richness of life through the dim and unfocused lens of victimization rather than in the light of freedom, personal power, and personal choice. What a sad state of affairs when some women can no longer even grasp the concept of free choice, consent, and self-responsibility.
>
> The truth is that S/M women and men mutually consent to our preferred sexual activities and thoroughly enjoy and need the mutual love, empowerment, and joy we find in our sexual preference.[47]

Ian Young, a gay male sadomasochist, makes a similar appeal to consent to prove the legitimacy of his sexual practice.

> I think, first of all, one has to make the absolutely essential point – and then make it over and over again for those who for one reason or another didn't grasp it the first time – that S&M is by its nature consensual. We are talking about mutually agreed upon activities ... People don't realize, or they forget, that in S&M, it's often the submissive partner who in effect controls and structures the scene.[48]

Young then goes on to apparently contradict himself. Some-times, he says, the activities may not be mutually agreed upon but decided upon by the S who will only find out later if the M agreed.

On the question of consent, there is this further point: the M may say he wants to go only so far. In fact, he wants his limits pushed a little further. A good S – that is to say, an empathetic and perceptive S – will pick up on how much further the M can in fact be taken without frightening him or freaking him out . . . Still, there's an underlying agreement, an unspoken understanding of what will have been consented to after the scene is over.[49]

This problem, that in S/M consent once given at the beginning of a scene is in effect considered irrevocable, does seem to parallel the situation of women in marriage or relationship rape who are considered to have given consent to sexual intercourse in perpetuity by virtue of their marriage or implied marriage contract. But here the principle is justified on the grounds of the sexual pleasure of the masochist.

But their use of consent as a justification does not necessarily serve them well in the courts. In February 1992 the idea of consent in relation to S/M became a cause célèbre because of the failure of the appeal in the Operation Spanner case in the UK. In this case a group of male homosexual sadomasochists who had 'willingly and enthusiastically participated in the commission of acts of violence' appealed against prison sentences for assault and aiding and abetting assault. The consent of the victims was the ground for the appeal. It was held that consent was no defence where actual bodily harm was inflicted for no good reason, that sexual pleasure was not a good reason, and where 'hurt or injury calculated to interfere with the health or comfort of the other party' was inflicted and the injuries were neither 'transient nor trifling'. The 'assaults' consisted of brandings, genital torture with pins, spiked gloves and stinging nettles, including nailing one penis to a bench, canings and strappings.[50]

Gay activists in the UK have campaigned against the convictions on the grounds that consensual sexual behaviour should not be a criminal offence. It is significant that the cases of sadomasochism in which the police have sought prosecutions involve homosexual men or prostitutes rather than heterosexual men practising upon women. There can be little doubt that the police could choose to pursue similar cases on similar evidence, in this case videos made of the men's activities, if they wished. In fact the prosecutions were discriminatory. In the case of heterosexual sadomasochism it is likely that the police could find numerous cases where consent was much more dubious than in the Spanner case, where the women victims were unwilling participants constrained to take part simply for the gratification of their male partners. It was stated at the appeal hearing that 'the function of the court is to mark its disapproval of these activities by imposing short terms of immediate imprisonment.' It rather looks as if such official disapproval only exists where men are the victims of sadomasochism, and where the accepted rules of sexual engagement are contravened. It seems that the consent of women to just about anything can be presumed or at least considered even in circumstances which would suggest a great deal of force whereas the consent of gay male sadomasochists will be considered immaterial even where consent on all sides is loudly trumpeted. There are clearly different rules in operation here.

The desire of the court to set up moral regulations may well have been hypocritical and misplaced but some limits on the indulgence of a masochism which can endanger life might be necessary. The Operation Spanner case demonstrates one of the problems inherent in the notion of consent as employed by sadomasochists. In one of the assaults considered at the appeal a victim was branded twice, once above the penis and once on the inner thigh. It is stated that 'There was some doubt about whether the victim consented to the second branding.'[51] The victim was in bondage and if he protested his protest was unheard or ignored. It may have been deliberately ignored. Sadomasochist literature, even the little theoretical literature which exists, suggests that despite the lauding of consent it has little importance in practice save to make its transgression exciting either for the masochist, the sadist or both.

Amongst lesbians who engage in S/M the problem of sexual assault and non-consensual abuse in general is now beginning to emerge. It is predictable that it would do so considering that consent is such a problematic notion as the basis for any sexual practice. One practitioner is quoted in a Sydney S/M magazine as saying 'If my tops were always consensual with me I'd be bored out of my mind.' There is now apparently a new phrase current among practitioners to cover the principle of consent once given being irrevocable. It is 'consensual non-consensuality', described as 'you consent to BE there – you consent to letting them do whatever they want to you. It's still your initial decision.'[52] As in the Ian Young example above consent now becomes something you can only judge the next day when you wake up, according to whether you feel uncomfortable.

> Many times in SM what turns us on or gets us hot is something we have NOT given our consent to, WOULD not if we were asked, but they do it anyway. If you do things that both partners feel OK about the next day, it's a good thing. If they're feeling fucked with, it's NOT OK.[53]

This is a concept that the judicial process would have trouble understanding and does create a problem for sadomasochists who do consider the next day that they have been seriously assaulted. The S might well feel he or she had been acting in good faith and according to the rules.

The concept of consent as used in S/M creates some problems for the feminist cause of seeking to get women's 'No's' taken seriously. The rebel sadomasochists who believe in such concepts as consensual non-consensuality show a not surprising anti-feminist lack of sympathy with women who do get badly hurt in S/M practice. Alix says that 'anybody who is stupid enough to run off with someone they don't even know, and let them chain them down and do God-knows-what-all, deserves whatever they get. It's evolution in action.'[54] A feminist perspective has always asserted that women do not deserve abuse however they behave, and that the responsibility for abuse lies with the abuser. Alix does not agree: 'If you've got the brains God gave a turnip, you can use your common sense and discrimination to keep yourself out of those really bad situations.' Presently the problem of violence in the S/M community is becoming so serious that the best known US proponent of S/M, sex educator Pat Califia, is writing about the need for the S/M community to develop a code of ethics.[55] She also asserts that lesbian S/M practitioners should be prepared to call the police to deal with persistent violence that cannot be stopped by any other means. In such a situation the problems deliberately created by sadomasochists for sexual kicks could provide difficulties in the way of their achieving justice in the courts.

The use of the idea of consent by sadomasochists may throw the problems associated with this concept into particularly sharp relief. What it also suggests is the importance of the idea of consent to the construction of sexual desire. In a male supremacist culture where sex is constructed from the eroticisation of the inequality between men and women, traditional heterosexual sex is, as MacKinnon puts it, 'aggressive intrusion on those with less power.'[56] Where sex is so constructed the idea of consent serves to smooth over the real barbarity that can take place in sexual practice. Catharine MacKinnon points out that though malestream thought on sexuality tends to see the woman's right to withhold consent as affording the woman a power equal to that which a man gains from his custom of sexual initiation, there is no equality in these practices. Where sex is constructed to be eroticised inequality, the idea of consent can be an incitement, both to men's violence and to sadomasochism. The idea of consent constructs a taboo to be broken. The transgression of consent becomes an exciting possibility. Sadomasochism exists because of the construction of male supremacist sexuality around consent. It then uses the same idea to justify its existence.

Now that the sexual revolution has come to lesbians we have all the problems associated with the practice of eroticised inequality, heterosexual desire, in our community. A pool of women is readily available to provide prostitution services to other lesbians. The results of women's oppression, the damage done by sexual abuse, by the use of women in the sex industry, by the hatred of lesbians has provided the raw material, the lesbians who will invent and model in the pornography, get beaten at S/M parties, perform live sex acts. Those who want 'equal opportunities' in sexuality hope that a code of ethics will prettify this scene. I suggest that the strong and healthy survival of our community requires the construction of a quite different sexuality, one based upon love of women and lesbians, a sexuality that will support our lesbian pride.

The lesbian sexual revolution has transformed the culture

and politics of lesbians already. Though the number of lesbians involved actually in using women in prostitution or in S/M practice may be limited, the promotion of erotica by feminist and lesbian presses seems to be having a general effect. Some of those lesbians who would find live lesbian sex acts in clubs distinctly tacky are prepared to prepare little entertainments for parties which include the reading and even enactment of erotica. Sex as performance, sex in public, sex for the titillation of an audience is the stuff of the sex industry. It is women's historic role. It isn't revolution. But some lesbians presently, even some who have strong connections with feminism, do see the representation and living out of lesbianism simply as sex, sex of any kind, as precisely the source of lesbian power. This is a mistake.

The American sex therapist, JoAnn Loulan, who has recently taken to promoting roleplaying to lesbians because it offers sexual thrills, writes, 'Our female power has a history of being based in sex.'[57] This is not a feminist insight. It would be more accurate to say that historically women have been given few choices if they wished to subsist other than selling themselves sexually whilst men have told them that this made them powerful. Feminist theory over the last 150 years has tended to see men as falsely categorising women as sex, and giving them no other role in order that they may use women sexually at their pleasure. Patriarchal ideology has traditionally told women that the fact that men desired them made them powerful despite their social disadvantages. Feminists have disagreed.

Christabel Pankhurst in 1913 wrote that men have propounded the doctrine that woman 'is sex and beyond that nothing.'[58] Another British pre-First World War feminist Cicely Hamilton charged men with having emphasised only the sex faculty in woman in order to gratify their desire. Sex 'assumed undue and exaggerated proportions' because for generations sex furnished woman 'with the means of her livelihood.'[59] Monique Wittig is a contemporary lesbian theorist who has explained how confining women to 'the category of sex' has contributed to the oppression of women. Wittig shows how women have been made into 'the sex', and are also 'sex itself'. Only women have a sex because men are the norm and do not have one. Women are the sex that is sex.

The category of sex is the product of heterosexual society that turns half of the population into sexual beings, for sex is a category which women cannot be outside of. Wherever they are, whatever they do (including working in the public sector), they are seen (and made) sexually available to men, and they, breasts, buttocks, costume, must be visible. They must wear their yellow star, their constant smile, day and night. One might consider that every woman, married or not, has a period of forced sexual service, a sexual service which we may compare to the military one, and which can vary between a day, a year, or twenty years or more. Some lesbians and nuns escape, but they are very few . . . [60]

Wittig explains that though women are 'very visible as sexual beings', as 'social beings' they are totally invisible. Lesbians who are accepting that their lives, identities, appearance and behaviour should be based upon sex and claim that this is revolutionary are misguided. They are the lesbians who do not escape the relegation of women simply to a sexual function. They are being religiously faithful to the precepts of male supremacy. Lesbianism has been seen as only sexual practice by male pornography and sexology. It is feminists who have given it another definition and made of lesbianism something more than a sexual deviation. The patriarchs are likely to experience nary a shudder at the threat to their power implicit in lesbians constructing themselves into a sort of home-made sex industry and imitating the forms of men's pornography. The heteropatriarchy will not crumble.

The lesbian sex industry represents a grand diversion of lesbian energies and for that reason alone it is necessary for lesbians to rethink the connection between sex and revolution. But the need to rethink sexuality stems from the need to change the whole way sex is constructed under male supremacy if women and lesbians are to have any genuine kind of liberation. Sex under male supremacy has been constructed to be the eroticised subordination of women and dominance of men, what I call heterosexual desire. The results of this construction of sexuality include the rape and murder of women and children and the restriction of where women may walk and what they may wear and even what areas of employment they may enter. One result is the abuse of women in the sex industry. The eroticising of women's subordination has been intended by the sexologists to make women submit to men not just in the bedroom but in all areas of their relationships with men. The eroticised inequality that is sex under male supremacy infuses our environment to such an extent that it can be difficult to see. It crucially informs the way that men relate to women in all those areas where men and women have contact. Eroticised inequality is fundamental to male supremacy and is, as I state in *Anticlimax*, 'the grease that oils the engine of male supremacy', that which makes it rewarding for men, and to some extent for women, and exciting.[61] The new lesbian sex industry institutionalises and commodifies the eroticised subordination of women. It is being sold back to us as our 'pleasure' and as revolution too.

1. See my books: (1985). *The Spinster and Her Enemies: Feminism and Sexuality 1880–1930*. London: Pandora. (1990). *Anticlimax. A Feminist Perspective on the Sexual Revolution*. London: The Women's Press. (1991). New York: New York University Press.

2. I use the term 'lesbianandgay' to describe those theorists who apparently make no distinction between lesbians and gay men in their theory. They avoid feminist insights about the different sex class positions of women and men and homogenise experience to create a universal gay theory in which lesbian specificity disappears. This approach is most generally taken by postmodernist scholars, some of whose work is considered in my chapter 'Return to Gender'.

3. For a discussion of sexual liberalism see the excellent collection: Leidholdt, Dorchen and Raymond, Janice G. (Eds.) (1990). *The Sexual Liberals and the Attack on Feminism*. Oxford and New York: Pergamon Press (now TCP).

4. For a discussion of male sexual violence as social control see: Brownmiller, Susan (1975). *Against Our Will: Men, Women and Rape*. London: Secker and Warburg, and Coveney, Lal *et al* (Eds.) (1984). *The Sexuality Papers*. London: Hutchinson. See the Introduction.

5. On heterosexuality as an institution see: Rich, Adrienne (1984). 'Compulsory Heterosexuality and Lesbian Existence.' In Snitow, Ann *et al* (Eds.). *Desire: The Politics of Sexuality*. London: Virago. (1983). Published as *Powers of Desire*. New York: Monthly Review Press. Wittig, Monique (1992). *The Straight Mind and Other Essays*. Boston: Beacon Press. Chapter 6 in my book.

(1990). *Anticlimax. A Feminist Perspective on the Sexual Revolution.*
London: The Women's Press.

For a good refutation of the idea of sexual preference see: Kitzinger, Celia
(1987). *The Social Construction of Lesbianism.* London: Sage Publications.

6. For a discussion of the 1967 Act see Weeks, Jeffrey (1977). *Coming Out.*
London: Quartet.

7. MacKinnon, Catharine (1987). *Feminism Unmodified.* Cambridge, MA:
Harvard University Press, p. 93.

8. Ibid. p. 101.

9. For a feminist critique of the concept of consent see Pateman, Carol (1988).
The Sexual Contract. Cambridge: Polity. (1988). Palo Alto, California.
Stanford University Press and Pateman, Carol (1989). Chapter on Women and
Consent. In *The Disorder of Women.* Cambridge: Polity. Also Hawthorne,
Susan (1991b). 'What do Lesbians Want? Towards a Feminist Sexual Ethics.'
Journal of Australian Lesbian Feminist Studies. Vol. 1. No. 2.

10. See my book (1985). *The Spinster and Her Enemies.* London: Pandora.

11. Hegeler, Inge and Stan (1963). *An ABZ of Love.* London: New English
Library. p. 252.

12. For a discussion of the impact of therapy language and practice on
feminism see: Kitzinger, Celia and Perkins, Rachel (1993). *Changing Our
Minds: Lesbianism, Feminism and Psychology.* London: Onlywomen Press.

13. Jeffreys, Sheila (1985). *The Spinster and Her Enemies. Feminism and
Sexuality 1880–1930.* London: Pandora. p. 182.

14. Quoted in (1990). *Anticlimax.* pp. 29–30.

15. See (1990). *Anticlimax.* Chapter 6 on Heterosexual Desire.

16. For the importance of sadomasochism in the eighties in heterosexual
practice see: Ehrenreich, Barbara *et al* (1987). *Re-Making Love: The
Feminization of Sex.* London: Fontana/Collins. (1986) New York: Doubleday.
For a critique of sadomasochism in lesbian practice see: Linden, Robin Ruth
et al (Eds.) (1982). *Against Sadomasochism.* Palo Alto, California: Frog in the
Well Press.

17. Steinem, Gloria (1980). 'Erotica and Pornography: A Clear and Present
Difference.' In Lederer, Laura (Ed.). *Take Back the Night.* New York: Quill.
p. 37.

18. Dworkin, Andrea (1981). *Pornography: Men Possessing Women.* New
York: Perigee. pp. 9–10.

19. Califia, Pat (1989). *Macho Sluts.* Boston: Alyson Publications.
Introduction p. 13.

20. Smith, Barbara (1988). 'Sappho was a Right-off Woman.' In Chester, Gail
and Dickey, Julienne (Eds.). *Feminism and Censorship.* London: Prism.
pp. 183–184.

21. MacKinnon, Catharine (1984). 'Not a Moral Issue.' *Yale Law and Policy Review*. Vol. 11, No. 2. p. 343.

22. Hayman, Amanda (1989). 'The Flame.' In Sheba Collective (Eds.). *Serious Pleasure*. London: Sheba. p. 163.

23. *On Our Backs* (1986). p. 2. Summer.

24. *Bad Attitude* (1985). p. 19. Winter.

25. Bright, Susie (1986). *On Our Backs*. p. 6. Winter.

26. Nestle, Joan (1988). *A Restricted Country*. London: Sheba. p. 142.

27. Bell, A. P. and Weinberg, M (1978). *Homosexualities: A Study in Diversity among Men and Women*. New York: Simon and Schuster. p. 109.

28. Bodacious Bitch (1986). 'Letter from a Mistress to her Pet.' *On Our Backs*. p. 8. Summer.

29. Susan M. (1986). 'The Phoenix Chair.' *On Our Backs*. p. 49. Summer.

30. O'Sullivan, Sue (1990). 'An Interview with Cindy Patton. Mappings: Lesbians, AIDS and Sexuality.' *Feminist Review* No. 34. p. 125. Spring.

31. Ibid. pp. 125–126.

32. Ibid. p. 126.

33. Ibid. p. 127.

34. For suggestions to lesbians about how to have fantasies about children see the Sydney lesbian S/M magazine *Wicked Women*. Vol. 2. No. 4. 1992.

35. Juicy Lucy (1982) 'If I Ask You to Tie Me Up, Will You Still Want to Love Me.' Samois (Eds.). *Coming to Power*. Boston: Alyson Publications. p. 30.

36. Penelope, Julia (1987). 'The Illusion of Control: Sadomasochism and the Sexual Metaphors of Childhood.' *Lesbian Ethics*. Venice, California. Vol. 2. No. 3. p. 89.

37. Ibid. p. 92.

38. *Sojourner* (1988). p. 5. June.

39. A letter in *Sojourner*, May 1988 calls for a group for women self-injurers.

40. Steinem, Gloria (1980). In Lederer, Laura (Ed.). *Take Back the Night*. New York: Quill. p. 37.

41. *On Our Backs* (1986). pp. 10–11. Fall.

42. See Pateman, Carol (1988). Chapter 7.

43. McLeod, Eileen (1982). *Women Working: Prostitution Now*. London: Croom Helm.

44. *Wicked Women* (1992). Vol 2. No. 4. p. 16. Sydney.

45. *Brother/Sister* (1992). 27 November. p. 20. Melbourne.

46. *Sojourner* (1988). p. 3. March.

47. *Sojourner* (1988). p. 7. May.

48. Young, Ian (1978). 'Forum on Sadomasochism.' In Jay, Karla and Young, Allen (Eds.). *Lavender Culture*. New York: Harcourt Brace Jovanovitch. p. 97.

49. Ibid. p. 98.

50. *The Weekly Law Reports* (1992). 27 March.

51. Ibid. p. 445.

52. *Wicked Women* (1992). Vol. 2. No. 4. p. 30. Sydney.

53. Ibid.

54. Ibid. p. 31.

55. Califia's article appears in the same issue of *Wicked Women*.

56. MacKinnon, Catharine (1989). *Towards a Feminist Theory of the State.* Cambridge, MA: Harvard. p. 127.

57. Loulan, JoAnn (1990). *The Lesbian Erotic Dance.* San Francisco: Spinsters. p. 21.

58. Christabel Pankhurst quoted in my book (1985) *The Spinster and Her Enemies.* p. 47.

59. Cicely Hamilton quoted in *The Spinster and Her Enemies* p. 47.

60. Wittig, Monique (1992). *The Straight Mind and Other Essays.* Boston: Beacon Press. p. 7.

61. Jeffreys, Sheila (1990). *Anticlimax.* p. 251.

Chapter 3

LESBIAN SEX THERAPY

Sex therapists are part of the growing lesbian sex industry in the US. The new libertarian lesbian sex therapists are involved in constructing lesbian sex to resemble the heterosexual version as nearly as possible. They are recycling the old shibboleths of male supremacist ideology to lesbians. They are telling lesbians that they are sexually deficient, that they are erotophobic, heterophobic and generally just not very good at sex, not compared with gay men anyway. Such lesbian sex therapists are involved in the reconstruction of lesbian sex by teaching lesbians how to develop what I call 'heterosexual' desire, that is desire which eroticises inequality.

The lesbian sex brokers try to give the impression that they are performing a vital and selfless service to the backward lesbian community. They see themselves as knights in shining armour, the bearers of a 'sexual revolution' to lesbians. But this lesbian 'sexual revolution' is no more positively linked with freedom for lesbians than the heterosexual revolution was with freedom for heterosexual women. The values and ideology of both are very similar. This should not be surprising. The lesbian sex therapists were trained in institutes run by men who trained heterosexual sex therapists to inculcate the values of sexology, male dominance and female submission, in reluctant heterosexual women. The lesbian sexual revolution is not coming from the separate space that lesbian feminists have, since the early seventies, tried to create. It is permeated with old-fashioned patriarchal woman-hating values.

It could be argued that the whole academic world is male

supremacist in its values and that institutes for the study of human sexuality and the training of sex therapists are no more hostile grounds for a lesbian to be trained in than, say, a history department. But if it is true, as I argue in my book *Anticlimax*, that sexual intercourse is the act on which all the social relations of male supremacy are founded and that the management and manipulation of that act play an important part in maintaining female subordination in and out of the home, then a sex institute becomes a slightly more worrying place than a history depart-ment for a lesbian to be trained in. The values of the male political science of sexology could simply be rejected by the aware lesbian trainee, but she would not earn her living that way. To practice sex therapy at all requires that the practitioners have accepted some basic sexological values and indeed you find their work littered with them.

SEXUAL LIBERALISM

Common to lesbian sex therapy practitioners is the notion that sex should not be subjected to political analysis. Sexual practice is seen as something entirely individual and private which has no relevance to the world outside the bedroom. We can see why this notion is vital to male supremacist sexology. Sex as it is constructed presently is in men's interests and any questioning is dangerous to their interests. This idea of the political neutrality of sexual practice is carried over into lesbian sexology. Lesbian and gay theorists who see themselves as progressive social con-structionists do not usually protect the present construction of sex by saying that it is 'natural', though this often seems to be the implication, but they are prepared to revert to an equally effective defence, i.e. that sex is 'private'. Lesbians who think that sex deserves as much rigorous feminist scrutiny as any other area of human activity can then be seen as the enemies of sex and even perhaps of lesbian liberation itself.

JoAnn Loulan is a lesbian sex therapist who tries to take a 'morally neutral' position. She introduces her 'What we do in bed' chapter in *Lesbian Sex* by stating:

Every possible sexual activity is judged by someone as: not

really sex, disgusting, insipid, unsanitary, wrong, male-identified, abnormal, repulsive, silly, too violent, too tame, too aggressive, too passive, too much like heterosexual sex, etc. Some people think that lesbians have to have sex a particular way to be lesbians. Lesbian sex is *anything* two lesbians do together. Monitoring our own and other's sexual behaviour is in no one's interest but our oppressors.[1]

'Monitoring' sounds like the activity of conservative moral majority pressure groups who might like to legally proscribe various sexual activities and lock up offenders. This is very different from feminist political analysis but Loulan is including such analysis here as part of the oppression of women. This deliberate confusion of feminist critique with right-wing censorship serves to discourage lesbians from engaging in political discussion of sexual practice. What lesbian would want to be called an oppressor of women?

Some lesbian therapists are prepared to go to considerable lengths to overcome the intrusion of a feminist political analysis into their work. Susan Hamadock in describing the problems encountered by lesbian therapists in dealing with sexuality mentions the obstacle feminism might pose to their work. 'For some, unresolved conflict between our radical feminist politics and particular forms of sexual expression such as S&M contribute to our reluctance to bring sexuality into our work as therapists.'[2] Hamadock wanted to develop the 'desirable qualities helpful to clients' which she identified as 'warmth, interest, objectivity, and acceptance.' To achieve this she took part in an 'invaluable training process' known as Sexual Attitude Reassessment which is 'an explicit multi-media presentation depicting all aspects of human sexual behaviour.'[3] The SAR seems to have relieved Hamadock of any uncomfortable remnants of feminist politics in the area of sexuality. It is convenient that conventional male supremacist sexology provides such a tool for therapists troubled by feminism.

But not all lesbian therapists aspire to moral relativism. Other lesbian sex therapists feel perfectly free to state their prejudices and, presumably, enforce them on their clients. Margaret Nicholls, who describes herself as a feminist, is proud to tell us that she repudiates what she sees as an incorrect feminist sexual practice.

> I repudiate politically correct lesbian lovemaking... Two women lie side by side (tops or bottoms are strictly forbidden – lesbians must be non-hierarchical); they touch each other gently and sweetly all over their bodies for several hours.[4]

It might be difficult at first sight to see what is so very wrong with this picture. But it does not fit with Nicholls' political agenda. It is not true that anything goes for lesbian sex therapists. They have their prejudices, often against what they identify as misguided feminism.

A very illuminating new book by Celia Kitzinger and Rachel Perkins called *Changing Our Minds: Lesbianism, Feminism and Psychology* examines the ways in which the ideas and practices of a burgeoning therapy industry have affected the language and concept of feminist thought to the detriment of developing political analysis. Therapists have brought moral relativism, they say, through an embargo in the therapy community on the words 'should' and 'ought' and 'right' and 'wrong' and on the making of moral judgements. Kitzinger and Perkins conducted an interview with JoAnn Loulan and another lesbian sex therapist from the US, Marny Hall, for the journal *Feminism and Psychology*. Marny Hall states 'But right and wrong is a patriarchal dualism... It's heaven and hell, it's sin and redemption' and '... eventually I think we trash each other because we think something's wrong.' Celia Kitzinger responds that the ability to speak of right and wrong is necessary:

> ... any attempt to build concepts of right and wrong, a lesbian ethics. That's all eroded by a psychological framework which says, 'whatever turns you on is okay', or 'different strokes for different folks'. Within a psychological framework it becomes virtually impossible to talk of right or wrong without your morality being described as some sort of psychological hangup.[5]

Some lesbian sex therapists promote eroticised inequality or what I call heterosexual desire. They have accepted wholesale the sexological principle that equality cannot be sexy. They support sadomasochism in lesbian sex magazines and in learned journals, providing an important pseudo-scientific justification for the practice. Such therapists tell women that they are prudes and unadventurous for objecting to any sexual practice whatsoever. They teach lesbian couples how to do S/M so that they can inject new eroticism into their relationships. Carolyn Stack explains the role of the therapist in *Bad Attitude*. She says that the problems with which lesbians come to a therapist are changing. The common problem used to be that one partner wanted sex more than the other. Now it was likely to be that one wanted to do S/M and the other didn't. She does not tell us how she helps the resolution of such a problem. We can surmise from what we know of sex therapy and from the obviously positive attitude she has to S/M in the article that she throws her authority behind the S/M lesbian rather than her reluctant partner.[6]

Stack advises us to see fetishism, pornography, sadomasochism and water sports as solutions for the dire condition of erotophobia. Erotophobia consists of any feelings of discomfort with these activities. Erotophobia is now coming into use as a general term to describe a woman's disinclination to engage in any form of sexual practice. Feminist political objections would qualify as erotophobia. Male sexologists have traditionally used the concepts of 'frigidity' or 'inhibition' for the same purpose in respect of heterosexual women, of undermining opposition to unwanted sexual practice.

Margaret Nicholls teaches sadomasochism to revive sexual activity in long-term relationships. She calls this being a sexual enhancer, 'it is critical that as therapists we play a role helping gay women renew and revive flagging sexuality.'[7] She describes the forms the enhancement might take.

> Written or visual erotica can help many couples enhance their sex lives . . . some couples will want to develop and encourage

fetishes; the playful use of leather, rubber, articles of clothing. Others will find it exciting to experiment with less usual, kinky techniques such as S/M, bondage, use of urine, and so on.[8]

She does not consider any possible contra-indications such as a client's history of sexual abuse, the possible existence of violence and coercion in the relationship, the impact of sexual practice on the dynamics of the relationship or the importance of safe sex and the avoidance of serious physical injury. She approaches sexual practice in a traditional sexological way, as if it exists in a timeless vacuum of harmless fun which has nothing to do with the rest of the practitioners' lives. Nicholls sees sadomasochism as so positive that even those who criticise it will benefit in the long run from its adoption within the lesbian community. It will be good for us all.

> ... it may represent a freeing of our sexuality, an attempt to open up, expand, and embroider our sexual technique and erotic potential, and as such, it may be just what we need right now. Even those lesbians for whom S/M and its variants hold no interest may eventually benefit from the sexual openness that this trend in our community may portend.[9]

Nicholls also advises the resumption of other dominant/submissive components of heterosexual practice to overcome the problem of flagging sexuality. Lesbians were 'less likely to pressure a reluctant partner to have sex ... compared to men' and were likely to see sexual pressure as 'male behaviour and thus assaultive and abusive.'[10] She suggests that 'contrary to our feminist beliefs, perhaps a little pressure is good for a relationship.' Thus Nicholls challenges the important feminist principle that 'Yes means yes, and no means no'. She also suggests that to be sexually healthy, lesbians needed to 'fight' with each other in a relationship more often. This would alleviate the problem of associating sex and love too closely. She explains that she uses 'lack of fighting in a lesbian relationship as a diagnostic clue to detect low-level sexuality when the partners have not directly told me of this problem, and I am almost never wrong.'[11] Battering, she seems to be suggesting, could be good for sex.

The ability of lesbians to be intimate with each other presented another difficulty for lesbian sexual frequency. It 'may hurt sexual desire' because sexual desire requires a 'barrier', 'some kind of tension, a taboo, a difference of some sort, a power discrepancy, romance, the excitement of newness or the thrill of the chase – some form of disequilibrium.'[12] Nicholls is giving a good description of heterosexual desire. Heterosexual desire is based upon eroticising otherness, in fact power difference. Lesbians have the difficulty that they are not members of different sex classes and the mechanics of domination and submission are not built into their relationships. Lesbians can therefore experience 'the softening or disappearance of individual differences' which American lesbian therapists have classified as a treatable relationship problem called 'fusion or merging'.

Instead of celebrating what distinguishes lesbians from the heterorelational world, of being proud of our ability to form close bonds, Nicholls criticises lesbians for falling short of the power dynamics of patriarchal culture. The cure for too great an intimacy is to 'introduce other types of barriers/tension/difference into our relationships.'[13] This could be done 'through the use of sex toys and props, through costume, through S/M (which maximises differences between partners), by developing sexual rituals with our partners, by introducing tricking into our relationships.' Lesbians, then should seek to reintroduce the power differences of heterosexuality into their relationships. These ideas seem to have become the conventional wisdom already within the lesbian community. Lillian Faderman in her book *Odd Girls and Twilight Lovers* states as fact that 'sexual desire requires some kind of "barrier".'[14] This shows the power of sex therapy to create lesbian ideas about sex.

Not surprisingly Nicholls is enthusiastic about butch/femme roleplaying as well since this would also offer the potential of eroticised power difference. JoAnn Loulan, who is the most popular lesbian sex therapist in the US embraces lesbian roleplaying in her latest book *The Lesbian Erotic Dance*. She thanks other lesbians for helping her to 'understand that I truly was a femme, and proud of it.'[15] Loulan asserts roleplaying as central to if not the only dynamic of lesbian sexuality. She criticises feminists for having analysed roleplaying politically and says that if lesbians say they do not see themselves as butch or femme in some way then they are simply in denial and not honest with themselves. We will return to her ideas on roleplaying in a later chapter.

SEXUAL NEED

Another concept generally accepted by lesbian therapists is that of sexual 'need'. Male sexologists who understand that sex is the mechanism through which men practice their dominance and women have their subordination reinforced are bound to see sexual activity as vital to human health. For the past hundred years sexologists have forecast terrible ills for women who did not engage in sex with men. Now lesbian sex therapists are giving us similar messages. In a section on menopausal women experiencing pain during sexual activity, Pat Califia states 'it's important to keep active sexually. A daily orgasm, either with a partner or with masturbation, will help keep the pelvic muscles in tone and the vagina healthy.'[16] 'Needs' are of course socially constructed. Sex is not a biological need like food or water. Presently sexual 'needs' are being constructed for lesbians by lesbian sex therapists.

The lesbian sex therapist Carolyn Stack explains in *Bad Attitude* what she sees as a tragic state of affairs for lesbians.

Statistics tell us that lesbians as a group have sex less often than gay men, straight men or straight women. It is common for lesbian couples to be together for years without sexual contact or with very infrequent sexual contact. A commonly held belief in our community is that sex, in any relationship, inevitably dies with the passing of the initial erotic bloom. Individual lesbians may spend years without partners and without sex.[17]

For Stack absence of sex is a self evident problem which needs therapy. It may not be a problem for the lesbians concerned until they meet the coercion of the lesbian sex industry. The absence of sex is diagnosed as 'erotic atrophy' by Stack which certainly doesn't sound very nice and no self-respecting lesbian would want to have it.

It is interesting that lesbians have become the new resisting constituency of women for sexology. For the last century it is the lack of enthusiasm shown by heterosexual women towards sexual activity and especially sexual intercourse with men that has preoccupied the sexologists and sex advice writers in general. Now it seems that lesbians share with heterosexual women a disinclination to place a sufficiently high importance on sex in their relationships. This should surely give feminists pause. Why should we assume that women are always the problem and that we must, heterosexual or lesbian, be retrained? It could be that we should be reflecting on sexuality in its entirety, questioning the notion of sexual 'needs' that always seems to find women deficient, and trying to understand sexual activity politically.

OBJECTIFICATION

Another fundamental concept of male supremacist as well as lesbian sex therapy is that of objectification. Feminists have long criticised men's pornography because it objectifies women, i.e. turns women into objects for men to consume. Men are taught that women are simply objects on whom they can act out their fantasies. Men can objectify women because women are the subordinate class and exist in the conditions of subordination which render them the victims of pornography and prostitution, rape and sexual abuse. In the act of objectification members of the oppressor class are able to remove the elements of common humanity which might enable them to identify with their victim. Such is the process involved in war when recruits are trained to objectify their enemy so that they can kill them, a process used for the war in Vietnam. Male sexuality is organised around objectification. Objectifying sexual desire exists in the head and the imagination. Men fantasise what they would like to do and who to and can go out looking for a suitable object.

The new lesbian sex industry and lesbian sex therapists have undertaken the task of constructing objectifying sex for lesbians. Lesbians are to have fantasies and pornography and to act out their fantasies on their lovers. Lesbians now must have objects too and know what they want to do to them. Pat Califia's book, *Sapphistry*, best exemplifies this model. Her book starts with a chapter on 'The Erotic Imagination' and is composed of selected extracts from the sexual fantasies of lesbians. She states: 'A sexual experience is produced by interactions between our fantasies, our emotional reactions and physical sensation.'[18] This is not necessarily true of sexuality, but only of objectifying sexuality. Lesbian sexuality can derive from a passionate emotional and physical interaction with another woman in which conscious fantasy and planning of sexual scenarios does not take place. In such sexual interaction lesbians might learn from and with each other about sex by exploring each others' bodies. This is a different model of sexuality. Califia is the leading US proponent of sadomasochism and objectifying sexuality is of course fundamental to that practice. Sadomasochists can relate to either gender, Califia makes plain, because all that matters is the scenario to be acted out. Animals can also be used, and she has a section on animals in the book.

Loulan is positive about objectification too. About fantasies she writes: 'Instead of rejecting fantasy because you feel it's wrong, try embracing it as a gift that enhances your sex life.'[19] She tells lesbians that it is a lesbian's right to fantasise that she is making love with someone else while she is with her lover. She says: 'Whether or not you tell your partner is up to you . . . Whichever way you go, remember that you are entitled to a secret fantasy life.'[20] Califia instructs the partner of the fantasising lesbian thus: 'if your partner confesses to indulging in erotic fantasies when she is with you, you may feel flattered instead of jealous.'[21] These lesbian sex therapists are very much in favour of objectification, a form of sexuality which is the basis of sexual abuse and exploitation.

One change these lesbian sex therapists want to see in lesbian behaviour is a cutting of the link lesbians tend to make between sex and emotion. Carolyn Stack explains:

> . . . I believe that it's important for women to learn to disentangle their emotional lives from their sexuality more than we characteristically do . . . The struggle for sexual liberation

in our community, evidenced by the recent publication of lesbian sex magazines and the controversies around pornography and sadomasochism, is one way that we are beginning to disentangle sex/love bonds and to name our eroticism.[22]

What Stack means is that we must separate sex from loving emotion. The activities she promotes are connected with emotions, of hate and rage, contempt, indifference, alienation. Sex cannot be performed without emotion because people are not machines. We can make a choice about the emotions we would like to see associated with sex and we can choose positive or negative ones. Some lesbian sex therapists advocate one night stands as a solution to atrophy for those involved in long term relationships. This requires that lesbians learn new and efficient forms of objectification.

ANTI-LESBIANISM

You might wish to describe all the sexological ideas expressed so far as anti-lesbian since it seems clear that they are not going to lead to the liberation of lesbians. But some lesbian sex therapists are more obvious in their contempt for lesbians. Margaret Nicholls in fact identifies herself as bisexual. According to her, lesbians are woefully deficient sexually. She writes that we are 'essentially sexually repressed.'[23] We fare particularly badly in comparison with gay men who are the least sexually repressed group in society.

We have more sexual conflicts than do men, gay or heterosexual, lower sexual desire, and fewer ways of expressing our sexual needs. Our relationships represent the pairing of two relatively sexually inhibited individuals; thus it is no wonder that the frequency of sex in our relationships is less than in gay male or heterosexual relationships ... Moreover, our sex is less diverse and varied than the sexual techniques of gay males and possibly even of heterosexual couples.[24]

According to this model sex would only be reasonably OK in situations where one or more men were involved. Only men really know how to do sex. And it's not just that only men have penises but somehow they have the essence of what is good sex in every way. Nicholls believes lesbians should imitate gay men. 'Lesbian sexuality needs to get more "male" in its orientation, with more emphasis on sex itself and perhaps less on romance.'[25] Surely any lesbian feminist would be able to see at a glance that an argument that assumed lesbians to be inferior to men either straight or gay was not pro-lesbian. But Nicholls scrupulously abjures any of the insights a feminist perspective could give her on the construction of sexuality. Lesbians are simply inferior to men and need to be more like them.

THE NEED FOR THE DILDO

Some lesbian sex therapists reject many of the male supremacist assumptions about sex, which is gratifying. Some reject the boom slump model. Loulan, for instance, rejects the tyranny of the idea that sexual activity should always be directed towards and result in orgasm. But in lesbian sex therapy there is considerable promotion of the use of dildos. The new lesbian sex magazines promote dildos and tell lesbians how to acquire them. Should any problems be encountered with their use then therapists will advise. The bizarre idea of treating women so that they could be penetrated with dildos appears in an article in the book *Women and Sex Therapy*, on how to cure women with vaginismus. Vaginismus is defined as 'a condition in females characterized by spastic, reflex contractions of the musculature investing the outer third of the vagina ... It can prevent intercourse or at best, make it uncomfortable.'[26] The woman sex therapist recommends the brutal treatment of using plastic vaginal dilators which are graduated in size. The woman is taught to use them on herself until 'able to painlessly accommodate a dilator that is equivalent to the girth of the object she and her partner use for vaginal insertion.'[27] Penile insertion is considered by sexologists to be crucial to the maintenance of male power. But the insertion of objects into lesbians is surely a voluntary activity. If an object was considered necessary in a particular relationship surely a smaller one could be used.

The lesbian sex therapists directly challenge lesbian feminist politics too. The sex therapist, Margaret Nicholls, attacks and satirises cherished principles of feminism for being unsexy and the source of lesbian erotophobia. She says lesbian feminists tend not to look attractive. She describes the 'lesbian-feminist clone look' as:

> ... work boots or Frye boots, jeans, work shirt or flannel shirt, man-tailored vest (with or without tie), short hair, no make-up, preferably unshaved legs and underarms, perhaps even facial hair that is emphasized rather than bleached or removed. In an attempt to reject male-defined concepts of women's beauty, many of us ended up looking like teenage boys.[28]

This was, she says, 'sexually boring' and positively describes the efforts of butch/femme proponents to 'recognize the import-ance to sexual desire of physical attractiveness and diversity of physical looks created by costume and adornment.' Of lesbian-feminist attempts not to be 'looks-ist' she writes 'what may be good politics may make for bad sex.'[29] She makes her priorities clear. But what is surprising is her assumption that lesbians in work shirts would necessarily be unattractive physically to other lesbians. Loulan also sees lesbian feminism as sexless. She explains that in the seventies:

> Flannel shirts, blue jeans, no make-up, no jewelry and short hair were all requirements of the club. Effectively, we became desexualized in our dress codes. It was not clear who was sleeping with whom.[30]

Such lesbian sex therapists are committed to the promotion of conventional, heterosexist notions of what is attractive and sexy. They find it difficult to recognise or imagine any erotic attraction in the absence of roleplaying or 'femininity' in some form and assume that their readers share this difficulty. The lesbian sex therapists have joined in the sexological task of deriding and burying feminist insight into the politics of sexuality. Sexologists from Havelock Ellis onwards have dedicated themselves to this task. Nicholls and Loulan are no exceptions. According to some lesbian sex therapists feminism is bad for sex and lesbians should get their priorities right.

POLITICISING SEX

Sex therapy, as conventionally understood and as practised by the lesbian therapists discussed here, depends upon the privatisation of sex. This conflicts with the feminist principle that the personal is the political. As feminists we should surely be suspicious of the argument that any area of 'private' life should be immune from political criticism. If the feminist pursuit of equality in personal relationships and an end to the eroticised inequality of gender fetishism endangers 'sex' as seriously as some lesbian therapists believe, then two choices are open. One is to privatise sex and exclude feminist insights in order to protect the heteropatriarchal construction of sexuality. The other is to understand that sexuality is fundamental to the oppression of women and to direct the courage and vision of lesbian feminist political analysis to what lesbians do in bed.

1. Loulan, JoAnn (1984), *Lesbian Sex*. San Francisco: Spinsters. p. 47.
2. Hamadock, Susan (1988). 'Lesbian Sexuality in the Framework of Psychotherapy.' In Cole, Ellen and Rothblum, Esther (Eds.). *Women and Sex Therapy.* New York: Harrington Park Press. p. 208.
3. Ibid. p. 211.
4. Nicholls, Margaret (1987b). 'Lesbian Sexuality: Issues and Developing Theory.' In Boston Lesbian Psychologies Collective (Eds.). *Lesbian Psychologies.* Illinois: University of Illinois Press. pp. 97–98.
5. Hall, Marny, Kitzinger, Celia, Loulan, JoAnn and Perkins, Rachel (1992). 'In Conversation.' *Feminism and Psychology.* Vol. 2. No. 1. pp. 7–25.
6. Stack, Carolyn (1985). 'Lesbian Sexual Problems.' *Bad Attitude.* p. 21. Spring.
7. Nicholls, Margaret (1987a). 'Doing Sex Therapy with Lesbians: Bending a Heterosexual Paradigm to Fit a Gay Lifestyle.' In Boston Lesbian Psychologies Collective (Eds.) p. 256.
8. Ibid. pp. 258–259.

9. Nicholls, Margaret (1987b). 'Lesbian Sexuality: Issues and Developing Theory.' In Boston Lesbian Psychologies Collective (Eds.) p. 113.

10. Ibid. p. 103.

11. Ibid. p. 104.

12. Ibid. p. 106. Here Nicholls is quoting Tripp, C. A. (1975). *The Homosexual Matrix*. New York: McGraw Hill.

13. Ibid. p. 107–108.

14. Faderman, Lillian (1991). *Odd Girls and Twilight Lovers. A History of Lesbian Life in Twentieth-Century America*. New York: Columbia University Press. p. 248.

15. Loulan, JoAnn (1990). *The Lesbian Erotic Dance*. San Francisco: Spinsters. p. ix.

16. Califia, Pat (1988). *Sapphistry: The Book of Lesbian Sexuality*. Tallahassee: Naiad Press. p. 80.

17. Stack, Carolyn (1985). *Bad Attitude*. p. 21.

18. Califia, Pat (1988). p. 1.

19. Loulan, JoAnn (1984). p. 62.

20. Ibid.

21. Califia, Pat (1988). p. 12.

22. Stack, Carolyn (1985). p. 21.

23. Nicholls, Margaret (1987b). 'Lesbian Sexuality: Issues and Developing Theory.' In Boston Lesbian Psychologies Collective (Eds.) p. 100.

24. Ibid.

25. Nicholls, Margaret (1987a). 'Doing Sex Therapy with Lesbians.' In Boston Lesbian Psychologies Collective (Eds.) p. 259.

26. Kessler, Jo Marie (1988). 'When the Diagnosis is Vaginismus: Fighting Misconceptions.' In Cole and Rothblum (Eds.) p. 176.

27. Ibid. p. 180.

28. Nicholls, Margaret (1987b). 'Lesbian Sexuality' in Boston Lesbian Psychologies Collective (Eds.) p. 114.

29. Ibid. p. 105.

30. Loulan, JoAnn (1990). p. 27.

Chapter 4

THE ESSENTIAL LESBIAN

Gay liberation activists and lesbian feminists in the 1970s opposed the idea that sexual orientation was biologically based. The sixties and seventies were the great decades of social constructionism. Social theorists vigorously opposed biological arguments about racial inferiority, gender differences, mental illness. It was recognised that biological explanations provided the scientific basis for conservative social engineering. Biological arguments, arguments from nature, could be used to assert the rightness and inevitability of women's subordination, of racial inequality, of heterosexual hegemony and of drugs and institutions for those suffering mental ill health. In the eighties the confidence in social constructionism was rocked by the adherence of some lesbians and gay men to a fresh wave of biological determinism to explain sexual orientation. Some lesbian theorists have even begun to assert that butch/femme roleplaying and masculinity and femininity in their stereotypical forms are natural, even unavoidable, for lesbians.

The belief in biology comes mainly from male gay theorists. This should perhaps not surprise us since gay activists did not subscribe to the slogan, 'Any man can be gay'. Traditional gay male politics continued to rely on the idea that homosexuality should be tolerated because gay men could not help themselves. They were an oppressed biological minority, or if biology were not to blame then there was a 'certain something' at least which made gay men inevitably different. Lesbians were often shocked to discover how deep the reliance on biology went among gay men, even sometimes those of otherwise progressive politics.

When teaching a lesbian and gay studies evening class in the early eighties I found that the gay male students were swift to express some belief in biology. The majority of lesbian students expressed complete rejection of the idea. The lesbians had very often been heterosexual, wives and mothers, and had often not thought of loving women until well past their teens. A biological explanation would not have made sense in terms of their experience or their politics.

The considerable difference over biology between male gay activists and lesbian feminist ones was evident in the campaign in the UK against Section 28 of the *Local Government Act 1988*. Prominent gay spokespersons went on television to argue that the amendment against the 'promotion of homosexuality' was a nonsense because homosexuality was innate and couldn't be promoted. Lesbian activists were amazed. This was the opposite of lesbian feminist politics and judging from debate on the amendment in the House of Commons it seemed that it was lesbian feminist efforts precisely to promote lesbianism that were causing alarm in conservative legislators. There seemed to be a fundamental political difference here, and even though some gay activists were critical of this biological position they were not in the ascendant.[1]

In 1987 there was a lesbian and gay studies conference in Amsterdam for which the theme was 'Essentialism versus social constructionism'. This seemed to be a controversy which was pressing for those who had planned the conference. The introduction to the collected papers states 'For a decade there has been a growing controversy among gay and lesbian scholars centring around two rival scientific theories and their implications for homosexuality: *essentialism* and *constructionism*.'[2] Lesbian feminists were merely puzzled that a question they thought had been answered twenty years before should excite so much interest in 1987. The fact that such a question could be seen as important enough to stage a whole conference around suggested that a belief in essentialism must be alive and well somewhere outside the lesbian feminist community. Lesbian feminist theorists were still busily challenging the institution of heterosexuality, suggesting that all women could make the choice to be lesbian save for the restrictions imposed by compulsory heterosexuality. Considering whether they were essentially lesbian was a non-question.

In the nineties a rollback of social constructionism in the gay community carries on apace. In 1991 the research findings of Dr Simon LeVay, characterised as a 'gay activist', were published in the US. LeVay studied the brains of gay men who had died from AIDS and of men who claimed they were not gay who had died from the same cause. He found that a tiny area of the hypothalamus was on average twice as large in heterosexual men as in either heterosexual women or homosexual men. He suggested that varying hormone levels before birth 'wired' the hypothalamus for either heterosexuality or homosexuality. Since then another study at the University of California Medical School has apparently backed his findings. LeVay sees his work as really positive for ending discrimination against gays. He had always believed that homosexuality was biologically determined and set out to prove it so that anti-gay discrimination might be opposed on the grounds that gays were condemned by nature to their behaviour and must be treated with the mercy that should be shown to any group who cannot help themselves. This is an old argument which harks back to the turn of the century. It is an idea that dies hard. But it does not fit lesbian experience or lesbian feminist theory. LeVay has not yet had access to the brains of lesbians but is convinced that he will find that their brains resemble those of heterosexual men in the crucial area.

It is significant that LeVay also believes that biology is responsible for differences between males and females in behaviour. He thinks that women are more verbally competent than men and men more spatially competent than women by reason of brain differences. He manages to associate these brain differences with the fact that gay men are 'less strongly right-handed than straight men.'[3] LeVay is clearly prepared to believe that any number of stereotypical differences between men and women are the result of biology with no evidence whatsoever apart from his hunches. Most worryingly he believes that 'male and female sex drives are biologically determined.' One fundamental insight of feminist theory is that male sexual behaviour is learned and not natural. There would be no hope otherwise of women's freedom from sexual violence. LeVay's wisdom suggests otherwise:

> In general, throughout the entire mammalian kingdom, men are more promiscuous than women. Males have the potential to father an unlimited number of offspring. It's cheap for them to inseminate a female, so it's in their interest to be as promiscuous as they can. For a female, it's quite different . . . There's no question in my mind that this characteristic is biologically determined. There's something in the brains of males and females that causes them to be this way. Now if you look at gay men and lesbians, this trait is not sex-reversed. In fact, this trait in gay men is no longer restricted by women's unwillingness – so the sky is the limit. Most straight men don't get as much sex as they want because women won't let them.[4]

LeVay shows us that biological arguments about 'gay genes' can lead directly into biological arguments that justify women's oppression.

It is worrying that the LeVay theory has been treated enthusiastically in some of the gay press and at least with sympathetic curiosity in the rest. The return to essentialism is in full swing it seems. Feminists have been particularly hostile to biological determinist explanations because the very idea of feminism, the possibility of its birth, depends on fighting the idea of biologically constructed psychological differences between the sexes. After a good grounding in such a battle it is not possible for lesbian feminists to be sanguine about biological explanations of homosexuality. Gay men can be because their freedom as men does not depend to the same extent on fighting biologism.

Women's 'difference' or femininity has been explained in lesbian feminist theory as a male invention, and the subjection of women to femininity as a projection onto women of men's fantasies, or as one separatist put it:

> Men project onto females all of their own deficiencies (cowardice, illogic, inanity, dishonesty, treachery, pettiness, etc.) and they push onto females an array of male-invented

feminine mannerisms and styles that encourage weakness, dependence, submissiveness and general fuckability.[5]

Femininity has been experienced by lesbian feminists simply as brutal restriction of freedom, as torture of the body. Lesbians have been freer to abandon its dictates and express total rejection. The same writer makes femininity sound quite brutal.

> ... we're supposed to believe it's natural to want to mince along on stilted shoes, face masked with stinking, lurid chemicals, nails bloody talons, dieted-jazzercized-depilated-plastic surgeried bodies encased in exposing dresses, voices unnaturally high, gestures 'cute' and aggressively flirtatious, and minds focused on pleasing men at all costs.[6]

Heterosexual feminists have demolished the myth of femininity effectively too, most notably Naomi Wolf in *The Beauty Myth*.[7] She, like other feminist theorists before her, shows how the fashion and beauty industries cause women to do grave damage to their bodies and even starve themselves to death through eating disorders. What is surprising then is that femininity is being re-introduced presently into lesbian culture as a new and revolutionary erotic possibility.

In the seventies lesbian feminists, myself included, wore badges saying 'Any woman can be a lesbian' and we believed it. We believed it not just on good political grounds such as our resistance to biological theories of gender or sexual behaviour, but because for many of us it was our experience. Thousands of women who had not knowingly considered lesbianism as a possibility, left men and committed all their emotional and sexual energies to women, and are still so committed today.[8] The idea of political lesbianism, as this phenomenon was generally called, was controversial at the time. Political lesbians were accused by some of being not 'real' lesbians since they were seen as turning to women for political reasons rather than out of a lifelong determination. But no lesbian feminists would have thought of arguing that lesbians and heterosexual women were simply two distinct biological categories.

Joan Nestle, the leading propagandist of the new lesbian roleplaying, does state categorically 'I think the phrase, *every woman is a potential Lesbian*, is no longer useful.'[9] She says it was simply a 'rhetorical device' and that now is the time for lesbians and heterosexual women to simply recognise their different 'choices'. Lesbians must now 'stop bullying women into sexual stances, to end the assumption that only Lesbians make choices.' The 'bullying' she has in mind probably comprises the exciting theoretical work by lesbian feminists such as Adrienne Rich and Monique Wittig who analyse heterosexuality as a political institution. A new determinism which reifies the sexual categories of the male supremacist sexual system has crept in here under the rhetoric of choice. It is from the pornographers of the new roleplaying, the therapists of roleplaying, that the new essentialism flows. This is not particularly surprising, I will argue here, because at the root of a belief in roleplaying there is inevitably an essentialist foundation.

Femininity and masculinity returned to the lesbian community in the context of the rehabilitation of roleplaying in the early eighties. Though there are lesbians who were unaffected by such developments, the lessening of gender fetishism in the sixties and the impact of feminism provided a liberation for many of those lesbians who had previously used roles. Julia Penelope is a lesbian theorist who had chosen to abandon butch roleplaying. She was horrified to see a revalidation and in 1984 she attacked the new roleplaying from a strong and clear radical feminist perspective.

> The impulse to revive the labels 'butch' and 'femme' and inject some political respectability into their meaning (however belatedly) by talking about 'gut feelings', 'intuitions', and 'power' is the lesbian manifestation of the contemporary right wing backlash, further encouraged by 50s nostalgia ('Happy Days'), and the illusion of security we get by going back to what we imagine to have been 'better days', (usually because we didn't live through them), and talking about 'reclaiming our heritage'.[10]

As Penelope points out the new roleplaying was legitimated with appeals to lesbian history, usually the fifties.

Another lesbian who abandoned the butch role explains that she defined herself in the mid-fifties as a butch and aspired to be a 'Big Bad Butch' who saw femmes as 'too sissy or too inadequate to be butch.' She is amazed that any lesbians today could 'plead ignorance of the woman-hating elements which permeated the traditional butch-femme identities.'

It's easy to feel nostalgia for the good old, bad old days . . . There's a thrill to conquest. There's a thrill to overpowering someone, either literally or figuratively. But for me those old roles were terribly crippling and it took a long time to free myself from their grip.[11]

She explains that the rigidity of roles were alleviated by the 'hippie sixties' which allowed men to wear beads and long hair. But what she describes as the 'big breakthrough' came with the Women's Liberation Movement through which she learned to 'combine strength with sensitivity, and to widen our conceptions of sexuality and sensuality.' She concludes:

At this point it seems mad to jeopardise this ethos for the cheap thrills of black leather jackets and dolly dresses . . . We no longer have any excuse for letting the popular punk culture define for us what is sexy, what is romantic, what is worth living for.[12]

But the pursuit of 'cheap thrills' through roleplaying within the lesbian community has burgeoned through the eighties and into the nineties and is indeed jeopardising the survival of the lesbian feminist critique of masculinity and femininity. The imitation of the political class system of heterosexuality demonstrates a staggering exactitude in recent roleplaying literature. The roleplayers see no humour in their project, even in its more unlikely manifestations, perhaps because humour would puncture the erotic buzz that is supposed to be one of the main benefits thereof. *The Persistent Desire*, a roleplaying anthology edited by Joan Nestle, reveals the extraordinary lengths to which the promoters of roleplaying are prepared to go in their imitation of some of the most politically oppressive aspects of heterosexuality. The roleplaying propagandists reject any suggestion that their practice could be politically constructed and derive from the oppression of women.

One article by Paula Austin, a 'black self-identified femme', gives a representative picture of the way this roleplaying imitates old-fashioned heterosexuality. Austin realises she is a femme whilst in a relationship with a lesbian named Rhon. Austin opines that 'I was convinced she had hidden somewhere in the recesses of her clothing a penis.'[13] Rhon is attractive because she is 'hard, the hardest dyke I had ever been with.' About another lover Buddy, she writes 'I love the hardness, the hint of power and violence, the strength, the inkling of being owned.'[14] Austin confesses to angst over her 'femme-ininity' and whether it is politically correct but clearly decides to disregard her concerns. This is her description of her 'femme-ininity'.

> Being femme for me means wearing a short, tight skirt, garters, and three-inch heels when I'm going out. It means standing in front of the mirror putting on mascara and reddish brown lipstick. It means shopping for a low-cut blouse to reveal a hint of cleavage some nights. It means smiling, or sometimes pouting, when my woman puts her arm around my waist and, with her other hand, turns my face up to kiss hers. It means whispering, 'I'm yours, own me,' when she makes love to me. It means feeling sexy.[15]

This like other descriptions of the new roleplaying has a Mills and Boon quality. But what is ironic is that within heterosexuality women are refusing such gendered inequality. A generation of heterosexual young women would find such material for a heterosexual audience frankly embarrassing and even Mills and Boon are having to market slightly more egalitarian models for the nineties. The 'hint of power and violence' that excites Austin is likely to mean real abuse in heterosexuality and often means such in lesbian relationships too.

The model roleplaying relationships described in the anthology have a flavour of down home, folksy, working class, heart of America, fifties heterosexuality. Femmes welcome their butches home after a hard day, usually performing manual labour but sometimes a professional occupation, and proceed to offer them comfort against a harsh world. As Nestle expresses this, 'When she comes home to me, I must caress the parts of her that have been worn thin, trying to do her work in a man's world.'[16] One wonders what the femmes are supposed to do all day, bake cakes? Then the femme is supposed to make her butch feel safe enough to let herself be vulnerable, revealed in being made love to, but her masculinity must be protected: 'I know how to make love to/Your woman's body/Without taking your masculinity away.'[17] The role of the femme, like that of the traditional housewife, is to nurture the power of her butch so that she can retain her place in the male ruling class and her power over her.

Though this might seem very perplexing from a feminist perspective, the idealisation of precisely the power dynamics that keep women subordinate and abused within heterosexual relationships is seen as positive by the new roleplayers. But then they seem to have asserted a declaration of independence from the feminist movement. Some repudiate their previous feminism, others say they have never been feminists. Lyndall MacCowan, a femme, explains in *The Persistent Desire* that she never identified with feminism or with being a woman. She says that when she came out in the seventies:

It would've been heretical then, as it still is now, to be a lesbian and assert that feminism has little meaning for me – imagine trying to be an atheist in fourteenth century Europe. Yet such a statement is true, and it's important to say it, because feminism has come to overshadow lesbianism's meaning. It's not that I don't believe women are oppressed, but I've never been able to identify myself with that all-encompassing group 'woman'. I've never been anywhere near being as oppressed as a woman as I am as a lesbian.[18]

MacCowan states that being a lesbian means 'knowing that I am not a woman'.[19] Yet being a lesbian femme actually subjects her directly to the oppression of women. Paula Austin writes about the difficulty of having to suffer men's sexual harassment because she looks like a heterosexual woman and one might have thought that MacCowan who favours similar apparel would have the same problem.

Angry statements about the authoritarian and bullying behaviour of lesbian feminists towards those in their ranks like MacCowan or JoAnn Loulan who really wanted to be femmes are common in this roleplaying literature. This approach relieves them of responsibility for having consciously espoused feminist ideas in the seventies. Rather than really being silent victims when they were in the lesbian feminist movement it is likely that they have simply changed their minds to fit the fashion of the conservative backlash.

It is in the explanations offered for roleplaying that the essentialism behind butch/femme ideology is clearest. Baldly biological explanations are not usually suggested though even these are returning in some areas. Loulan suggests that homosexuality is hereditary, an idea abandoned even by most sexologists once psychoanalysis caught on before the Second World War.

> Some of us are just born that way. It probably *is* genetic, homosexuality does run strongly in some families. I know a woman who has six brothers and sisters and all but one are gay.[20]

She says 'we can depend' on stories of homosexuality running in families 'to prove that yes, one of the components is our DNA.'[21] It does seem surprising that the fact that the vast majority of lesbians and gay men have heterosexual parents does not shake the appeal of the heredity argument. Interestingly she wants to use a combination of explanations using both genetics for some and 'choice' for others. The genetic variety are apparently self identified, if you say you are a genetic then you are. This combination is reminiscent of the old sexological idea that homosexuals were divided into inverts and perverts. Inverts were the congenitals who couldn't help it and deserved sympathy and the perverts had deliberately chosen to be bad. It is interesting that the thinking of someone like Loulan who did have a brush with feminism in the seventies could revert so easily to traditional sexology. It suggests a deeply rooted conservatism which her experience of feminism was not sufficient to alter.

Loulan has anxieties about suggesting that all homosexuality is genetic because she is aware this could be used to suggest a 'genetic defect' and she does not think lesbianism is 'pathological'.

In explaining roleplaying Loulan opts for a psychological explanation in terms of archetypes. She says that lesbians have certain archetypes buried deep within their collective unconscious which cannot be argued with. Each one is 'an image that determines behaviour and emotional responses unconsciously.'[22] Roleplaying is then not the result of a biological but a psychological determinism. The commonest lesbian archetypes are 'the concepts of butch and femme and then recently androgyny as well.'[23] Archetypal roleplaying is apparently so determining that all lesbians are somehow connected into roleplaying even if they won't admit it. She describes 'this lesbian eroticism of butch and femme' as something 'which each of us has a connection to, which each of us has been made to deny, put down, and be ashamed of . . .'[24] This leaves those who still want to deny it in some sort of false consciousness. Her audiences tend to be in this benighted state. She says that when she asks audiences whether they have ever rated themselves on a butch/femme scale, 95% say they have, but when asked if roleplaying is important to them then 95% say it is 'unimportant in their lives'.[25] The only explanation, for Loulan, is that 95% of lesbians are in denial and it is Loulan's sad duty to try to open them up to the delights of roleplaying. Sexologists have traditionally taken on such awesome responsibilities and not quailed at the idea of having to change women's sexual behaviour en masse to fit into their prescriptions.[26]

Joan Nestle, in a 1985 panel on roleplaying offered a version of the archetype theory. She says that when she met a butch she experienced 'some kind of basic, prehistoric foreknowledge of each other.'[27] Another panel participant, Jewelle Gomez, asseverates that roleplaying is natural and inevitable. She sees butch and femme as representing the 'two poles that nature presents each of us with.'[28] As evidence she presents folk wisdom and the yin and yang of eastern religion. She considers that this ancient wisdom was lost in Western European puritanical religion which caused people to forget that 'there are two sides within individuals.' Presumably feminism, which questioned the folk wisdom of all patriarchal ideologies about the essential nature of gender, shared in this tragic forgetting. This essential dualism she describes as 'a natural principle, a natural, psychological, biological, emotional, physiological principle.'[29] This doesn't leave much space for conscientious objectors.

There are lesbian academics as well as sex therapists involved in promoting the new essentialism of roleplaying. Saskia Wieringa is an anthropologist who claims once to have made the mistake, because of a feminist consciousness, of seeing butch/femme culture in the west as 'rather outdated'. Then she experienced the lesbian bar culture of Jakarta and Lima and realised 'how narrow my own so-called *political lesbianism* was.'[30] The discovery of something similar to western roleplaying in other cultures convinced her of the poverty of social constructionist approaches to lesbianism. She decided that psychobiological factors must be involved. The existence of roleplaying in cultures outside the west could be used to support a feminist social constructionist approach. If lesbian roleplaying is related to heterosexual roleplaying then we would expect it to be particularly strong in periods and in cultures in which gender differentiation was enforced most strictly within heterosexuality. This might explain the bar culture of Jakarta and Lima more easily than the invention of some roleplaying essence.

Feminist explanations of roleplaying which link it to male supremacist sex roles are roundly rejected by its proponents. Loulan attributes the feminist idea that roleplaying lesbians are 'mimicking male/female roles' to lesbian self-hatred, our fear that lesbians are just an inferior version of heterosexuality. She says that 'somewhere in our deepest homophobic selves, we agree that lesbians are an ersatz version of the heterosexual model,' whereas in fact 'butch and femme have nothing to do with male and female.'[31] Roleplaying is 'something profoundly female' which instead of deriving from male/female derives from some other root, an archetype or principle which both male/female roles and lesbian ones stem from, a dualism in nature. This means that rather than imitating a heterosexual original, lesbians get their roles independently and from the same source in nature as heterosexual men and women do. It's quite surprising then that the great original dualism in nature should be so specific about who does the vacuuming and gossiping but it does seem to be. This is Loulan's description of 'femme energy'.

> A certain lightness, a certain sparkle, a certain interest in every single little detail about what my best friend said to that person she met in the grocery store. A connection to gossip columns filled with people I don't know and will never meet.[32]

Presumably lesbians suffering from depression could not be femmes, since they would lack the required sparkle. Respondents to her survey who identified as femme annoyed Loulan by being 'most likely to initiate cleaning and decorating the house, doing childcare, organizing social activities, and doing the actual socializing.'[33] She feels this is too like male/female roles. It might even suggest that femmeness has something to do with learnt female subordination rather than the great archetypes in the sky.

Lyndall MacCowan asserts that masculinity and femininity in heterosexuality are just two genders and really there could be many more. Butch and femme are genders too, 'lesbian-specific genders' and part of the potentially great variety. She believes that 'Gender systems are a cultural universal' and that it is not true that 'a gender system always implies sexism or homophobia.'[34] Gender is only oppressive if limited in a particular society to two and 'rigidly correlated' with biological sex. According to this unusual interpretation of gender as simply an erotic category, she sees 'androgyny' as a lesbian gender too. Clearly role-players have to repudiate a feminist analysis of gender if they are to have self-respect and believe their games are harmless. So they seek to create confusion about what gender is.

A feminist analysis would see gender as being a political category, indeed a political class, into which human beings are placed in accordance with possession or non possession of a penis. Those possessing the masculine gender form not simply an interesting erotic category, but the ruling class in the system of oppression called male supremacy in which women are suffering and dying. The power difference between these two gender classes is eroticised to be what is understood as sex under male supremacy. Therefore, for many, to have sex they need to have a gender and relate to someone of the opposite gender. 'Gender' as a way to get sexual kicks is directly derived from gender the regulating mechanism of the class system of male supremacy. MacCowan ends her piece by saying it is 'time we reclaim the right to fuck around with gender.'[35] But it is difficult to see how the slavish repetition of the feminine role to which a woman has been brought up, trying to live as a Mills and Boon heroine, is 'fucking around' with anything at all. And the opportunities for heterosexual woman to thus 'fuck around' seem even more limited. If they try femininity no one will notice and if they try masculinity they might meet some opposition from men.

Lesbian feminists who oppose roleplaying are called 'androgynes' in roleplaying literature. Lesbian feminists do not generally use this word to apply to themselves because it does not mean the elimination of masculinity and femininity which is the feminist project. Androgyny represents the combination of masculinity and femininity in one person. Janice Raymond sees the idea of androgyny as fundamental to justifying heterosexuality as a political institution.

> ... hetero-reality and hetero-relations are built on the myth of androgyny. 'Thou as a woman must bond with a man' to fulfill the supposed cosmic purpose of reunifying that which was mythically separated into male and female. Arguments supporting the primacy and prevalence of hetero-relations are in some way based on a cosmic male-female polarity in which the lost halves seek to be rejoined.[36]

Androgyny is a concept that lesbian feminists reject. It can be no accident therefore that roleplayers use it to refer to feminists. They are seeking to draw those who specifically reject and seek to dismantle gender within its poisonous rule. Loulan calls the feminist project of demolishing hierarchies of power and seeking equality the 'androgynous imperative'.[37] She is particularly dismissive of any pursuit of equality in sexual relationships.

> The lesbian who subscribes to the androgynous imperative idealizes a relationship that has no differences in power ... There is no way to keep a relationship of any sort power-free.

The fact that there are two people exchanging energy means that they are passing power back and forth.[38]

It is the exciting erotic possibilities offered by the power differences being introduced to or formalised in lesbian relationships through roleplaying that explains its new popularity. It does not derive from nature, psychological imperative or tradition. The new roleplayers appeal to lesbian history to legitimate their practice, as if they are simply continuing an honourable tradition. I have argued elsewhere that those seeking to rehabilitate roleplaying in the eighties were doing so for rather different reasons, specifically erotic ones.[39] The new roleplaying is a variety of the newly fashionable sadomasochism. It does not resemble its historical counterpart because gender roles have been exploded by feminist theory and are no longer compulsory, certainly not for those now promoting them who are well versed in such theory. The political repression of the fifties had made roleplaying a form of protection when one of a lesbian couple could 'pass' in the street, and had made it difficult for some lesbians to think beyond gender difference because of the blanket propaganda of separate spheres and women's difference that pervaded that decade. The eighties and nineties are a very different time. A far reaching feminist critique of heterosexuality from Jill Johnston to Adrienne Rich and Monique Wittig has spelled out the emptiness of traditional heterosexuality and named it as an institution of political control of women. An imitation of the rules of this institution could not be performed out of ignorance in the eighties by those who had been steeped in feminist theory.

Roleplaying in the eighties is the soft pornography compared with the hard core pornography of lesbian S/M. It provides the thrill of eroticised power difference without the extremes of violence and vulgarity. Merrill Mushroom describes the advantages of roleplaying using the catchwords of S/M such as vulnerability, trust and power.

The basic dynamics of butch-femme relating involve power, trust, vulnerability, tenderness and caring. When I as a butch demand of my lover 'Give it to me, baby, now', being as deep

87

inside her as I can penetrate; and she completely releases herself and flows out to me ... Sometimes I want her to take me right away, and then I seduce her the way a femme seduces a butch – seduce her into taking me instead of wanting me to take her. Sometimes her own butch streak will dominate, and she will Have Her Way with me, and I will let her.[40]

Mushroom still sees herself as a butch despite a little controlled role swapping. The disadvantages of roleplaying are forgotten in this new version which is supposed to be just playing rather than for real. There are other reasons for the revitalisation of roleplaying. Lesbians are wanting to describe problems in their relationships, particularly around sexuality, and in the absence of a feminist language, now that feminism is so despised and discarded, the language of roleplaying appears useful.

The sex therapist JoAnn Loulan in her book *The Lesbian Erotic Dance* expresses her view that roleplaying is about the construction of erotic categories. Butch/femme for her is about how to choose a sexual partner and what to do with them. For her lesbianism is a sexual practice and it is the sexual practice itself, doing it, which makes lesbianism revolutionary. Feminist criticism of roleplaying is referred to by its propagandists as 'desexualising' lesbianism. Loulan feels she 'can't help commenting on the desexualizing of our culture.'[41] Contributors to *The Persistent Desire* make the same argument. Madeline Davis remarks:

Frankly, I don't understand not being role identified. Sure, I believe them when they say that they are not, but it all seems so 'the same' to me and sort of boring. They're too busy holding hands and swaying and singing about 'filling up and spilling over'.[42]

Arlene Istar complains about feminism, 'We have limited our options by desexualizing our community.'[43] Lyndall MacCowan explains that 'butch and femme are gender constructions that arise from a sexual definition of lesbianism'[44] and that 'Butch-femme has been made invisible because lesbian sexuality has been made invisible' and goes on to an explicit repudiation of lesbian feminism's temerity in giving lesbianism a political meaning.

> It is time to explicitly say that the lesbian-feminist analysis linking women's oppression with gender, sex roles, sexuality, and sexual orientation is both simplistic and inaccurate, and has long outlived its ability to fuel a movement for women's – let alone lesbians' – liberation.[45]

Roleplaying sexuality as demonstrated in collections such as *The Persistent Desire* imitates classic heterosexual fellatio and intercourse fairly religiously in order to realise the potential of these practices for sadomasochistic satisfactions. One butch helpfully explains the excitement of penetration for her: '. . . fucking between equals is passionless . . . When we fuck we possess. When we get fucked we become the possession.'[46] Joan Nestle describes being fucked with a dildo, '. . . she reaches down and slips the cock into me . . . she starts to move her hips in short strong thrusts.'[47] Pat Califia has a poem in the collection about wishing she had a cock with lines like 'Imagining the swell and rigid length/shoved into you', 'Fucking you until I come,/Staying in you until I get hard again.'[48] The words used for fucking in the poem are 'shove and thrust and hump', 'drill', 'hurt and fill and punch into you.'[49]

More surprising than the imitation of brutal sexual intercourse is the practice of cocksucking. This means performing the act of fellatio on a dildo. Jan Brown explains that the reason for this practice is that it is the ultimate in dominance and submission. 'It is about the urge to dominate, take, and degrade. It is about the fierce need to submit. To serve somebody.'[50] Nestle also describes cocksucking. Lest it lack erotic potential for the woman strapped into it Nestle invents a variation. 'I take one of her hands and wrap it around the base so she can feel my lips as I move on her . . . licking the lavender cock.'[51]

The roleplaying practices described, in their determination to imitate traditional heterosexual sex, include non-consensual violence. The Pat Califia poem above about drilling and hurting also mentions the butch's alcoholism and violence. Scarlet Woman writes about what would in a heterosexual context be liable in some jurisdictions to the charge of marital rape. The woman wakes 'Under fast hands alarmed into instant arousal' and 'You move in faster than I can trust you' while 'My brain is asleep'.[52] But this is represented as acceptable because the victim does get aroused in the course of the event. It is perhaps not surprising that when the dynamics of heterosexuality are imitated down to the very dynamics of activity and passivity then rape is likely to become a real possibility between women.

It is an open secret among proponents of lesbian sadomasochism that the sexuality of cruelty is linked with childhood sexual abuse. Practitioners defend S/M by stating that it is the only way they can experience sexual pleasure because their abuse has tied abuse and pleasure so closely together for them that any possibility of an eroticism of equality is locked out. From the writings of roleplayers it seems fairly clear that there are similar links between the compulsiveness of the mild S/M practice it involves and women's oppression. Jan Brown, in *The Persistent Desire*, tells us that she worked as a street prostitute at seventeen. As an adult butch she tells us that she and her roleplaying friends lied to feminists to try to make their sexual practices appear respectable. 'We explained to them that even though many of us might jerk off to gang rape, torture, daddy in our beds, and other undeniably incorrect imagery, it was really nothing to lose sleep over.'[53] They emphasised the difference between fantasy and reality and that they were in control of their fantasies. But she says, 'we lied'. In fact it is the lack of control that is attractive. The power of the fantasies lies:

... in the lust to be overpowered, forced, hurt, used, objectified. We jerk off to the rapist, to the Hell's Angel, to daddy, to the Nazi, to the cop, and to all the other images that have nothing to do with the kind of lesbian sex that entails murmurs of endearment, stroking of breasts, and long, slow tongue work. And, yes, we also dream of the taking. We dream of someone's blood on our hands, of laughing at cries for mercy. We wear the uniform and the gun; we haul our cocks out of our pants to drive into a struggling body. Sometimes we want to give up to the strangler's hands. Sometimes, we need to have a dick as hard as truth between our legs, to have the freedom to ignore 'no' or to have our own 'no' ignored.[54]

Brown explains that the fantasies arise directly from the oppression of women because 'many of us have graduated from the university of self-destruct.' They are 'street survivors, incest survivors', have lived with 'abusive boyfriends' or 'substance abuse' and 'carry many kinds of scars'. But the sex that is eroticised cruelty is their salvation and 'keeps us alive – out of prisons and locked wards, abusive relationships, and bad-odds fights in bars.'[55] Brown explains quite straightforwardly how roleplaying eroticises the real material experience of brutality.

A poem in the *Femme-Butch Reader* makes the same point. Sonja Franeta's poetical narrator explains that she would listen to the sounds of her father beating and abusing her mother and 'discovered how to rub/the hurt away directly on myself.'[56] She was beaten herself. Once again eroticised cruelty is seen as the answer in which 'our pain will turn to pleasure' and is expressed this time in belt buckle, boots, leather jacket, knife and being 'tough'. The idea that roleplaying sexuality like other forms of S/M is some kind of religious ritual of masochism that will save or compensate for real pain is a common refrain.

It is not just libertarian roleplayers who fall into the essentialist fallacy. Three radical separatist lesbians living in Oakland, California, who have unimpeachably feminist perspectives on sadomasochism and femininity, are using the idea of butchness and femmeness in ways which share some of the deeply problematic implications of the libertarian perspective we have seen above. Bev Jo, Linda Strega and Ruston attack what they see as the oppression of butches by femmes. They do not see butch and femme as erotic categories at all. Their definitions are political. They see butches as 'those who, as girls, rejected feminization, and refused to play the role designed by men for women' and femmes as 'those who accepted the feminine role, to various degrees, as girls.'[57] They reject the idea of roleplaying entirely and believe that lesbians should be eschewing any 'masculine' or 'feminine' behaviour. But they believe that butch and femme are categories that all lesbians fall into without exception, that they are the 'basic core identities' that 'all Lesbians have'.[58] They ask 'Is it possible to be neither Butch nor Fem' and reply 'no'.[59]

They seem to have decided to use the roleplaying vocabulary in order to address a significant political question. This is the difference in experience between lesbians who have always looked like lesbians and suffered punishment for lesbian visibility and those lesbians who 'passed' by adopting feminine clothing or came out as lesbians after some time of living as heterosexual and gaining the privileges that long-time lesbians were unable to acquire. They define the lesbians who carried the standard of lesbian visibility as brave heroes of lesbian liberation and as butches. Joan Nestle, who comes from a very different politics, makes the same point. Indeed the admiration for the visible butches expressed by the new femmes seems to emanate from some understandable guilt about their assumption of the privileges of passing. Femmes, as many of them point out, are only visible when on the arm of a butch. Jo, Strega and Ruston have a very different approach. They call upon all lesbians to simply relinquish the privileges of passing and give up femininity so that 'butches' would no longer suffer for their visibility. That is a more dynamic lesbian positive solution.

But their use of roleplaying vocabulary in situations in which it hardly seems appropriate does undermine the important political points they are making. To say that children as young as two by making a decision to accept or reject femininity are locking themselves into a system whereby they will all their lives be oppressing butches or be oppressed as butches does smack of essentialism. It rigidifies butch/femme categories and does not allow for change. They seek to reverse what they see as the oppression of butches by femmes but in doing so create a new hierarchy. Butches, who they see as fairly rare, possibly only 5 in 100 lesbians, are 'much closer to our inborn, natural state' of being female. Femmes will never be able to become that 'natural' and so are relegated to being in an inferior category all their lives. The creation of such unnecessary divisions cannot help the building of lesbian feminist community. Two lesbians who look and behave identically, both in plaid shirts, jeans and boots may in fact, according to this analysis, remain in different status categories all their lives.

According to this analysis butches and femmes can be recognised by the congnoscenti on sight even if they do not themselves know what they are, 'You can usually tell when you first meet someone whether she's Butch or fem.'[60] Some clues to recognition are provided under the heading 'One Honest Fem's Self-Recognition List'. Said femme explains that when she meets other lesbians she feels 'less difference with fems' and with a butch she feels a 'potential barrier'. She feels herself 'moving like a Fem, and automatically using some feminine gestures.'[61] What is more she finds that 'feminine activities like sewing, needlecrafts, cooking, and other things designated as "women's work" ' feel like things that belong to her and to her 'sphere of activity'. It seems that the great archetype in the sky is at work again.

Yet the work of these three lesbians contains much clear and cogent feminist analysis such as Linda Strega's of the movement towards femininity in the lesbian community in the eighties. Linda Strega calls lesbian femininity the 'Big Sell-Out'. She explains that other lesbians have 'verbally assaulted' her at social gatherings about why she wanted to 'wear a uniform'.[62] This social assault on what lesbian feminists had always tended to wear, shirts and jeans, is the parallel of the literary assault carried out by the roleplayers such as JoAnn Loulan and sex therapists like Margaret Nicholls. As Strega points out, those who might with more justice be seen as wearing uniforms are surely the lesbians who choose to imitate traditional male-designed femininity. Somehow the newly feminine lesbians see themselves as truly courageous to challenge that tiny fraction of the western world that does not enforce compulsory femininity on women, lesbian feminists. Strega suggests that rather than being an act of heroism, the return to femininity is about 'passing' to gain privilege.

In the late eighties it became more and more difficult to state that such and such a woman 'looked like a lesbian'. Angry lesbian protestors would say that there was no such thing as 'what a lesbian looked like'. Well, like Strega, I think that is not so. There has been a historical tradition of lesbians rejecting femininity in different ways and to different extents but the rejection of femininity has been, I would suggest, a common theme. Lesbians have tended to assert human dignity against the social indignities of male-designed femininity. The lesbians at feminist discos in the seventies and early eighties did not look vastly different from the lesbians at traditional lesbian discos: shirts, T-shirts and jeans predominated, and short hair. The political strategy of looking like lesbians is more than just a personal desire to be warm and comfortable and possessed of freedom of action, very useful in a world where men attack women. It is an important strategy for the creation of lesbian freedom. In the workplace, in their families of origin, on the street, lesbians who 'look like lesbians', and their attackers do know what that means, are at risk. The more that lesbians and heterosexual women reject femininity the easier it becomes for other women to escape degrading feminine norms and the more difficult it becomes to discriminate against lesbians.

The new roleplaying is the fundamentalism of lesbianism. As fundamentalism in all patriarchal religions is founded upon and designed to maintain the oppression of women through the enforcement of male dominance and female submission, so too is lesbian roleplaying. It requires the same enthusiastic self abasement from women and achieves it. It is explained by the same mythology of biology or yin and yang. Lesbian roleplaying needs to be explained as part of the very grave worldwide backlash against the liberation of women in which some women are indeed embracing their oppression with slavish obedience and compulsive repetition, but plenty more are rebelling. The erotic dance of roleplaying, the rhythm that Loulan rhapsodises about, is the rhythm of slavery, of male dominance and female submission, an old rhythm indeed but not natural.

---

1. See Alderson, Lyn and Wistrich, Harriet (1988). 'Clause 29: Radical Feminist Perspectives.' In *Trouble and Strife*. No. 13. pp. 3–8. (During its passage Section 28 became, at one point, Clause 29.)
2. Altman, Dennis *et al* (Eds.) (1989). *Which Homosexuality?* London: Gay Men's Press. Introduction p. 6.
3. *Campaign* (1992). 'Are We Born to Be Gay?' No. 199. p. 69. October. Australia.
4. Ibid.

5. Jo, Bev, Strega, Linda and Ruston (1990). *Dykes-Loving-Dykes*. Oakland, California: Battleaxe. p. 168.

6. Ibid.

7. Wolf, Naomi (1990). *The Beauty Myth*. London: Vintage.

8. For a description of my decision to become a political lesbian see: Holdsworth, Angela (1988). *Out of the Doll's House*. London: BBC Publications. My reasons are quoted in chapters 7 and 8.

9. Nestle, Joan (1988). *A Restricted Country: Essays and Short Stories*. London: Sheba. p. 124.

10. Penelope, Julia (1984). 'Whose Past Are We Reclaiming?' *Common Lives, Lesbian Lives*. No. 13. p. 42.

11. Koertge, Noretta (1986). 'Butch Images 1956–86.' In *Lesbian Ethics*. Vol. 2. No. 2. p. 103.

12. Ibid.

13. Austin, Paula (1992). 'Femme-inism.' In Nestle, Joan (Ed.). *The Persistent Desire*. Boston: Alyson Publication. p. 362.

14. Ibid. p. 363.

15. Ibid. p. 365.

16. Nestle, Joan (1992b). 'My Woman Poppa.' p. 348.

17. Califia, Pat (1992b). 'The Femme Poem.' p. 418.

18. MacCowan, Lyndall (1992). 'Re-collecting History, Renaming Lives: Femme Stigma and the Feminist Seventies and Eighties.' p. 309. In Nestle, Joan. p. 309.

19. Ibid. p. 311.

20. Loulan, JoAnn (1990). *The Lesbian Erotic Dance*. San Francisco: Spinsters. p. 193.

21. Ibid. p. 194.

22. Bolen, Jean Shinoda quoted in Loulan, JoAnn (1990). p. 17.

23. Ibid. p. 20.

24. Ibid. p. 29.

25. Ibid. p. 43.

26. See chapter on 'The Invention of the Frigid Woman' in my book (1985). *The Spinster and Her Enemies*.

27. Quoted in Loulan, JoAnn (1990). p. 98.

28. Ibid. p. 49.

29. Ibid. p. 50.

30. Wieringa, Saskia (1989). 'An Anthropological Critique of Constructionism: Berdaches and Butches.' In Altman, Dennis *et al* (Eds.). *Which Homosexuality?* p. 215.

31. Loulan, JoAnn (1990). p. 48.

32. Ibid. p. 102.

33. Ibid. p. 102.

34. MacCowan, Lyndall (1992). p. 318.

35. Ibid. p. 323.

36. Raymond, Janice G. (1986). *A Passion for Friends: Toward a Philosophy of Female Affection*. London: The Women's Press. p. 12. Boston: Beacon Press.

37. Loulan, JoAnn (1990). p. 73.

38. Ibid. p. 76.

39. See my chapter (1989). 'Butch and Femme: Now and Then.' In The Lesbian History Group (Eds.). *Not A Passing Phase*. London: The Women's Press.

40. Mushroom, Merrill (1983). 'Confessions of a Butch Dyke.' *Common Lives, Lesbian Lives*. No. 9. p. 43.

41. Loulan, JoAnn (1990). p. 203.

42. Davis, Madeline (1992). 'Epilogue, Nine Years Later.' In Nestle, Joan (Ed.) p. 270.

43. Istar, Arlene (1992). 'Femme-Dyke.' In Nestle, John (Ed.) p. 382.

44. MacCowan, Lyndall (1992). p. 306.

45. Ibid. p. 306.

46. Brown, Jan (1992). 'Sex, Lies and Penetration: A Butch Finally "Fesses Up".' In Nestle, Joan (Ed.) p. 411.

47. Nestle, Joan (1992). 'My Woman Poppa.' p. 350.

48. Califia, Pat (1992). 'Gender Fuck Gender.' In Nestle, Joan (Ed.) p. 423.

49. Ibid. p. 424.

50. Brown, Jan (1992). p. 413.

51. Nestle, Joan (1992). 'My Woman Poppa.' p. 349.

52. Scarlet Woman (1992). 'Roll Me Over and Make Me a Rose.' In Nestle, Joan (Ed.). *The Persistent Desire*. p. 352.

53. Brown, Jan (1992). p. 411.

54. Ibid. p. 412.

55. Ibid.

56. Franeta, Sonja (1992). 'Bridge Poem.' In Nestle, Joan (Ed.). *The Persistent Desire*. p. 375.

57. Jo, Bev, Strega, Linda, and Ruston (1990). pp. 140–141.

58. Ibid. p. 139.

59. Ibid. p. 157.

60. Ibid. p. 147.

61. Ibid. pp. 150–151.

62. Ibid. p. 163.

Chapter 5

RETURN TO GENDER: POSTMODERNISM AND LESBIAN AND GAY THEORY

There has been a sudden enthusiasm for and incorporation of the work of the Masters of postmodernism, Lacan, Foucault, Derrida into feminist theory in the eighties. Feminist critics have argued that this has led to a depoliticising of feminism.[1] In the area of lesbian and gay theory the work of postmodernist male icons and of theorists inspired by them has been greeted with even more enthusiasm. This is not surprising since that which is called lesbianandgay theory, i.e. theory which homogenises lesbians and gay men, must be palatable to gay men. Anything which smacks too outrightly of feminism is regarded with suspicion. The project of creating independent lesbian feminist theory is now seen by many as bizarrely separatist. The stars of the new lesbianandgay theory, Judith Butler and Diana Fuss, are women but involved in recycling a feminism founded on postmodernist mainly gay Masters, which does not irritate male gay sensibilities. This is not an easy task. How, for instance, is the phenomenon of drag to be made not just acceptable but even seen as revolutionary in lesbianandgay theory when it has stuck in the craw of feminist theory ever since lesbians dissented from gay liberation? It is to be accomplished by a return to gender, an invention of a harmless version of gender as an idea which lesbians and gay men can endlessly play with and be revolutionary at the same time.

The version of gender the lesbianandgay theorists are presenting is a far cry from the understanding of gender which other

97

feminist theorists might have. It is gender depoliticised, sanitised and something difficult to associate with sexual violence, economic inequality, women dying from backstreet abortions. It is gender reinvented as play for those who see themselves far removed from the nitty gritty of women's oppression. It goes down well in the world of lesbianandgay theory because it is feminism as fun instead of feminism as irritatingly challenging.

Let us first look at who the new lesbianandgay theorists are since this might help us to understand why they have chosen their particular politics. Whilst the heavy feminist politicos of the seventies are likely to have had backgrounds in politics, history and sociology, the new variety come from literary and cultural studies and film studies. Let us take as an example the book, *Inside/Out. Lesbian Theories, Gay Theories*, edited by Diana Fuss.[2] Judith Butler teaches in a Humanities Center and is therefore not necessarily in the area of cultural criticism. The other eighteen authors are and cover literature, media, film, photography, art history. There is no reason why a literary critic should not make a valuable contribution to the development of political theory but when all that is seen as 'theory' by a whole new generation of lesbian and gay students and teachers emanates from the arts rather than the social sciences then there may be reason for alarm. This might help to explain why this new theory has little time for old fashioned talk of material power relations, for economics, for power that does not just play around but resides in the hands of particular classes and elites. Postmodernist theory elevated language to a pre-eminent place in the political, the word became reality, the cultural critic became the political activist by wielding a pen and the housewife who gets beaten up by her husband because she leaves one cobweb in a corner becomes strangely invisible.

Let us now look at the authorities cited by the new lesbianandgay theorists. The notes to Diana Fuss's introduction cite Judith Butler, Lacan, Derrida more than once, Foucault, nine more men and two more women. You might feel that this was truly surprising since such a huge body of original lesbian feminist theory exists which could be an inspiration, but this theory does not exist for the new lesbianandgays. There are no references to Mary Daly, Audre Lorde, Janice Raymond, Julia Penelope, Sarah Hoagland, Charlotte Bunch. These separatists of the intellect who posit a lesbian theory into which gay men are not easily assimilated have been disappeared.

At the root of the gender problem in the new lesbianandgay theory lies the idea of the dominance of language and of binary oppositions therein which comes from Lacan and Derrida. Language is seen as overwhelmingly important. Whilst other feminists might see language as important in a landscape of other oppressive forces in maintaining the oppression of women, such as economic constraints, male violence, the institution of heterosexuality, the new postmodernist lesbianandgay theorists see language as primary. Language operates through the construction of false binary oppositions which, by some mysterious process, control the way people are able to think and therefore act. Masculinity/femininity is supposed to be one of these binaries, the one which is most fundamental to the oppression of women and lesbians and gays.

The postmodernist feminist drops men out of the analysis. Power becomes, in a Foucauldian sense, something that just floats about constantly reconstituting itself for no real purpose and with no real connection with real human beings. Thus, Judith Butler ascribes power to 'regimes' as in 'the power regimes of heterosexism and phallogocentrism seek to augment themselves through a constant repetition of their logic . . .'[3] Elsewhere she continues to anthropomorphise heterosexuality.

> That heterosexuality is always in the act of elaborating itself is evidence that it is perpetually at risk, that is, that it 'knows' its own possibility of becoming undone.[4]

This is a 'heterosexuality' with a postgraduate degree! A feminist analysis might generally ask in whose interests these regimes were set up and operate, a *cui bono* question might not seem out of place. Then men might pop into the picture.

Butler's understanding of gender is similarly removed from a context of power relations.

> Gender is the repeated stylization of the body, a set of repeated

acts within a highly rigid regulatory frame that congeal over time to produce the appearance of substance, of a natural sort of being.[5]

She says elsewhere that 'gender is drag'. Gender then becomes a way of holding the body, clothing, appearance and it is not surprising that Butler is able to come to the conclusion that all forms of swapping gender about, such as drag and lesbian roleplaying, are revolutionary. But it is unclear where the actual vulgar oppression of women fits into all this. When a woman is being beaten by the brutal man she lives with is this because she has adopted the feminine gender in her appearance? Would it be a solution for her to adopt a masculine gender for the day and strut about in a work shirt or leather chaps? When gender is seen as an idea, or a form of appearance, then the oppression of women does disappear. The tendency of the idea of gender to invisibilise the power relations of male supremacy has been commented upon by radical feminist theorists.[6] Gender as a concept has always been more popular amongst liberal and socialist feminist theorists and now postmodernists.

When feminist theorists of any political persuasion have written about gender in the past they have seen it as something which might be overcome, superseded. Feminists, whether heterosexual or lesbian, have been quite reasonably insulted by being called either feminine or masculine. They have seen themselves, as most still do, as conscientious objectors to gender who were refusing to have any truck with it and refusing to act it out. Some pursued the track of androgyny but the limitations of this approach have also been pointed out by radical feminist theorists.[7] Androgyny, as an idea, has been seen as depending on a continued notion of masculinity and femininity, since it is supposed to combine traits associated with both these concepts and therefore to reify them rather than leaving them behind. This project that feminists and lesbian feminists have been engaged in for up to twenty years or more of exploding gender by refusing to behave according to the laws of gender, has now been declared not just ill-conceived but impossible by some postmodernist feminists. Butler identifies the 'pro-sexuality' movement within feminist theory as saying that sexuality is 'always constructed within the terms of discourse and power, where power is partially understood in terms of heterosexual and phallic cultural conventions'. She agrees with this and states that it is impossible to construct a sexuality which is outside these conventions.

> If sexuality is culturally constructed within existing power relations, then the postulation of a normative sexuality that is 'before', 'outside', or 'beyond' power is a cultural impossibility and a politically impracticable dream, one that postpones the concrete and contemporary task of rethinking subversive possibilities for sexuality and identity within the terms of power itself.[8]

Feminism as it has been generally understood has been declared impossible. Postmodern theory has been enlisted to support the sexual libertarian and specifically sadomasochist project.

Most feminists of the seventies and eighties will probably have seen themselves as engaged in the task of eliminating gender and phallocentric sexuality. We have been involved in the creation of something new and different. Now we discover that we were trying to do something impossible. I have young lesbian students who will say to me 'Surely you have gender in your relationship.' They do not know that they are being insulting by discounting more than twenty years of struggle by lesbian feminists to have no such thing. It is nearly as frustrating as when men used to tell me as an embryo feminist, that there was such a thing as 'natural' femininity and masculinity. Men don't tend to tell me that any more, only postmodernists of both sexes. Such students accept, as a result of high ingestion of postmodernist theory, that it is impossible to sidestep gender. You cannot break out of a binary opposition, according to Derrida, you can only give more weight to the weaker half of the binary and cause it stress and strain.

To imagine that you can sidestep it is said to be essentialist. A quite new meaning of the word essentialist has been invented so that it can be used against all those who maintain some belief in the possibility of social action to create social change. Once upon a time we might have known where we were with essentialism. It represented the belief that men and women were naturally and biologically different. This was not a belief of radical feminists who have always been missionaries of social constructionism, though it has suited feminist theorists of other faiths to pretend to the contrary. Chris Weedon is one postmodern feminist who reiterates in her work the puzzling assertion that radical feminists who want to transform male sexuality in the interests of women's freedom are really biological determinists who believe it cannot be changed![9] What is now called essentialism is the belief that a lesbian can eschew gender, or the belief that it is possible to practice a sexuality not organised around the penis or power imbalance. Such beliefs are said to be essentialist by postmodernists because they rely on the existence of an unknowable essence of lesbianism. All that is known or that can be thought is gendered and phallocentric, and only playing within the rules of this system can alter it. It would be possible to reverse the game and accuse those who tell lesbians that they cannot get out of gender or phallogocentrism of essentialism with rather more justification one might think. But inventing and hurling around new versions of essentialism is something I would like to avoid. Suffice it to say that the idea of the inevitability of gender and phallogocentrism is brutally determinist, pessimistic, and manages to wipe the feminist project of the last twenty years off the map. It fits into the general postmodernist tendency to regard political activism and the belief that political change is possible as suspicious, derisory and somehow vulgar.

Let us look more closely at what Butler sees as the revolutionary possibilities of drag. The social construction of gender is a very old and basic tenet of feminism. But to postmodernists, this, like other traditional and very well worn feminist insights is seen to be new and exciting. And indeed it may well be that they are seeming exciting to a whole new generation of young women who don't have any access to feminist literature of the sixties and seventies because that literature does not appear on their courses and is nowhere referenced. The revolutionary potential of drag and roleplaying, Butler asserts, lies in the ability of such practices to illuminate the fact that gender is socially constructed. They reveal that gender has no essence or ideal form but is all just drag whether put on by feminine heterosexual women or masculine heterosexual men or roleplaying lesbians or male gay drag artists or clones.

> Drag constitutes the mundane way in which genders are appropriated, theatricalized, worn, and done; it implies that all gendering is a kind of impersonation and approximation. If this is true, it seems, there is no original or primary gender that drag imitates, *but gender is a kind of imitation for which there is no original* ... [10]

Gender, inasmuch as it comprises gestures, costume and appearance, can indeed be seen as drag, or as Butler also calls it 'performance'. The 'performance' is supposed to show up the fact that there is no 'inner sex or essence or psychic gender core.' If this is to be a revolutionary strategy then how would it effect change? This is not very clear.

> How then to ... engage gender itself as an inevitable fabrication, to fabricate gender in terms which reveal every claim to the origin, the inner, the true, and the real as nothing other than the effects of *drag*, whose subversive possibilities ought to be played and replayed to make the 'sex' of gender into a site of insistent political play?[11]

Apparently the audience of the gender as drag performance is to realise gender is not 'real' or true'. But what do they do having made this realisation? Will heterosexual women and men witnessing drag shows rush home and throw off gender, proclaiming to their spouses that there is no such thing as masculinity and femininity? This doesn't seem terribly likely. If gender were indeed an idea, if male supremacy only managed to carry on because little lightbulbs of realisation of the falsity of gender were failing to be illuminated in the heads of men and women, then Butler's strategy might be destined for success. But she has a liberal and idealist understanding of the oppression of women. Male supremacy does not carry on just because people don't realise gender is socially constructed, because of an unfortunate misapprehension that we must somehow learn how to shift. It carries on because men's interests are served thereby.

There is no reason why men should give up all the real advantages, economic, sexual, emotional, that male supremacy offers them because they see that men can wear skirts. Similarly the oppression of women does not just consist of having to wear makeup. Seeing a man in a skirt or a woman wearing a tie will not be sufficient to extricate a woman from a heterosexual relationship when she will suffer socially, financially and quite likely physically, in some cases with the loss of her life, if she decides to slough off her oppression.

According to those who celebrate playing with gender it is not just the assumption of a gender that might seem incongruous, i.e. femininity by a man or masculinity by a woman, that is potentially revolutionary. Apparently the performance of the expected gender role can be too. This idea has been around in gay male theory for some time. Gay male commentators on the development of the seventies phenomenon of the masculine clone, leather man have disagreed over the revolutionary potential of this development. Many gay theorists have been understandably dismayed. They have seen gay masculinity as a betrayal of the principle of gay liberation which sought to break down gender stereotypes and saw masculinity as a concept that was oppressive to women.[12] Others have argued that the masculine gay man is revolutionary because he questions the effeminate gay male stereotype. It has been pointed out that the revolutionary potential of the masculine gay man might well not be realised because the unsuspecting passer-by would not realise the man was gay and might just think he was masculine. How after all was anyone to know? The argument that masculinity donned by gay men could be politically progressive seems in the end simply to be a way of seeking to justify what some gay men wanted to do, or were attracted to. The right-on-ness was invented after the fact, perhaps because some gay men realised the retrogressive nature of the masculinity they adopted to 'pass', to feel powerful or to be sexually attractive, and needed to reassure themselves.

The return to gender which has been taking place in the gay male community since the late seventies in terms of a renewed enthusiasm for drag shows and a newly masculine style has had its analogue rather later in the lesbian community. It was not until the eighties that the return to gender became obvious in the lesbian community with the phenomenon of a rehabilitated roleplaying and lipstick lesbianism. It was convenient that there were ideas in the works of the postmodern masters which would provide an intellectual justification and allow feminist objections to be overridden and derided in the academy. Judith Butler demonstrates in *Gender Trouble* that old fashioned psycho-analysis in the form of a Joan Riviere paper from 1929 plus Lacanian utterances on femininity as masquerade and parody can be deployed by the new lesbianandgay theorists of cultural studies to support the performance of femininity by lesbians as a political strategy. This strategy is elsewhere called 'mimicry' although that is a word not well suited to Butler's analysis since it would suggest that some original exists which can be mim-icked and indeed she does not use it. Carol-Anne Tyler explains the idea of mimicry using Luce Irigaray.

> To be a mimic, according to Irigaray, is to 'assume the femi-nine role deliberately . . . so as to make "visible", by an effect of playful repetition, what was supposed to remain invisible . . .' To play the feminine is to 'speak' it ironically, to italicize it . . . to hyperbolize it . . . or to parody it . . . In mimicry, as in camp, one 'does' ideology in order to undo it, producing knowledge about it: that gender and the heterosex-ual orientation presumed to anchor it are unnatural and even oppressive.[13]

But Tyler is critical of this idea. She points out that if all gender is masquerade then it must surely be impossible to distinguish the parody from the 'real'. There is no real. Thus, the revolution-ary potential must be lost.

It is the idea of mimicry which lies behind some of the acclaim by cultural critics of Madonna. Madonna is supposed to under-mine ideas of the fixity and reliability of gender by assuming femininity as performance. Mimicry requires that the femininity to be assumed be exaggerated. This is apparently how innocent observers are to know that a revolutionary strategy is being engaged in. The over the top degree of make-up or height of shoe heel would reveal that gender as performance was being undertaken. Cherry Smyth, exponent of 'queer' politics, tells us that traditional female clothing can be revolutionary when discussing the work of lesbian photographer Della Grace:

> Some of the iconography is indeed robbed from women sex-trade workers and post-punk fashion, which injects a violent autonomy into femme chic, making it trashy and threatening, rather than vulnerable and submissive, to wear a mini-skirt and revealing bodice.[14]

This style is best personified, she says, in 'Madonna herself, who is probably one of the most famous examples of queer transgression.'[15] Feminist theorists who are neither 'queer' nor postmodern have a great deal of difficulty in seeing Madonna as transgressing against anything but feminism, anti-racism and progressive politics in general. bell hooks, the black American feminist theorist, explains that Madonna obeys and exploits the rules of white male supremacy rather than challenging them. She says that black women cannot see Madonna's change of hair colour to blonde as 'merely a question of aesthetic choice' but arising from white supremacy and racism. In *Truth or Dare: In Bed With Madonna* she sees her using the 'position of outsider' to 'colonize and appropriate black experience for her own opportunistic ends even as she attempts to mask her acts of racist aggression as affirmation.'[16] She points out that Madonna in using the motif of innocent female daring to be bad 'relies on the continued production of the racist/sexist sexual myth that black women are not innocent and never can be.'[17]

hooks quotes Susan Bordo at the head of her article as saying that the ' "destabilizing" potential of texts' can only be determined in relation to 'actual social practice.'[18] If we look at the 'destabilizing potential' of mimicry in this way then we are forced to recognize that there are many examples around us all the time, on public transport, at office parties, in restaurants, of women assuming exaggerated femininity. It is hard to know how to tell the difference between thoughtless, common or garden femininity and sophisticated femininity as masquerade. There is snobbery involved here too. There is clearly a distinction of value being made between women's choices to wear precisely similar clothes according to whether they are ignorant and unenlightened or whether they have done cultural studies and read Lacan and made a deliberate and revolutionary choice to wear lacy lowcut bodices.

Why is there such excitement about all this? It is difficult to believe that the postmodernist lesbian theorists are serious in seeing mimicry or roleplaying generally as a revolutionary strategy. But the theory does allow women who want to use gender fetishism for their own purposes, whether erotic or just traditional, to do so with a smug sense of political self-righteousness. Playing with gender and all the traditional paraphernalia of dominance and submission, power and powerlessness that male supremacy has ever produced, seems like fun. Whereas to a generation of women who grew up in the sixties make-up and high heels meant pain, expense, vulnerability, and a poor sense of self, a new young generation are telling us that these things are wonderful because they are choosing them. There is a new generation who seem to puzzle about how we manage to have fun without plucking our eyebrows and shaving our legs. Meanwhile the construction of gender seems unthreatened. We simply have the phenomenon of lesbians joining in to help shore up the facade of femininity. There was a time when lesbian feminists saw it as consciousness raising to appear in public or on the television in a guise which deliberately eschewed femininity. We believed that this would show women that an alternative to femininity was available. Now we are told by the parodists, mimics, performance artists that for a lesbian to appear dressed up in the way that might be expected of an extremely feminine heterosexual woman is more unsettling to male supremacy. It's hard to see why. Those most likely to be unsettled are surely the feminists and lesbians who feel completely undermined and even humiliated by having a lesbian show and tell the world that she wants to be feminine too.

Apart from the return to gender there is another aspect of the postmodernist approach to lesbian and gay studies that does not appear to be an obviously useful revolutionary strategy. This is the radical uncertainty about lesbian and gay identity. Both male and female theorists are adopting radical uncertainty. Naming and the creation of an identity were seen as fundamental political tasks for the emergent lesbian and gay movements of the seventies. Naming was particularly important to lesbian feminists who were well aware of the many ways in which women generally were disappeared from history, scholarship, from the records as soon as they married and lost their names. We knew it was important to place ourselves on the map and struggle to remain there. It was crucially necessary to adopt and promote the word lesbian because it established for lesbians a separate identity from gay men. Lesbian feminists in the western world then sought to flesh out this identity. We were constructing for ourselves a conscious political identity. Lesbian feminists have always been radical social constructionists in their approach to lesbianism. A lesbian identity which would defeat hostile and controlling stereotypes of lesbians and form the basis of our political work was constructed through poetry, works of theory, our conferences, collectives and everyday political work. It is an historically specific identity. The lesbian identity currently being constructed by sexual libertarians, queer nation theorists is quite different. The identity which is chosen and constructed will fit the political strategies undertaken.

Postmodernist lesbianandgay theorists seek to throw overboard any concept of even temporarily stable identity. Three political concerns seem to underlie this endeavour. One is a concern to avoid essentialism. This is a concern which does not seem particularly relevant to lesbian feminists who are pretty well aware that their lesbian identity is a deliberate and clearly intentional social construction. But it is a concern in particular for gay male theorists who are faced with a gay male culture far more anchored in ideas of essential identity than that of lesbians. The gay male concern with essentialism has dictated that lesbianandgay theorists in general should be very absorbed in this issue. As Richard Dyer expresses this in *Inside/Out* the 'notion of the homosexual'

> ... seemed to sail too close to the wind of the kind of biological etiologies of homosexuality that had been used against same-sex relations and, by holding up a model of what we inexorably are, to deprive us of the political practice of determining what we wanted to be.[19]

The other political concern underlying the desire for radical uncertainty is that of avoiding ethnocentrism. It was felt by the radically uncertain that a stable concept of what a lesbian or gay man is would be bound to reflect the ideas of the dominant racial or ethnic group and fail to allow for the considerable differences in experience and practice of those of other cultures. As Dyer writes:

> Work that sought to establish the continuity of lesbian/gay identity across time and culture seemed to be imposing the way lesbian/gay sexuality is for 'us' now upon the diversity and radical differences of both the past and 'other' (non-white, Third World) cultures and often eliding the differences between lesbians and gay men.[20]

Within women's liberation and lesbian feminism in general considerable work has been done by black and ethnic minority women to assert their own different identities without radically destabilizing the idea that there is such a thing as a lesbian. This work has been done by Black lesbians, Jewish lesbians, Chicana lesbians, Asian and indigenous lesbians, all of whom have been asserting a lesbian identity. This common identity does probably arise from western urban culture and would not necessarily transfer outside of that arena. Indigenous lesbians in Australia, for instance, have questioned the relevance of a word based upon a Greek island for their identity, and have pointed out that woman-loving in traditional indigenous culture does not allow room for an urban lesbian identity. But the importance for lesbian organising in urban western culture of a recognisable identity has seemed important to political lesbians across the board. The fact that the identity might make no sense to indigenous peoples or non-urban peoples in general does not negate its importance as an organising tool in its own context.

Another reason for suspicion of the lesbian or gay identity was based upon Foucauldian notions of 'the very operation of power through the regulation of desire that lesbian/gay politics and theory were supposed to be against.'[21] If the categories of homosexuality were invented as tools of social control then, Dyer suggests, we should be careful of the ways in which our use of them could contribute to this regulation. It is good and useful to be reminded of how we should interrogate our political practice and even what we take for granted politically, such as that we call ourselves lesbians, to check that we have not slid into politically unhelpful or even damaging ways. But when we look at the way that radical uncertainty is practiced in lesbian writing then we might wonder if this spring-cleaning has gone too far. Postmodernist writers are keen on the importance of making their subject position known lest they should be seen as pretending to universality or objectivity. Lesbian feminists quite unaware of postmodernist theory developed their own version of this in newsletters in the the eighties where they would identify themselves in biographical notes as 'Ex-het. middle class, fat-oppressed, fem, Libran' and so forth but they tended to be certain of all these aspects of their identities. Elizabeth Meese gives us an example of the postmodernist version of radical uncertainty:

Why is it that the lesbian seems like a shadow – a shadow with/in woman, with/in writing? A contrastive shape in a shadow play, slightly formless, the edges blurred by the turns of the field, the sheets on which a drama is projected. The lesbian subject is not all I am and it is in all I am. A shadow of who I am that attests to my being there, I am never with/out this lesbian. And we are always turning, this way and that, in one place and another. The shadows alone, never mind the body, make such a complex choreography in our struggle to make sense.[22]

Many pieces of postmodernist writing on lesbian themes begin with several pages of this kind of introspection on the writer's lesbian identity. Similarly when postmodernist academics give speeches they tend to spend the first twenty minutes interrogating their own subject position, leaving little space for the content that the audience is patiently waiting for. It may well be that many lesbian readers have never felt like a shadow or felt that they had a huge struggle to make sense, but in postmodernist feminist writing there is much agonising on how hard it is to speak or to write. There is an anguished agony of the artist here which many of us who simply seek to express ourselves as simply and frequently as we can, just cannot afford in ordinary political struggle. Judith Butler begins her piece in *Inside/Out* with just such anguished introspection on who she is being when she is asked to go and give a speech as a lesbian.

At first I considered writing a different sort of essay, one with a philosophical tone: the 'being' of being homosexual. The prospect of *being* anything, even for pay, has always produced in me a certain anxiety, for 'to be' lesbian seems to be more than a simple injunction to become who or what I already am. And in no way does it settle the anxiety for me to say that this is 'part' of what I am. To write or speak *as a lesbian* appears a paradoxical appearance of this 'I,' one which feels neither true nor false. For it is a production, usually in response to a request, to come out or write in the name of an identity which, once produced, sometimes functions as a politically efficacious phantasm. I'm not at ease with 'lesbian theories, gay theories,' for ... identity categories tend to be instruments of regulatory regimes ... This is not to say that I will not appear at political occasions under the sign of lesbian, but that I would like to have it permanently unclear what precisely that sign signifies.[23]

I find this kind of writing politically worrying. Butler uses the word homosexual in the first sentence in application to herself which is not something that the average lesbian feminist would feel able to do. The word homosexual has even more specifically male connotations than the word gay for most lesbians who became political in the seventies and who would not see themselves as being in an identical category with gay men which could be covered by such a single word. This suggests that Butler is one of the new lesbianandgay theorists who has chosen to abandon a separate lesbian politics. The use of particular words may help us to place Butler politically but it is her great angst about where she places herself which forms a problem for lesbian or gay politics. It's not exciting or inspiring to be faced with radical uncertainty but that's not sufficient as a criticism. What needs to be asked, and many heterosexual feminists, black

111

writers as well as lesbians are beginning to ask, is whether it is politically useful to become so doubtful about the word lesbian or other political categories such as woman or black when the oppressed groups making use of these identity categories are only just beginning to make space for themselves historically, culturally, and in the academy.

The point of postmodernist questioning of subject positions was that members of dominant groups should acknowledge their biases so that readers could more easily recognise certain writing as being part of regulatory systems. This is all fine and good but it is not the members of dominant groups who have taken up this opportunity to be radically uncertain and there is no good reason to expect that they would wish to. It is not the vice-chancellors of traditional universities who begin orations with twenty minutes of agonising over their subject positions and their right to be saying what they are about to say. Male, heterosexual, white academics are not taking up the opportunity in droves either. It seems to be mainly women, lesbians, gays and members of ethnic minority groups in general who are feeling under pressure to be radically uncertain. Whilst the certainties of regulatory regimes remain in place it may be that the best political way to fight them is to have some certainty ourselves about who we are and what we are doing. It could be that the requirement to be uncertain is simply feeding into the general difficulty the oppressed have with feeling confident and assertive in opposition to the dominant myth-making machinery. It could be helping us to feel powerless.

Diana Fuss devotes a whole chapter to the question of lesbian and gay identity politics in her book, *Essentially Speaking*. She suggests that lesbian theorists have been more committed than gay men to the idea of an essentialist identity.

> In general, current lesbian theory is less willing to question or to part with the idea of a 'lesbian essence' and an identity politics based on this shared essence. Gay male theorists, on the other hand, following the lead of Foucault, have been quick to endorse the social constructionist hypothesis and to develop more detailed analyses of the historical construction of sexualities.[24]

Now this will be a surprise to lesbian readers. The opposite has been our common experience. As a teacher I have discovered over and over again that the idea that male homosexuality is socially constructed is anathema to some male gay students and difficult to accept for many more, but not difficult for lesbians. Many lesbians, after all, have chosen to love women for political reasons, very often after half a lifetime of wifehood and motherhood in which they never thought of being attracted to women. Gay men do not often have this experience. It is difficult to find any who will say that their sexual preference is political and the result of consciously choosing to leave women or heterosexuality. Maybe, then, Fuss means that Lesbian writers have not promoted the idea of social construction even though most lesbians at the level of experience have accepted it. But this seems an unreasonable suggestion too. There is a quite massive literature on political lesbianism and the idea that heterosexuality is a political institution, constructed as the foundation of women's oppression. But Fuss ignores this literature apart from mentioning Adrienne Rich on several pages, perhaps has never seen it, though much is actually taught on women's studies courses. She explains that lesbians subscribe to essentialism more enthusiastically than gay men because as women we are more marginal and the certainty of an essentialist identity therefore seems more important to our security. This really seems like the opposite of the question that is really interesting to ask, which is why gay men who have less need of an essentialist identity in terms of their security subscribe so much more tenaciously to such.

According to Fuss, and other postmodernist lesbianandgay theorists, it is Foucault who has taught the world that sexuality is socially constructed. Particularly it is he who has taught us that sexual identities are differently experienced in different historical periods. So, Fuss speculates, it might be because of lesbians' greater need to adhere politically to essentialism that there has been a 'scarcity of Foucauldian analyses on lesbian sexuality compared to the plethora of such studies on the gay male subject'.[25] This is a distinctly surprising statement. Quite apart from the inaccuracy of attributing essentialism to lesbian theory, there is another problem here. Why should lesbians do

Foucauldian analysis? Why should they use the work of a gay man who did not really notice women let alone lesbians in his theory, to describe their experience, and one whose insights were antedated considerably by lesbian feminism? Lesbian feminists, in particular Lillian Faderman, have done their own excellent and groundbreaking work on the changing forms and development of woman-loving in history. But Fuss does not reference Faderman.

How can she manage to overlook lesbian feminism and believe that lesbians cannot do theory if they are not striving to fit themselves into the unsuitable concepts of a gay man? This must be because Fuss's starting point is not in lesbian theory or lesbian feminism. She does realise that male gay theory cannot entirely encompass lesbianism. For instance, when talking about the importance of social constructionist theories of lesbian and gay identity she suggests that these will help in theorising the differences between lesbians and gay men but does not seem to regard these as large.

> . . . invention theories allow us to make important distinctions between male homosexuals and lesbians, two groups which are frequently conflated in the research on sexual minorities (research noticeably skewed in the direction of the gay male subject) but which, in fact, are not constructed in precisely the same ways.[26]

One might even wish to be a little stronger than that and say that lesbians and gay men were actually constructed in very different ways but Fuss, being resolutely lesbianandgay in her approach, prefers to be much more mild and tentative. It is interesting considering that postmodernist theorists see themselves as unmatched in their attention to 'difference' that they sometimes reveal themselves as very timid in acknowledging such differences as those that are politically constructed between men and women. Fuss's starting point is in gay male theory, and in postmodernist men in general. At the same time as not referencing Faderman she has nineteen works by Derrida in the bibliography.

It does seem to be his work which has sent some lesbian and

feminist theorists into a tizzy over essentialism. She tells us of his 'recent efforts to deconstruct "essence" '.[27] It is clear that the word essentialism is not being used in the traditional ways in these postmodernist writings. Many detractors of radical feminist theory do, with little evidence, accuse it of being essentialist in its old fashioned sense of biological determinist. Anti-pornography campaigners are accused, for instance, of believing that male and female sexuality are essentially different. But Fuss does not use the word in the same way. She, like other postmodernist theorists, tends to use the word to describe any politics based upon any concept of identity, constructed or otherwise, or any politics which believes that there is any similarity amongst a class of people on which political theorising or action can be based. It is a concept of essentialism so often directed against anyone who believes in or suggests political action that some feminists and other activists have come to believe that the word is just a way of saying that political action is vulgar. It may be that postmodernists have committed verbicide on this term and that it can no longer be used usefully.

The struggles which theorists like Butler and Fuss are having with concepts like gender, identity and essence arise from the works of their male authorities. These lesbian theorists are not situated within lesbian or feminist politics but are seeking to forge a unified lesbianandgay politics based on male gay theory. They criticise lesbian feminist politics, when they mention it at all, for its failure to measure up in terms of their postmodernist male masters, and wrestle to fit lesbian politics seamlessly into the pockets of gay postmodernists. Meanwhile lesbian feminist theorists are engaged in a strange shadow play of seeking to criticise these intrusions of what is clearly a rather inappropriate theory onto the stage without being familiar with its origins. Not many of us have read nineteen works of Derrida and many will not want to, but we are expected to struggle to answer his questions, introduced by his women followers.

I would like to suggest that however daring postmodern theorists see themselves to be they are actually simply placing a fashionable intellectual gloss on old fashioned liberalism and individualism. A good example of this is the effect that exposure to postmodern theory can have on straightforward political analysis in respect of pornography. Kobena Mercer is a former member of the Gay Black Group in London and is now teaching art history at the University of California, Santa Cruz. Whilst in the Gay Black Group he used the insights of feminist anti-pornography activists to critique the work of the white gay American photographer, Robert Mapplethorpe. Much of Mapplethorpe's work focused on black male nudes. Mercer interpreted the photo entitled 'Man in a Polyester Suit' which showed 'the profile of a black man whose head was cropped – or "decapitated", so to speak – holding his semi-tumescent penis through the Y-fronts of his underpants' as perpetuating 'the racist stereotype that, essentially, the black man is nothing more than his penis.'[28] He saw such photos as perpetuating 'racial fetishism,' an 'aesthetic idealization of racial difference that merely inverts and reverses the binary axis of colonial discourse.'[29] Then, he says, he became aware of conflicting readings of Mapplethorpe's work as a result of becoming familiar with poststructuralist theory. Indeed once in the academy, and he is now an academic, it is not easy to hold on to positions which can be seen as vulgarly political. The ideas of postmodernist cultural studies made him realise:

> The variety of conflicting interpretations of the value of Mapplethorpe's work would imply that the text does not bear one, singular and unequivocal meaning, but is open to a number of competing readings.[30]

He decides that the question of whether Mapplethorpe's black male nudes 'reinforce or undermine racist myths about black sexuality' is 'unanswerable' because of the 'death of the author' argument in poststructuralist theory. He now interrogates his own subject position as he views the photographs and wonders whether 'my anger was also mingled with feelings of jealousy, rivalry or envy', the 'anger and envy' being the effects of his 'identification with both object and subject of the look.' Cultural criticism of this variety depends on the individual. It is just opinion and people have different ones. 'A great deal depends on the reader and the social identity she or he brings to the text.'[31] Mercer has become radically uncertain and is now as apologetic about his earlier clear anti-racist stand on Mapple-thorpe as we have seen many lesbians become about their earlier embarrassing feminism in this volume.

Another example of the way in which postmodernist-speak serves to leach out political meaning is the blurb for a conference entitled 'Forces of Desire' at the prestigious Humanities Research Centre at the Australian National University in Canberra in June 1993.

The key issues here will be the examination of sexuality without the dominance of a master model, and the structuring and restructuring of desire. Speakers will be invited to address a range of topics, such as: multiple sexualities as practices and life-styles beyond the dominant models with investment in reproductive sexuality; the costs of sustaining such models; the varieties of sexuality – masochism, sadism, perversions, heterosexualities, gay sexualities; sexuality as normative and the possibilities and purposes of resistance to and transformation of these norms; knowledge as implicated in sexual practices – the erotics of knowledge production, the desire for knowledges; the interactions of sexuality, knowledge, power and violence.[32]

It may be that lesbian feminist readers are already feeling rather puzzled about how their analysis would fit in here. In fact lesbians are not mentioned. They seem to have been disappeared into 'gay sexualities'. How many are there of these? The varieties of sexuality start off with masochism and sadism and nowhere seem to include anything specifically egalitarian. The lesbian feminist critique of heterosexuality as an institution does not seem welcome since in this 'model' we only have 'heterosexualities', this plural form somehow not lending itself to such an analysis. S's have appeared on all sorts of things as we might expect with a certain postmodern approach which seeks to cover all eventualities with plurals which end up excluding lesbians and feminists and much that could be called political analysis. In favour of 'difference' everything has been homogenised here. I always wonder how the plurals and singulars are decided upon. For instance there are singulars of masochism, sadism, desire and power but plurals of everything else. There is a politics here of course, even a 'master model' perhaps. I suspect that the politics is a sexual libertarian one of sexual minorities, mainstream gay male politics of the moment. It could be that the 'gay sexualities' are supposed to include pedophilia, transsexualism and so on, all represented as somehow equal to 'lesbianism' if that fits anywhere here at all. There do not seem to be any radical or revolutionary feminists on the list of research fellows or speakers invited. But they do include Gayle Rubin, proponent of lesbian sadomasochism and butch lesbian transsexualism, Jeffrey Weeks, Foucauldian gay historian, Carol Vance, a leading libertarian lesbianandgay theorist and Cindy Patton, who we met in Chapter 2 bemoaning the amount of seriousness given by feminists to the issue of sexual abuse. Surely it must be difficult for sadomasochists, dwellers on the 'sexual fringe' such as Rubin, to maintain that they are really daring, when they are invited, and financially supported, by a prestigious institution in this way.

Postmodernist lesbian and gay theory performs the useful function of permitting those who simply wish to employ the tools and trappings of sexism and racism to feel not only justified but even revolutionary. Lesbian roleplaying, sadomasochism, male gay masculinity, drag, Madonna's mimicry, her use of black men and black iconography, Mapplethorpe's racist sexual stereotyping, can be milked for all the pleasure and profit that they offer in a male supremacist culture in which inequality of power is seen as all that sex is or could be. The enjoyment of the status quo is then called 'parody' so that it can be retrieved by intellectuals who might otherwise feel anxious about the excitement they experience. For those postmodern lesbianandgay theorists who have no interest in taking their pleasures in these ways, the ideas of radical uncertainty, of the utopian or essentialist nature of any project for social change, provide a theoretical support for a gentlemanly liberalism and individualism.

---

1. See Brodribb, Somer (1992). *Nothing Mat(t)ers: A Feminist Critique of Postmodernism*. Melbourne: Spinifex Press.

2. Fuss, Diana (Ed.) (1991). *Inside/Out. Lesbian Theories, Gay Theories.* London and New York: Routledge.

3. Butler, Judith (1990). *Gender Trouble. Feminism and the Subversion of Identity.* London New York: Routledge. p. 32.

4. Butler, Judith (1991). 'Imitation and Gender Insubordination.' In Fuss, Diana (Ed.) p. 23.

5. Butler, Judith (1990). p. 33.

6. For a good exposition of radical feminist politics and the idea of gender see: Thompson, Denise (1991). *Reading Between the Lines. A Lesbian Feminist Critique of Feminist Accounts of Sexuality.* Sydney: Gorgon's Head Press.

7. On the idea of androgyny see Raymond, Janice G. (1986). *A Passion for Friends.* Boson: Beacon Press. p. 12.

8. Butler, Judith (1990). p. 30.

9. See Weedon, Chris (1987). *Feminist Practice and Poststructuralist Theory.* Oxford: Basil Blackwell.

10. Butler, Judith (1991). p. 21.

11. Ibid. p. 29.

12. See Humphries, Martin (1985). 'Gay Machismo.' In Metcalf, Andy and Humphries, Martin (Eds.) *The Sexuality of Men.* London: Pluto Press. Kleinberg, Seymour. (1987). 'The New Masculinity of Gay Men and Beyond.' In Kaufman, Michael (Ed.) (1987). *Beyond Patriarchy. Essays by Men on Pleasure, Power and Change.* Toronto and New York: Oxford University Press.

13. Tyler, Carol-Anne (1991). *Boys Will Be Girls: The Politics of Gay Drag.* p. 53.

14. Smyth, Cherry (1992). *Lesbians Talk: Queer Notions.* London: Scarlet Press. p. 44.

15. Ibid.

16. hooks, bell (1992). *Black Looks: Race and Representation.* Boston: South End Press. Chapter entitled: 'Madonna. Plantation Mistress or Soul Sister?' p. 159.

17. Ibid. p. 160.

18. Ibid. p. 157.

19. Dyer, Richard (1991). *Believing in Fairies: The Author and the Homosexual.* p. 186.

20. Ibid.

21. Ibid.

22. Meese, Elizabeth (1990). 'Theorizing Lesbian: Writing – A Love Letter.' In Jay, Karla and Glasgow, Joanne (Eds.). *Lesbian Texts and Contexts. Radical Revisions.* New York: New York University Press. p. 70.

23. Butler, Judith (1991). pp. 13–14.

24. Fuss, Diana (1990). *Essentially Speaking. Feminism, Nature and Difference.* London and New York: Routledge. p. 98.

25. Ibid. p. 99.

26. Ibid. pp. 108–109.

27. Ibid. p. 102.

28. Mercer, Kobena (1992). 'Just Looking for Trouble: Robert Mapplethorpe and Fantasies of Race.' In Segal, Lynne and McIntosh, Mary (Eds.). *Sex Exposed. Sexuality and the Pornography Debate.* London: Virago. p. 96.

29. Ibid. p. 99.

30. Ibid. p. 102.

31. Ibid. p. 105.

32. Publicity material about visiting fellowships for the Humanities Research Centre at ANU's 1993 theme 'Sexualities and Culture'.

Chapter 6

THE LESBIAN OUTLAW

In the eighties and nineties many lesbians have sought to rebel against feminism rather than into it. One reason for this is the lesbian romance with outlaw status. The lesbian's status as outlaw is, for many lesbians, one important source of the satisfaction to be gained from lesbianism. Alongside all its disadvantages in social disapproval and penalties, lesbianism offers the glamour and excitement of outlawry. This is not perhaps a sufficient compensation for loss of social approval for those who want a quiet life rather than the delights of daredevilry, but even when entirely confined to the head rather than to lived experience, outlawry appears to offer some kind of solace. Both lesbian feminists and lifestyle lesbians can gain satisfaction from outlaw status. Lesbian feminists gain the dubious advantage of being outlaws both in the heterosexual world and in the lesbian one by virtue of their politics. Serious challenge to the political institution of heterosexuality provides the experience of outlawry and even martyrdom to its exponents but this version of outlawry is not as exciting now as it was to young lesbians a decade ago.

Lifestyle lesbians who would not dream of offering a challenge to the world domination of hetero-reality because they see sexual orientation as simply a matter of preference, can gain outlaw status through the adoption of what is seen as 'outlaw sexuality' e.g. sadomasochism. The new 'sexual outlaw' lesbians can compensate for the problems posed by lesbian feminism and the growth of lesbian culture for outlaw status. Where once outlawry could be assured simply by adoption of lesbian sexuality and lifestyle it seems that the apparently greater social possibilities gained for lesbians by lesbian liberation have made things too easy. A character in Sarah Schulman's novel, *After Delores*, expresses this sentiment:

> ... It's too easy to be gay today in New York City. I come from those times when sexual excitement could only be in hidden places. Sweet women had to put themselves in constant danger to make love to me. All my erotic life is concerned with intrigue and secrets. You can't understand that these days, not at all. Lesbians will never be that sexy again.[1]

An expanded lesbian scene has been created largely by the efforts of lesbian feminists. Lesbians who revolt against the possibility of relatively cosy lesbian lives and who are lesbians mostly because of the transgressive sexual excitements offered by outlawry can now only recoup their excitement by turning to a style and practice designed to shock the very lesbian community which is giving them too easy a time. Ruby Rich argues that lesbian S/M originates in an attempt to regain such a sexual excitement. She describes the excitement that some lesbians could see themselves as losing as a result of the success of lesbian feminism.

> ... The lesbian moved from a position of outlaw to one of respectable citizen. Yet in the pre-Stonewall era prior to 1969, the lesbian was a far more criminal figure, her very sexuality criminalized in many laws, her desires unacceptable, and her clothing taboo (at least for the butch, who was the only visible lesbian in this period). For many women, the drive toward lesbianism was not only sexual but also a will to be the outlaw, the same drive that moved other subcultures, like the Beats, to cross to the 'wrong' side of the tracks, if only metaphorically. Thus, there was a very real sense of loss associated with the hard-worn respectability: a loss of taboo and with it eroticism.[2]

Outlawry and decadence have been an important theme in twentieth century lesbian culture. There was a time when the lesbian bar was the place where the delights of outlawry could be easily appreciated. Surprisingly little has been written about the importance and meaning of the bar in lesbian culture. Karla Jay has written a short piece on this theme entitled *Life in the Underworld: The Lesbian Bar as Metaphor*. Jay points out that the bar has survived the developments that might have been expected to presage its disappearance such as gay liberation.

> . . . It is time to admit that if we cannot praise the lesbian bar, so too are we unable to bury it. Much as in the days before the current gay liberation movements, bars play a large part in the lives of lesbians and gay men . . . Far from being obliterated by gay liberation, the subculture of the bars has proliferated in the years since the 1969 Stonewall rebellion.[3]

It may be that some lesbian bars today, especially with the development of the Sunday afternoon tea-dance, have become too respectable and removed the delights of outlawry, but seedy bars remain and new imitations are being created around the theme of sadomasochism. There are lesbians who abjure the bar and lesbian bar culture but for many the bar has a continuing allure which derives from much more than decadence. The bar offers self-affirmation, particularly to lesbians who are not 'out' but even to those who are thoroughly and publicly out. The bar offers lesbians a place to be themselves. As Jay puts it, 'It is the one theater where the actors can play themselves, for it is in the outside world that they wear masks and play strange parts.'[4] The bar offers support. Lesbian novels and folk history are replete with references to the support gained, particularly over broken love affairs, from other lesbians at the bar. The bar can offer practical support in the form of new lovers, solicitors or house painters.

But it is ironic that the bar has been able to offer self-affirmation when the atmosphere and facilities of the bar were often so apparently hostile. Jay explains her reaction on going into a lesbian bar for the first time.

> . . . I was appalled by the dinginess and the glaring appraisals from the women posing against the bar, their hands on jutting

123

hips. I never thought I would overcome the feeling of being an outsider in a world supposedly mine. And I never have.[5]

As Jay also points out, the problems associated with the lesbian bar include serious abuse of alcohol. Lesbian bars have traditionally been sited in cellars or basements with backed up toilets, crush, smoke, and terrible food. In one particularly seedy bar at King's Cross in London in the late seventies the disco took place in either the cellar there, which we called the urinal because of the persistent smell and the decor, or up many flights of steep stairs with malodorous toilets on the landings. Some bars are less seedy these days but usually fall rather short of the kind of places one would choose to eat or drink in. The seediness is the result of the exploitability of lesbians. Venues depend on the goodwill of landlords who recognize that lesbians drink and are prepared to accept them on the premises, though not usually protect them from ambush and male violence whilst there. Used to such places we are genuinely astonished when we enter a lesbian venue which is so comfortable that we feel just like regular folks, but such places can sometimes be found, usually outside Britain.

But despite all this, black lesbians and white lesbians, lesbians from different walks of life and class backgrounds do mingle on the same turf in the bars. Even seriously seedy bars are able to appear glamorous because of the decadence they embody. The concept of outlawry is steeped in the love of decadence which is a powerful lesbian and gay motif. This is revealed in the love/hate relationship many lesbians have with the bar scene. It is in the bars that the lesbian outlaw finds a home and decadence is supposed to reign. A classic description of the lesbian and gay bar is provided by Radclyffe Hall in *The Well of Loneliness*.

... As long as she lived Stephen never forgot her first impressions of the bar known as Alec's – that miserable meeting-place of the most miserable of all those who comprised the miserable army. That merciless, drug-dealing, death-dealing haunt to which flocked the battered remnants of men whom their fellow-men had at last stamped under; who, despised of the world, must despise themselves beyond all hope, it seemed, of salvation. There they sat, closely herded together at the tables, creatures shabby yet tawdry, timid yet defiant – and their eyes, Stephen never forgot their eyes, those haunted, tormented eyes of the invert.[6]

It seems that Hall was here trying to persuade her readers that such a scene was undesirable. But she was not particularly effective. For those to whom outlawry is attractive this is not necessarily unalluring.

This romance with decadence and outlawry exists in heterosexual culture too and particularly in gay male culture. Rebellious counter-cultural heterosexuals who gain satisfaction from living in opposition to surburban values can get decadent kicks from a sleazy jazz nightclub. For heterosexuals decadence is a chosen path which can be swapped at any moment for a regular *Neighbours*-type lifestyle. For lesbians and gay men the sordid nature of our social venues is the result of our oppression. Lesbians are not usually destined to follow a decadent grail by whim but because of the circumstances of lesbian life, pressures to be hidden and secretive and the difficulties of finding lesbian company in an anti-lesbian world.

Lesbians may not choose to be outcasts but find that they are given the status of pariahs by a lesbian-hating society. It is possible that the lesbian romance with outlawry is a way of adapting to and making the best of the situation which results from oppression. Lesbians who may be forced to seek the company of others of their kind in seedy bars can learn to appreciate the courage, humour and culture of the lesbians they find there. Exiles forever from suburban comforts, they can learn to take comfort from their outlaw status. Rebelliousness, courage, eccentricity all have their glamour, especially when there is no alternative. Most lesbians probably don't really want to be like 'regular folks' anyway. Lesbian existence, let alone the bar, is a rebellious thumbing of the nose to heterosexual society and to a family of origin which may have been lost.

Another possible motive for the attraction some lesbians feel towards the bars might be *nostalgie de la boue*, an expression coined in the end of century decadence of the 1890s to denote a fascination with 'low-life' amongst the bourgeoisie. This fasci-

125

nation was acted out by middle-class straight men mainly through consorting with prostitutes in London bars. It is a hobby not really open to women because of the risks to physical safety and of sexual exploitation. It is women's work to meet men's demand for decadence rather than our pleasure to pursue it. But for lesbians the delights of *nostalgie de la boue* are available to some extent. Oscar Wilde was fascinated with his favourite version of *boue* i.e. use of young working class male prostitutes and drugs and not just in practice but in art. In *The Picture of Dorian Gray* Wilde painted a romantically decadent picture of the opium den. On his way to visit one such Gray mused:

> . . . Ugliness was the one reality. The coarse brawl, the loath-some den, the crude violence of disordered life, the very vile-ness of thief and outcast, were more vivid, in their intense actuality of impression, than all the gracious shapes of Art, the dreamy shadows of Song. They were what he needed for forgetfulness.[7]

The opium den Gray finds is suitably sordid.

> . . . The door opened quietly, and he went in without saying a word to the squat misshapen figure that flattened itself into the shadow as he passed. At the end of the hall hung a tattered green curtain that had swayed and shook in the gusty wind which had followed him in from the street. He dragged it aside, and entered a long, low room which looked as if it had been a third-rate dancing-saloon. Shrill flaring gas jets, dulled and distorted in the fly-blown mirrors that faced them, were ranged around the walls.[8]

There are some similarities here with the London lesbian bar of the seventies. Maureen Duffy's description of a London Lesbian bar in her 1966 novel, *The Microcosm*, conjures up something of the same sinister, doomed atmosphere.

> . . . And this too is wonderland, the world turned back to front through a glass darkly. The tourists stand about, backs

to the wall in defence, amazed, amused at the underwater life trapped in this hazy aquarium whose thin, transparent walls might break under a probing finger, letting these strange forms of life swim free among the plump goldfish in the garden pond.[9]

Duffy catches the romantic melancholy often associated with the lesbian scene, too, in her description of one of the habituées of the bar.

> ... Brilliant, sad, surrounded by a whirl of satellites who are drawn closer or spin pale, disconsolate moons away on the fringe of light as her eyes flash negative or positive, she passes to the bar. They revolve anxiously, hovering to see who will be summoned for their sun's warmth this chilly evening while the rest are left to reflect in each other's eyes or slip away into the shadows by the wall.[10]

Duffy chooses to express the sadness of the lesbian bar scene here. The positive virtues of support and friendship and rebelliousness that bars offered are not so often expressed in print. In print we have many examples of the lesbian and male gay scene described as uniformly depressing before the seventies. It is described as a world in which relationships are inevitably brief and tragic and poor suffering victims cut their wrists in the bathroom and when they grow old, live out unwanted and unfulfilled lives. The bar is seen as a haven for social misfits.

Ann Bannon offers us such a view of lesbian and gay culture through the eyes of Jack in *Women of the Shadows*. This is the most pessimistic of her novels as can be guessed from the title. Jack is depressed about the gay scene himself because of the heartbreak he routinely suffers and tries to turn Laura away from it so that she will agree to marry him in a marriage of convenience and move uptown to respectability.

> ... We don't know anything about a love that lasts or a life that means something. We spend all our time on our knees singing hosannas to the queers. Trying to make ourselves look

good. Trying to forget we aren't wholesome and healthy like other people.[11]

His image of growing old in the lesbian community is even more negative.

> . . . Have you seen the pitiful old women in their men's oxfords and chopped-off hair, stumping around like lost souls, wandering from bar to bar and staring at the pretty kids and weeping because they can't have them any more? Or living together, two of them, ugly and fat and wrinkled, with nothing to do and nothing to care about but the good old days that are no more?[12]

Lesbians greeted the new and positive lesbian novels from 1969 onwards such as *Patience and Sarah* and *Rubyfruit Jungle* with enthusiasm.[13] It is understandable that we believed and hoped that novels about doomed lesbians were a thing of the past. But this was not to be the case.

In a changed and pessimistic political climate lesbian culture in the nineties offers us some fictionalised accounts of lowlife which are receiving critical acclaim such as the American novel, *After Delores*, and the film, *Kamikaze Hearts*. The romance with lowlife, doom and despair that has formed a motif of lesbian and gay culture for most of the twentieth century is having a revival. The novel takes place in seedy bars in rundown areas of New York such as the following.

> . . . Some guy with an Iron Maiden tattoo vomited in our direction as Coco led me past all the new condominiums and few remaining flophouses left on the Bowery. We passed the shelter for homeless men, the lobster place with singing wait-resses, putrid Phebe's and walked through the grimy doorway of CBGB's, the punk palace.[14]

The novel's narrator is deep in the pain of a relationship breakup and one would not expect the novel to be upbeat. But the depressing tone of the novel derives from much more than this. The sex industry is a major background theme. But instead of any criticism we find the narrator cheerfully joining in the use of a woman in the sex industry,

> ... I drank some more beer and tried to decide whether or not to tip the dancer ... I stretched out over the bar ... and held out a dollar ... that little darling, bless her heart, gave me a big one-dollar smile, took the cash and stuffed it into her panties like I was a regular anybody.[15]

The choice of a lesbian identity is not made to sound positive in the novel. The narrator describes her choice as a lesser of two evils: 'Once I realized women could be pretty nasty I actually considered boys for about five minutes until I remembered that they bored me very quickly ...'[16] The sex described in the novel is a lesbian rape scene which the heroine is described as wanting though it causes great pain and lacerations to the vagina.

Novels of this type are defended as realistic, a welcome chance for lesbians to 'tell it like it is' instead of having to put on a good face for the sake of public relations. But it seems that we are back to the depressing world of the doomed lesbians, but a world in which there is no happiness or laughter, none of the gritty humour or courage of an Ann Bannon novel. What is different now is that there has been feminism. Lesbians do not have to feel quite so badly about themselves and feminist presses such as published *After Delores* in Britain would probably publish a positive novel. It is not enough to argue that this novel is 'realistic', men argue the same thing about *Lolita* or *American Psycho*. Novel writing, and particularly lesbian novel writing is a political endeavour. The choice to represent lesbians as failed, doomed, desperate, sadomasochistic is a political one.

The film, *Kamikaze Hearts*, was promoted as a 'lesbian romance'. In it two women, one showing some resemblance to a male-to-female transsexual, have a tortured relationship. Both work in the pornography industry. Mitch pouts and postures in teetering heels and bright red lipstick, looking like a drag queen, gets fucked in the porn movie within a movie and professes to love the work. Mitch sees sex on screen and sex off screen as just the same, all an act. Mitch is addicted to heroin. After suffering agonies of unrequited loyalty, Tigr succumbs to Mitch's charms and becomes re-addicted to heroin. This is the final scene. Mitch holds up a syringe and says 'I fucked her with my prick and she loved it'. The film gives a false picture of pornography modelling since women do not really work in the industry just for kicks and because they enjoy the sex, but for money. But when decadence is romanticised the sex industry is generally glamourised in this fashion. The film shares common themes with *After Delores*: drugs, sadomasochism, prostitution and despair.

Prostitution is an ever present element in the decadent scene. The power balance of male supremacy dictates that when men have dreams of decadence they do not usually see themselves as the prostitutes but as using the prostitutes. When lesbians take to decadence they do so according to their gender prescribed role. Like the men, they can see prostitution as glamorous and sexually fulfilling for its exponents, but women's fantasies and practice are mostly limited as yet to being the objects rather than the subjects of the sex industry. In the course of seeking to rehabilitate prostitution as a form of legitimate sexual outlawry for women, Joan Nestle tells us of the identity of interest between lesbians and prostitutes, who have shared a common history and oppression. Her essay, *Lesbians and Prostitutes: An Historical Sisterhood*, aims to 'show how Lesbians and prostitutes have always been connected, not just in the male imagination but in their actual histories.'[17] She explains that prostitutes and lesbians shared a common turf before the birth of lesbian feminism.

> ... In the bars of the late fifties and early sixties where I learned my Lesbian ways, whores were part of our world. We sat on barstools next to each other, we partied together, and we made love together.[18]

This seems to have been just as true of the London bar scene at that time. Then, says Nestle, this happy sisterhood was broken apart by lesbian feminism, in which the viewpoint or presence of 'working women' was not welcome. In the course of reclaiming the sisterhood of lesbians with prostitutes Nestle tells us that she has chosen herself, in recent years, to work as a prostitute.

130

... I write sex stories for Lesbian magazines, I pose for explicit photographs for Lesbian photographers, I do readings of sexually graphic materials dressed in sexually revealing clothes, and I have taken money from women for sexual acts.[19]

Somehow one cannot see Oscar Wilde indulging his *nostalgie de la boue* in such a fashion but then he was a middle class man and used others in prostitution rather than being used.

Nestle romanticises prostitution and falls victim to the lure of decadence. Prostitution has such glamour for Nestle that she chooses to dabble in it herself. It is not likely that lesbians historically have mixed socially with prostitutes because they found it titillating or that lesbians have worked as prostitutes because it was sexually exciting or glamorous. But prostitution, glamourised into a titillating fantasy, plays a part in the sexual life of many women straight and lesbian. This is because women are well trained to eroticise their own subordination and being used as a prostitute can be seen as the epitome of sexualised subordination.

A political movement of sexual outlawry has developed in the eighties amongst lesbians of which the glamourising of prostitution is but one part. The new lesbian politics of transgression is an offshoot of an older tradition in gay male culture and politics. John Rechy in *The Sexual Outlaw* explains how, by a happy coincidence, traditional male gay sexual practice happens to be revolutionary.

... Promiscuous homosexuals ... are the shock troops of the sexual revolution. The streets are the battleground, the revolution is the sexhunt, a radical statement is made each time a man has sex with another on a street.

What is it to be a sexual outlaw? Archetypal outsider, he is a

... symbol of survival, living fully at the very edge, triumphant over the threats, repression, persecution, prosecution, attacks, denunciations, hatred that have tried powerfully to crush him from the beginning of 'civilization'.[20]

131

But it is possible no one will notice him being revolutionary under a bridge or in the bushes. The excitement of his transgression depends precisely upon its being furtive. The rebellion Rechy is engaged in is not new or even specifically gay. He was once a writer on the Beat circuit which included, besides the homoeroticism of heroes such as Jack Kerouac and William Burroughs, a fierce rebellion by all of them against respectability and the 'rule' of women. Rechy has exchanged one form of rebellion for another.

Traditionally lesbians have not engaged in the same practices. There are some obvious reasons for this. Women would be extremely unsafe in such behaviour on the street. But also lesbian sexuality has tended to be constructed on the same model as that of heterosexual women. It has tended to be more concentrated on relationship and intimacy because women are not the ruling class and do not have a subject class to use sexually to prove their status. Lesbians, like heterosexual women, do not generally gain in status by sexually acting out, so engaging in repeated sex acts for their own sake with strangers has not been highly valued. Lesbians have had no masculinity to affirm even though some are now trying hard to acquire such and this may cause changes in sexual behaviour.

But we now have a situation in which some lesbians are seeking to construct a lesbian sexuality which will more clearly mirror that of the sexual outlawry of gay men. The sexual hopelessness of lesbians, judged by their difference from gay men, has become a new political truth in some areas of lesbian and gay studies. Thus Catherine Saalfield and Ray Navarro in the 1991 collection *Inside/Out* refer cheerfully to the 'lesbian sex panic' as if this was a well accepted concept '. . . lesbian sex panic (timidity, repression, and "feminine manners") existed long before AIDS' they tell us.[21] Chris Bearchell, a Canadian lesbian, gives us an example of the way that some lesbians seek to reconstruct lesbian sexuality in order to overcome this problem. She writes:

Many dykes, including those who call ourselves feminists, are compulsive rule-breakers. We take women to beaches, or find them there, and head for the dunes, or take bar-room tricks to bathroom cubicles for quickies. We reject *Playboy* lesbianism because it isn't hot enough and get our polaroids out instead. We seek out lovers we can trust for SM theatre, or choose to play sexual games *because* they involve certain risks. We are irresponsible tomboys who refused to grow up and who now refuse to leave out of our lives, including our love and sex lives, a kindred spirit because she happens to be 15 or 16 years old. It isn't true that public sex, porn, S/M and child-adult sex are not lesbian issues.[22]

The practices she is describing are not traditionally lesbian ones but she seems to hope that their adoption will gain for lesbians the excitements of sexual outlawry that she sees gay men enjoying. The politics of this sexuality are anti-feminist. Ruling class male sexuality is dangerous to the interests of women and has traditionally relied upon the sacrifice of a large section of the class of women to sexual slavery. This uncomfortable truth is subsumed here beneath one lesbian's search to be an equal sexual outlaw.

The theorists of lesbian sadomasochism have adopted the clothes of the outlaw in rage against feminism and all its works. The language of sexual outlawry may originate in gay male culture but S/M proponents such as Pat Califia and Gayle Rubin have adopted it. Rubin deliberately makes an analogy between 'coming out' as a lesbian and coming out as a sadomasochist. She felt cheated of the delights of outlawry when coming out as a lesbian:

... to be a baby dyke in 1970 was to feel great moral self-confidence. One could luxuriate in the knowledge that not only was one not a slimy pervert, but one's sexuality was especially blessed on political grounds. As a result, I never quite understood the experience of being gay in the face of unrelenting contempt.[23]

Rubin gives to sadomasochism the most romantic outlaw status she can imagine by comparing the experience of being a sadomasochist in 1980 with that of being a communist homosexual in 1950. She deliberately makes an analogy with the experience of

133

coming out as gay in order to invoke the sympathies of those with liberal feelings towards the oppression of homosexuals. Finding the sadomasochist community she describes thus:

> The routes of access to it are even more hidden. The aura of terror is more intense. The social penalties, the stigma, and the lack of legitimacy are even greater.[24]

Does this not remind us of the opium den? The outlawry of sadomasochism is a political outlawry according to Rubin. She sees sadomasochists as simply one of a list of sexual minorities in which most of the categories are only applicable to gay men. These sexual minorities are one moment seen as religious heretics and then as political dissidents. Always they are 'outlaws'.

> The sexual outlaws – boy-lovers, sadomasochists, prostitutes, and transpeople, among others – have an especially rich knowledge of the prevailing system of sexual hierarchy and of how sexual controls are exercised. These populations of erotic dissidents . . .'[25]

To the lesbians who are dedicated to being sexual outlaws feminism is boring and part of the repressive hierarchy of straight society. Gayle Rubin characterises 'femininism', the name she gives to feminists who campaign against male violence and pornography, as the enemy in *Coming to Power*.

> By a series of accidents, and through the mediating issue of pornography, S/M has become a challenge to this entire political tendency, which has ridden to power by manipulating women's fears around sex and around violence.[26]

She has set up such anti-pornography feminists as the mother figures she can have an adolescent rebellion against. She states that 'I, for one, did not join the women's movement to be told how to be a good girl.'[27] Such libertarian lesbians can gain considerable satisfaction from transgressing in the relatively safe surroundings of the women's movement, seeking to call forth a delicious opprobrium.

It is surprising in the end that sadomasochists should choose a form of outlawry which is much more acceptable to the straight world than lesbian feminism and certainly radical lesbianism or lesbian separatism could ever be. In Britain the nascent cult of lesbian sadomasochism gained flattering media coverage. It is titillating to the men who run the newspapers and the television programmes. In a sado-society leather and lace are more photogenic than a band of lesbian separatists and the message, that women can abuse other women and love their subordination, altogether more palatable. At an ACT UP demonstration of safe sex practices in the Bourke Street Mall, a pedestrianised shopping street, in Melbourne in May 1992, a lesbian wearing leather chaps and no knickers simulated oral sex and the use of dental dams with a woman in a skirt on her knees in front of her. Apparently the audience cheered and it is to be expected that men used to consuming simulated lesbian sex in their porn magazines would find this exciting but perhaps not revolutionary. It is difficult to see how the fulfilment of men's pornographic fantasies can explode the male supremacist construction of sexuality.

There are difficulties for lesbians in appropriating transgression as a philosophy that arise from the very different sex class position that women are in. Women have been offered under modern male supremacy either the sexual role of good girl or bad girl. Neither path led to freedom for women. Women who chose or were forced into the bad girl route to prostitution are unlikely to have seen the excitement of revolutionary transgression as one of its joys. Being bad boys, for men, was always a more liberating experience and generally carried out through the bodies of women or powerless men and boys. Men could realise themselves through sexually acting out in a way that women, who were the bodies through which they achieved liberation, could not. I would suggest that choosing to be bad girls in rebellion against feminist ethics and politics of sexuality will turn out to be just as restrictive as the bad girl role under male supremacy has always been.

The romanticising of outlawry for gay men and lesbians has

been given academic legitimacy by a postmodern theory which valorises outlaw behaviour. Gayle Rubin, for instance, is seen as a Foucauldian. Postmodern theory, especially its lesbian and gay varieties, is full of the revolutionary potential of transgression. Jonathan Dollimore chooses to set the scene for his book, *Sexual Dissidence*, with the transgressive heroism of Oscar Wilde. Dollimore shows how Wilde sought to explode the respectable categories of middle-class Victorian life. One example given of his transgression is the way in which he helped Andre Gide to come to terms with his homosexuality, or pederasty as he called it. In Algeria in 1899, Wilde arranged to buy a young boy musician Gide had evinced an interest in. As Dollimore describes it, 'Gide's experience in Africa is one of the most significant modern narratives of homosexual liberation.'[28] It does seem unlikely that the boy experienced such a liberation but rather simply another act of exploitation by rich white colonialists. But the incident is a good example of the way not just Wilde and Gide, but Dollimore in the present, can fail to notice that one person's sexual liberation may be another's oppression. And it demonstrates again the asymmetrical way in which men and women are likely to be able to indulge the decadence of prostitution. Transgression here for Wilde and Gide was an individualistic and ruthless masculine philosophy.

The rebelliousness that upper class white men have engaged in historically has not hurt them. It has been a rite of passage. They journey to the underworld composed of women and boys in prostitution, dabble in drugs and exploitative and abusive sex, then succeed to the family business or Harley Street. This form of rebellion is specifically masculine and has generally been carried out at the expense of women. The underworld is a necessary flipside which provides light relief as well as a reminder of the reasons to pursue respectable marriage. Presently some lesbian and gay theorists tell us that the underworld can be a place of rebellion, that if queer people are outrageous enough then the centre cannot hold, lesbians, gays, transsexuals, pedophiles, prostitutes, sadomasochists, will march from the margins and overturn the straight, limited nuclear family world. Reverse affirmation by which the sexually deviant reclaim sexological categories and turn them into revolutionary movements, will create massive social change. But there is no reason to believe that this will work, that a heteropatriarchal system that has required a sexual underworld for its survival will turn up its toes just because the characters it has created to populate this underworld go marching in the street. It is a handicap for transgression theorists that the success of their politics will precisely remove the pleasure of their practice by removing its transgressive element.

The 'high' theory which is used to justify transgression as a revolutionary possibility is poststructuralist. Foucault and Derrida are used to give theoretical support to the practitioners of lesbian roleplaying and sadomasochism. Searching lesbian feminist theory for such support would be a fruitless task. Derrida is enlisted for his notions of how to explode binary oppositions by the subversive appropriation of the less powerful side. Dollimore refers to Derrida to support his own notions of the subversive value of transgression.

> Derrida has insisted that metaphysics can only be contested from within, by disrupting its structures and redirecting its force against itself. He defines the binary opposition as a 'violent hierarchy' where one of the two terms forcefully governs the other, and insists that a crucial stage in the deconstruction of binaries involves their inversion, an overturning, which brings low what was high. In effect inversion of the binary is a necessary stage in its displacement . . . he adds that the political effect of failing to invert the binary opposition, of trying simply to jump beyond it into a world free of it, is simply to leave the binary intact in the only world we have.[29]

According to such theory inversion is necessary and revolutionary and the lesbian feminist project is worthy of derision. The feminist project of wishing, for instance, to move beyond gender instead of bringing it back in S/M or roleplaying, is made to seem simplistic and doomed to failure. The feminist critique of what postmodernists describe as binaries such as masculine and feminine genders, good girls and bad girls, dominance and submission suggests that reproducing them does not break down oppressive power structures but gives them oxygen. The postmodernist justification of transgression and inversion has arrived in a very conservative time when feminism is being almost universally attacked, and conveniently re-inscribes traditional forms of gay male practice as revolutionary. The only political change necessary in order to be part of the revolutionary project, according to this analysis, is for lesbians to be more like gay men. Feminism was about releasing women from the prison of gender and good girl/bad girl dichotomies. Being a feminist meant, and still means to many, being a conscientious objector who wilfully and rebelliously refuses to enter the games of gender and dominance and submission, and believes, despite postmodernist scepticism, that it is possible to live outside them.

The politics of transgression form the basis of the new 'Queer' politics. They are the politics of those gay men and lesbians who are responding with reasonable anger to the murderous inactivity of the US government in respect of AIDS and the wave of hatred expressed in the media, and by doctors, to HIV positive gay men. The word 'queer' is promoted as a more useful word than gay or homosexual because of its inclusivity, the fact that it does not just refer to white men. As far as lesbians go, this idea is deeply problematic and I have addressed that point elsewhere in this volume. But a particular problem of a queer politics founded upon transgression is that lesbians can find themselves with some very inappropriate bedfellows. A London 'Queer Power' leaflet defined queer thus:

> Queer means to fuck with gender. There are straight queers, bi-queers, tranny queers, lez queers, fag queers, SM queers, fisting queers in every single street in this apathetic country of ours.[30]

The word 'queer' as this definition demonstrates, represents a politics in which all those who are similarly transgressive share an affinity and equality. This politics stresses the revolutionary potential of the 'sexual minorities' as defined by the sexologists, who, when they organise together for their rights, are supposed to constitute a force for sexual revolution. Jeffrey Weeks, the British gay historian, expressed this politics as early as 1982:

So, willy nilly, the defence of choice and sexual freedom is falling to those who until recently seemed on the outer fringes of the sexual spectrum: s/mers, lesbians and gay men into role-playing, pedophile activists, as well as the more conventional libertarian socialists and radicals.[31]

So the politics of 'queer' are not new. Weeks and others see the roots of these politics in Foucault and of course the concept of 'reverse affirmation' considered in Chapter 1. Sexological categories which may have been created to enhance social control and exclude and stigmatise sexual minorities are transformed into affirmative politics which then challenge the sexual system.

Lesbians have at times employed such strategies. But accepting this politics means accepting that lesbianism is simply a way of being naughty with the genitals on a par with pedophilia. Quite apart from the fact that lesbian feminism has reconstructed lesbianism into very much more than a sexual practice, the other sexual practices included are deeply problematic for feminists. Apart from the category gay, they represent forms of sexuality which are indicted by feminist theorists as dangerous to the interests of women and as forming a crucial foundation of women's oppression. The other practices to be included in 'queer' are about gender fetishism and dominance and submission. Supposing the most unacceptable categories were left out such as pedophilia, this would require a reconstruction of 'queer' politics from a feminist perspective which might well remove the guts of the movement. Once anyone apart from lesbian feminists is left out then the inclusivity would seem to be damaged and it would be hard to say 'we are queer but not as queer as pedophiles etc' when one of the causes for celebration of the new politics is precisely their transgressive nature.

Many lesbians enjoy being outlaws. If we were not rebels we might not have the courage and strength to continue being lesbians in a lesbian hating world. Where is the most fruitful channel for this rebellious outlawry which gives lesbians much fun and satisfaction? The lesbian sexual outlaws might outrage suburban living rooms by practising S/M on Channel 4 television programmes but it does seem unlikely that this is going to change the world. Lesbian feminism offers the delights of outlawry too but in ways that are likely to be more efficacious in changing the condition of women and lesbians. Monique Wittig expresses the outlaw politics of the lesbian separatist very well.

> We are escapees from our class in the same way as the American runaway slaves were when escaping slavery and becoming free. For us this is an absolute necessity; our survival demands that we contribute all our strength to the destruction of the class of women within which men appropriate women. This can be accomplished only by the destruction of heterosexuality as a social system which is based on the oppression of women by men and which produces the doctrine of the difference between the sexes to justify this oppression.[32]

This is a rather different strategy from wearing black leather in shopping centres. Sexual outlawry effectively diverts lesbian rage from providing any challenge to male power. Those who live and expound lesbian feminist politics in the heteropatriarchy will find that all their desires for excitement and opprobrium can be met without any necessity to imitate the lesbians portrayed in men's pornographic imagination.

---

1. Schulman, Sarah (1990). *After Delores*. London: Sheba. p. 57.
2. Quoted in Creet, Julia (1991). 'Daughter of the Movement: The Psychodynamics of Lesbian S/M Fantasy.' *Differences: A Journal of Feminist Cultural Studies. Queer Theory Issue*. p. 147. Summer.
3. Jay, Karla (1986). 'The Lesbian Bar as Metaphor'. *Resources for Feminist Research*. Vol. 12. No 1. p. 18.
4. Ibid. p. 19.
5. Ibid.
6. Hall, Radclyffe (1982). *The Well of Loneliness*. London: Virago. p. 393. (1990) New York: Doubleday.
7. Wilde, Oscar (1975). 'The Picture of Dorian Gray.' In *The Complete Works of Oscar Wilde*. London: Collins. p. 141.
8. Ibid. p. 142.
9. Duffy, Maureen (1967). *The Microcosm*. London: Panther. p. 15. First published 1966.
10. Ibid. p. 11.

11. Bannon, Ann (1970). *Women of the Shadows*. London: Sphere. p. 78. First published 1959.

12. Ibid. p. 79.

13. Miller, Isabel (1973). *Patience and Sarah*. Greenwich, Connecticut: Fawcett Publications. (1979) London: The Women's Press. Brown, Rita Mae (1973). *Rubyfruit Jungle*. Plainfield, Vermont: Daughters Inc.

14. Schulman (1990). p. 106.

15. Ibid. p. 26.

16. Ibid. p. 35.

17. Nestle, Joan (1988). *A Restricted Country*. London: Sheba. p. 158. (1987) Ithaca, New York: Firebrand Books.

18. Ibid.

19. Ibid. p. 159.

20. Rechy, John (1979). *The Sexual Outlaw*. London: Futura. p. 299.

21. Saalfield, Catherine and Navarro, Ray (1991). 'Shocking Pink Praxis: Race and Gender on the ACT UP Frontlines.' In Fuss, Diana (Ed.) *Inside/Out. Lesbian Theories, Gay Theories*. London and New York: Routledge. p. 356.

22. Bearchell, Chris (1983). 'Why I am a Gay Liberationist: Thoughts on Sex, Freedom, the Family and the State.' In *Resources for Feminist Research*. Vol 12. No. 1. pp. 59–60.

23. Rubin, Gayle (1982) 'A Personal History of the Lesbian S/M Community and Movement in San Francisco.' In Samois (Ed.) *Coming to Power. Writings and Graphics on Lesbian S/M*. Boston: Alyson. 2nd Edition. p. 209.

24. Ibid. p. 221.

25. Ibid. p. 224.

26. Ibid. pp. 215–216.

27. Ibid. p. 214.

28. Dollimore, Jonathan (1991). *Sexual Dissidence. Augustine to Wilde, Freud to Foucault*. Oxford: Clarendon Press. p. 12.

29. Ibid. pp. 65–6.

30. Quoted in Smyth, Cherry (1992). *Lesbians Talk: Queer Notions*. London: Scarlet Press. p. 17.

31. Quoted in Jeffreys, Sheila (1990). *Anticlimax. A Feminist Perspective on the Sexual Revolution*. London: The Women's Press. p. 212. (1991). New York: New York University Press.

32. Wittig, Monique (1992). *The Straight Mind and Other Essays*. Boston: Beacon Press. p. 20.

Chapter 7

A PALE VERSION OF THE MALE: LESBIANS AND GAY MALE CULTURE

The gay historian Jeffrey Weeks when describing fin-de-siècle Paris and Berlin, wrote 'A lesbian sub-culture of sorts did exist, but was a pale version of the male . . .'[1] A feminist analysis cannot accept that lesbians are simply gay men of smaller growth, less glamorous cultural forms and with inadequately developed libidos. It has been an important part of feminist theorising to point out the extent to which the cultures men create routinely exclude women and depend for their identity on the oppression of women. Gay male culture is not necessarily any more pro-feminist or woman-loving than malestream culture in general. And yet we see the phenomenon in the eighties and nineties of some areas of the lesbian community seeking slavishly to imitate male gay cultural forms, however inappropriate to lesbian experience.

In the gay culture of the twentieth century male influence and money have ensured that gay men have hegemony. The articulation of a separate lesbian consciousness has been difficult and lesbians have been routinely submerged. Since gay men were the only 'homosexuals' of interest to sexologists, the media and other men generally, homosexuality has come to mean male homosexuality. There is plentiful evidence of the way that lesbians have been disappeared. The historian A. L. Rowse's well known contribution to gay history is entitled *Homosexuals in History*.[2] He does not include lesbians. Innumerable examples could be adduced of this process. In sexological literature on

142

homosexuality, lesbians, if mentioned at all, have been added in at the end or appeared in a footnote.

With the emergence of lesbian feminism in the early seventies it seemed to many of us that the lesbian voice had at last arrived and would be here to stay. Lesbians abandoned the position of little sisters they had occupied in homosexual organisations, separated deliberately from gay men to set up their own organisations, and started to create a specifically lesbian culture. This separation was based upon a feminist consciousness which illuminated the anti-women aspects of traditional male gay culture and demonstrated that lesbians and gay men had quite different and in some ways contradictory political agendas. Lesbian feminists devoted their energies to the development of women only spaces and services which offered the new generation of lesbians a very different starting point. It seems now that the separate lesbian culture which embodies specifically lesbian values is being strangled in its cradle. A new generation of lesbians are cheerfully adopting the values and practices of gay male culture to the extent, as some of them are prepared to admit, of wishing that they were gay men. The lesbians who are submerging themselves into gay male culture and politics are also attacking lesbian feminists in general and separatists in particular. Certain gay male sexual practices are being imitated with great effort and attempted verisimilitude by some lesbians, but not well enough according to the new lesbian sexologists who are still telling us that we do not measure up to gay men sexually.

There are similarities in the experience of oppression suffered by lesbians and gay men and on this basis many lesbians have repeatedly embarked on mixed gay and lesbian politics, gay liberation in the early seventies, queer politics today. Lesbians and gay men suffer discrimination at work, in relation to tax and insurance, harassment on the street, on public transport. Lesbians and gay men suffer the assault upon pride and self-worth created by the need to hide love relationships and conceal affection in public. Lesbians and gay men suffer loss of their families of origin and need to build friendship and community for our survival. The general gay-hating public does not discriminate greatly between lesbians and gay men in the expression of that hatred. Lesbians have suffered too from the avalanche of gay-hating that accompanied the AIDS epidemic in countries like Britain and the US. The passage of hostile legislation that has been justified by this new atmosphere has been of equal concern to lesbians and gay men. Measures such as Section 28 of the *Local Government Act* against the 'promotion of homosexuality' in Britain are fought, quite reasonably, by lesbians and gay men together. It can seem therefore that gay men and lesbians have a great deal of common ground politically. But the history of this political relationship has been fraught with difficulty and lesbians have made the decision time and again to separate.

Lesbians have tended to be restrained in their criticism of gay male politics because of a sensible awareness that to the heterosexual world lesbians are seen as just an inferior version of gay men and any political criticism of gay men would reflect upon us. Also as attacks have increased recently on the gains in civil rights made by lesbians and gay men since 1970, criticism of gay men has seemed even more dangerous and churlish. It has seemed wise to maintain the possibility of a united front against legislation and discrimination which treats lesbians and gay men as the same. Gay men do after all have more money, political clout and visibility than lesbians. Few lesbian feminist theorists, then, have sought to articulate the political differences that bedevil the relationship between lesbians and gay men. This task becomes more urgent as the imitation of gay male forms becomes more influential within the lesbian community.

The American lesbian philosopher, Marilyn Frye, is one of the few lesbians who has approached the task of criticising gay male politics.[3] She states that the differences between lesbians and gay men 'turn out to be so profound as to cast doubt on the assumption that there is any basic cultural or political affinity' 'upon which alliances could be built.'[4] She suggests that gay and straight male cultures share the same general principles of phallocracy such as the presumption of male citizenship; worship of the penis; male homoeroticism or man-loving; contempt for women, or woman-hating; compulsory male heterosexuality; and the presumption of general phallic access. She sees lesbian revolutionary potential as residing in their rejection of these principles.

144

Man-loving is one rather obvious way in which gay men diverge from lesbians. Gay men desire and love members of the ruling class of men. In this respect gay men are loyal to the basic principle of male supremacy, man-loving. Manhood and masculinity, the symbols and behaviour which denote membership of the political class status of men are celebrated in many aspects of gay male culture. Gay male theorists have explained that there was a transition in the seventies in western male gay culture which some have called the 'butch shift'. They explain that whereas before gay liberation when homosexuality was associated with effeminacy gay men might routinely seek sexual partners who were seen as 'real men' from the heterosexual world, post gay liberation gay men began to seek sexual partners from the now visible and more confident gay community. The attraction to the trappings of masculinity remained and now had to be recreated by gay men themselves.

Non-gay men used to be a desired object – our equivalent of the unattainable? – but the 'butch shift' has redirected our attention to ourselves. By creating amongst ourselves apparently masculine men who desire other men we are refuting the idea that we are really feminine souls in male bodies.[5]

This meant the taking up of weight-training, check shirts, faded blue jeans, bovver boots, short hair and moustaches or all-leather or denim looks. A passion for men can take the form of a wish to incorporate the power bestowed by masculinity, a power which gay men can feel is lacking to them because of their failure to take part in the usual dynamics of heterosexuality such as ownership of a woman. The appropriation of the symbols and forms of masculinity can be even more exaggerated than in male heterosexual culture. It can also take the form of masochism and worship of the aggressive, authoritarian aspects of the masculinity principle. Ingestion of the semen of the powerful can be seen as empowering.[6] Heterosexual women are also expected to worship men and the masculinity principle. The difference is that this role is not chosen voluntarily as in the case of gay men, and is often resisted most strongly as the literature of sexology teaches us. Heterosexuality for women is an institution of control maintained by force. Heterosexual women have a disadvantage compared with gay men in their worship of masculinity. They can never be men, or masculine, however much semen they ingest. Frye explains:

If man-loving is the rule of phallocratic culture, as I think it is, and if, therefore, male homoeroticism is compulsory, then gay men should be numbered among the faithful, or the loyal and law-abiding citizens, and lesbian feminists are sinners and criminals, or, if perceived politically, insurgents and traitors.[7]

Lesbians are in a very different position. Against all the odds lesbians choose to love members of the inferior sex class. In this way they are disloyal to male supremacy. Where lesbians can be seen to have overcome all the training they have received about women's innate disgustingness and unloveableness in order to love women, those gay men who worship masculinity reveal a woman-hating quite consistent with the woman-hating of straight society. The radical political potential of lesbianism rests upon precisely lesbian love of women. It is only lesbians in hetero-relational culture who can value women unequivocally and on this basis fight for the liberation of those they love and value. Heterosexual feminists too have seen the importance of loving and valuing women but they reserve their most important emotional and sexual energies for men. The love and respect lesbians have for women inevitably creates a serious tension in the relations between lesbians and gay men revealed particularly clearly in lesbian attitudes to such aspects of gay male culture as drag. Frye explains that it is the lesbian's love for women which most clearly differentiates her from gay men.

She does not love men; she does not preserve all passion and significant exchange for men. She does not hate women. She presupposes the equality of the female and male bodies, or even the superiority or normativeness of the female body. She has no interest in penises beyond some reasonable concern about how men use them against women. She claims civil rights for women without arguing that women are really men with different plumbing. She does not live as the complement to the rule of heterosexuality for men. She is not accessible to the penis; she does not view herself as a natural object of fucking and denies that men have either the right or the duty to fuck her.[8]

It is in the area of sexuality that the differences between the political agendas of lesbians and gay men are clearest. Liz Stanley in Britain and Denise Thompson in Australia have written of the great difficulties created for mixed lesbian and gay organising by differences around sexuality.[9] Feminist theorists have explained that male sexuality, including male gay sexuality, is constructed through and exercised to reinforce masculine identity. The gay male theorist John Stoltenberg expresses this analysis with particular forcefulness.

> So much of men's sexuality is tied up with gender-actualizing – with feeling like a real man – that they can scarcely recall any erotic sensation that had no gender-specific cultural meaning ... Acculturated male sexuality has a built-in-failsafe: either its political context reifies manhood or the experience cannot be felt as sensual ... [10]

Aspects of gay male behaviour such as casual sex, numbers of sexual partners and sexual compulsiveness can then be given a political rather than biological explanation. Frequent sexual activity is necessary to reinforce male sexual identity. Gay male politics often tends to accept that gayness is limited to sexual activity, limited to the sexological definition of what constitutes homosexuality. Seymour Kleinberg in an interesting duo of articles about gay masculinity before and after AIDS suggests that sexual activity took over from politics in the late seventies, early eighties.

> The more that sex dominated the style of life, from discos to parades, with rights secured or not, the less need most men felt they had for politics – and the less others, such as lesbians, feminists, and minorities, felt the gay movement offered them. For gay men sexual politics became oddly literal. Both before and after the movement, promiscuity was honoured as the

sign of an individual's aggressiveness (no matter how passive he was in bed). To fuck was to defy, as bad girls of the past did, dismantling some of society's dearest notions above virtue.[11]

The more radical demands of gay liberation about changing the world got diverted into the demand for greater phallic access.

Marilyn Frye describes male sexual behaviour, gay and straight, as involving a presumption of general phallic access. She explains that this presumption manifests itself in:

> . . . the almost universal right to fuck – to assert his individual male dominance over all that is not himself by using it for his phallic gratification or self-assertion at either a physical or a symbolic level. Any physical object can be urinated on or in, or ejaculated on or in, or penetrated by his penis, as can any nonhuman animal or any woman . . . [12]

The only serious limitation on this, apart from those imposed by property rights and local social mores, is that males are not supposed to 'fuck other males, especially adult males of their own class, tribe, race etc . . .' Inasmuch as gay men do violate this limitation they are truer to the principle of universal phallic access than straight men and carry it further. Frye explains the prohibition on men fucking each other as a way of enabling the masculinity principle to rule the world. She sees it as so destructive if men were routinely permitted to do sexually to each other what they do to women that male bonding would be damaged and male supremacy destroyed.

> The proscription against male-male fucking is the lid on masculinity, the limiting principle which keeps masculinity from being simply an endless firestorm of undifferentiated self . . . The straight male's phobic reaction to male homosexuality can then be seen as a fear of an unrestricted, unlimited, ungoverned masculinity.[13]

It could well be argued in response that the act of fucking another man would in fact strengthen male bonding rather than

148

destroy it. That can be seen as a problem for a feminist analysis too since it is male bonding that forms the scaffolding of male supremacy and it is not in women's interests necessarily that it should be stronger.

Marilyn Frye sees gay male politics as being 'antithetical' to lesbian feminism because:

The general direction of gay male politics is to claim maleness and male privilege for gay men and to promote the enlargement of the range of presumption of phallic access to the point where it is, in fact, absolutely unlimited. The general direction of lesbian feminist politics is the dismantling of male privilege, the erasure of masculinity, and the reversal of the rule of phallic access, replacing the rule that access is permitted unless specifically forbidden with the rule that it is forbidden unless specifically permitted.[14]

Frye does not dismiss the possibility that some gay men can break ranks and identify with the feminist struggle. Gay men are after all, she says, privileged with the possibilities of real knowledge and perception bestowed upon the outsider who can see the features of male supremacy particularly clearly. This could be turned to advantage and gay male culture could expand 'its tendencies to the pursuit of simple bodily pleasure, as opposed to its tendencies to fetishism, fantasy and alienation, it seems that it could nurture very radical, hitherto unthinkable new conceptions of what it can be to live as a male body.' But Frye saw no signs that this radical development was taking place when she wrote this piece in 1983. The forms of gay male culture can only be changed by a radical pro-feminist movement of gay men which seems not a great deal nearer yet in the nineties.

It is not hard to see how lesbians fall under the sway of gay male politics and culture. Malestream politics tends to throw lesbians together with gay men as in the funding of the London Lesbian and Gay Centre. This centre, which opened in 1984, received funding to the tune of £100,000 for lesbians specifically. This was to fund a lesbian floor in a building in which all other facilities including the bar were mixed. Lesbian feminists of a radical or revolutionary feminist persuasion did not see it as a priority to be involved in this enterprise since we would have preferred a lesbian centre. When sadomasochists demanded to meet at the building and the collective decided to allow them to, then lesbian feminists became involved to fight the decision. We felt that it was important to the lesbians using the building, especially since some of that money was earmarked for lesbians, to make it an S/M free space. We lost, predictably, since the vast majority of lesbian members of the centre voted against and the gay men, who outnumbered us, voted overwhelmingly for the right of the sadomasochists to meet.

This is a useful demonstration of the difficulty of lesbians and gay men seriously organising together without accepting gay male priorities. Gay men are generally in a majority in mixed organisations. Lesbians Against Sadomasochism, of which I was a member, was a lesbian feminist group set up to challenge the development of lesbian sadomasochism in London. Its work revealed some of the serious contradictions which tend to emerge in mixed lesbian and gay organising. Lesbian mothers en masse attended one of the general meetings at the new Lesbian and Gay Centre to make their views against sadomasochism known. They made points such as not feeling able to bring their children to a centre in which men and women in black leather and S/M regalia were present since they were struggling hard to rear their children in a way which resisted the sado-society. The lesbian mothers brought their children with them, partly from problems of childcare, but also to make a point. To a background of babies crying some gay men and lesbians sought to hold an abstract intellectual discussion of their right to pursue their pleasures in any way they wished.

Lesbian mothers and lesbian feminists in general found that similar difficulties arose around the issues of transsexualism, bisexuality and pedophilia. Lesbians did not see why they should accept transsexuals in the lesbian toilets since they did not see surgery as having made them women. The bisexual issue presented another difficulty. Though lesbians might have felt able to accept the presence of gay men in the centre since they would not harass them sexually, they did not feel happy with bisexual men who were potentially just as bothersome to women as any heterosexual men. This argument was obscure to many male gay members of the centre who were committed to supporting sexual minorities, seeing their own homosexuality as just one more perversion in a list of increasingly exotic sexual types. Where some gay men seemed able to be liberal about pedophilia, lesbians with a consciousness of the reality of sexual abuse could not. In the end the only choice open to lesbians who wanted to use the facilities of the centre was to accept or cease to criticise gay male sexual politics. Those who found them indigestible girlcotted the centre.

When lesbians are forced by state funding or commercial pressures to use mixed facilities there is no doubt that male priorities rule. This is true of mixed publications too. It was because of this understanding that mixed facilities were basically male facilities that feminists and lesbians originally argued for separate organisations, dances, journals in this wave of feminism. Mixed i.e. male facilities incorporate and support a version of lesbianism which does not threaten the interests of gay men. We could hardly expect them to do otherwise. So we find there is little sympathy for feminist opposition to sadomasochism and pornography in the mixed gay press. The stigmata of gay male commercial culture, i.e. black leather, slavemarkets and drag tend to dominate such publications because that is what pays for them. Lesbian feminism becomes an object of derision. Lesbians are seen as not having the money to provide a good market for the advertisers who keep the gay media in print and only the power of money would give lesbians a say. Meanwhile lesbian feminist publications struggle to survive as duplicated newsletters with small circulations, or fail for lack of money and resources.

In the early seventies not just lesbian feminists but many theorists of gay liberation analysed the phenomena of camp and drag critically and pointed out the ways in which they could be seen to be predicated upon womanhating. Lesbians left mixed organisations because of the difficulty many political gay men had in directing any critical gaze at such aspects of gay male culture. Now something very different is happening. These very practices themselves are being admired by some lesbians who are seeking to find versions of them for lesbians. It is a long journey from criticism to admiration and suggests just how conservative and anti-feminist the times have become and how low the confidence of lesbians has sunk.

A good example of someone who made this journey is the lesbian novelist Fiona Cooper who was one of four lesbians and gay men chosen to provide 'different perspectives on the last twenty years' for a special feature on gay pride in the London magazine *City Limits* in 1989. Cooper took the opportunity to repudiate feminism. When she became a feminist she apparently 'cut my hair short, wore a bomber jacket, dungarees, DMs, drank Guinness, played pool, stood around with mouth open absorbing this year's role models stalking around this brave new world.' Then she saw the light and realised feminism was 'rule-and-regulation-ridden' and she didn't want to be 'told what to do.'[15] So Cooper chose to rebel against feminism and adopt a male gay reality as if that was really revolutionary, at a time when many others were making the same journey. The malestream world doubtless welcomed such recusants warmly and they were relieved of the difficulties attendant upon holding feminist ideas in the hostile present.

Cooper was converted to gay male reality by seeing a male gay drag artist who intoxicated her with the glamour of male gay culture.

Then at the age of 25 my dear friend Maureen took me to see *Polyester*, where I discovered camp, trash, schlock, sleaze and Divine . . . I saw Divine on stage seven times and screamed myself hoarse. For weeks after I sashayed around with Divine's gracious 'Fuck you all, fuck you 40 times!' – the nearest to a nonphilosophy that has ever made sense to me. I found that I didn't need anyone else to OK things for me. If I wanted to wear glitter and tat and nail varnish and slap – so fucking what?

I got mind blown by today's drag queens with their anarchic humour bellowed from the back of a sleazy bar. I felt at home. I've often been asked to explain why I am so nuts about drag so here it is: I think it's funny. It's also brave, bold, anarchic, magnificent, tacky, weird and wonderful. And who do you think started Stonewall?[16]

She discovered that gay men were often nicer than feminists 'with a gentleness and warmth and a camp factor of 10' whereas feminists had 'miserable carping humourless analyses.' Her praise for gay male culture implies a serious discontent not just with feminism but with lesbian culture. Lesbians have not traditionally been very enthralled with the exclusively gay male phenomenon of drag. Drag artists wear the clothes that are imposed on women in male supremacy – clothes that symbolise the inferior status of women. The language and performances of drag artists are often the most clear manifestations of gay male womanhating.

Marilyn Frye recognises that some lesbians have been taken in by the argument of gay male apologists that drag shows a love of women and refutes this most vigorously.

... gay men's effeminacy and donning of feminine apparel displays no love of or identification with women or the womanly.

For the most part, this femininity is affected and is characterized by theatrical exaggeration. It is a casual and cynical mockery of women, for whom femininity is the trappings of oppression, but it is also a kind of play, a toying with that which is taboo ... What gay male affectation of femininity seems to me to be is a kind of serious sport in which men may exercise their power and control over the feminine, much as in other sports one exercises physical power and control over elements of the physical universe. Some gay men achieve, indeed, prodigious mastery of the feminine, and they are often treated by those in the know with the respect due to heroes. But the mastery of the feminine is not feminine. It is masculine. It is not a manifestation of woman-loving but of woman-hating. Someone with such mastery may have the very first claim to manhood.[17]

It is being suggested in some circles by lesbians anxious to have a 'drag' of their own, that dressing in masculine attire might provide a substitute. But this does not work politically. Women dressing up in traditional male clothing does not cause the immediate hilarity that men dressing in traditional female clothing does. This should alert us to the differences of political status represented by this clothing. Women's clothing represents powerlessness whilst men's clothing represents the opposite. Lesbians, like many heterosexual women presently, routinely dress in what were historically seen as men's clothes because they offer all the comforts and advantages which might be expected of clothes traditionally adopted by the ruling class. There is no shock value in a lesbian in a pair of trousers. There are suggestions from some quarters that lesbians might adopt effeminate clothing themselves to provide lesbians with an equivalent of drag but that provides problems since 'women's' clothes on women are not funny.

The phenomenon of 'camp' does not rely simply on effeminacy. Susan Sontag in her *Notes on Camp* represents it as a much wider cultural style.

> Indeed the essence of Camp is its love of the unnatural: of artifice and exaggeration. And Camp is esoteric – something of a private code, a badge of identity even, among small urban cliques.[18]

As a form of language and behaviour which identified gay men to each other and provided them with a humour of resistance, 'camp' played an important role in the history of gay survival in a hostile culture.

Camp in this form does not seem to have been employed by lesbians. The American lesbian historians Elizabeth Lapovsky Kennedy and Madeline Davis who have collected the oral history of lesbians who were engaged in roleplaying in New York State in the fifties and sixties found that 'the lesbian community had no parallel to the camp culture that developed around queens in male homosexual communities.'[19] The phenomenon of drag had no equivalent in lesbian entertainment since 'few butches performed as male impersonators.' No 'cultural aesthetic' they suggest 'developed' around male impersonation. Lesbians did not develop the sexual argot or provocative style associated with camp either. When lesbians seek to acquire camp or drag for lesbian culture presently they are simply taking over male gay cultural forms. A feminist analysis would reveal that drag, and to the extent that it is associated with effeminacy, camp too, are phenomena which arise from women's oppression and cannot be simply appropriated by lesbians.

The straightforward imitation of gay male masculinity is now being adopted by some lesbians. Gayle Rubin is a lesbian theorist who is particularly enthusiastic about the masculinity of gay male culture. It is the subject of her research which is on the gay male leather scene. She is sufficiently enamoured of gayness to think it quite reasonable for lesbians to have transsexual operations, as apparently they are doing in California, so that they may become gay men. Imitation can go to considerable lengths, it seems, far beyond the 'artifice' and 'parody' beloved of the postmodenist apologists of male gay culture and politics. Surgery is rather serious and permanent. Gayle Rubin is a proponent of sadomasochism. She remains famous in women's studies circles for a seventies article called *The Traffic in Women*. Rubin repudiates this article in the volume *Pleasure and Danger* in which she explains that she used to think that sex and gender were inevitably interconnected but now accepts the existence of a separate system of sexual oppression in which sexual minorities such as practitioners of 'intergenerational sex' suffer, a system which cannot be analysed by feminists whose theory had only limited usefulness for looking at sex.[20] It seems important for a new lesbian avant garde to set themselves apart from 'women' or the 'gender system' lest their chosen practice of roleplaying or sadomasochism appear politically suspect. In this way they can feel more justified in indulging erotic predilections based on inequalities of power without considering how these might impact upon the condition of women.

Gayle Rubin has travelled even further recently from her earlier feminist insights. In an anthology on roleplaying she writes on 'butch, gender, and boundaries'. She defines butch as 'a category of lesbian gender that is constituted through the deployment and manipulation of masculine gender codes and symbols'. It includes, she says, those who are gender 'dysphoric' or 'dissatisfied with the gender to which they were assigned' and seeking transsexual surgery. She explains that 'many butches have partially male gender identities.' The iconography of the butch in the lesbian community shares, she says, the same roots as the identical figure in the male gay scene of the 'outlaw leather biker'. These roots are in the motorcycle and street gangs of the early fifties. The styles are based on 'white, working-class, youthful masculinity.'[21] Rubin identifies this image of male aggression, one which strikes fear into many women, with rebelliousness. It would seem from such theory and practice that male gay revalidation of aggressive masculinity has permeated some areas of lesbian culture.

Rubin tells us there are many varieties of masculinity adopted by the butch apart from the biker. There is a great variety of 'recognizably male styles' and 'butches who express their masculinity within each symbolic assemblage.'

> There are butches who are tough street dudes, butches who are jocks, butches who are scholars, butches who are artists, rock-and-roll butches, butches who have motorcycles, and butches who have money. There are butches whose male models are effeminate men, sissies, drag queens, and many different types of male homosexuals.[22]

But the variety of masculinity to which Rubin directs particular attention is the FTM or female-to-male transsexual. She is angry that male-to-female-transsexuals have been regarded with suspicion in the lesbian movement in the past since she sees transsexualism as politically unproblematic. She exhorts lesbians to show support for the increasing number of FTMs because, she says, 'their numbers are growing and awareness of their presence is increasing.'[23] If she is right, even about San Francisco, then this is a bizarre aspect of the backlash against feminism. Where once feminists sought to construct the possibility of women being proud to be women and proud to be lovers of women we now have a phenomenon, not only of tremendous admiration for masculinity, which represents the oppressive power of our enemies, but a desire to cease being women altogether in order to assume male power. It does suggest that feminism has been unsuccessful in helping women to be happy in their bodies if increasing numbers are now approaching mutilating surgery because of their urgent desire not to be women.[24]

Rubin explains that many lesbians will be disturbed at the FTM phenomenon but that they should learn to be more sympathetic and helpful.

> When a woman's body begins to change into a male body, the transposition of male and female signals that constitute 'butch' begins to disintegrate. A cross-dressing, dildo-packing, bodybuilding butch may use a male name and masculine pronouns, yet still have soft skin, no facial hair, the visible swell of breasts or hips under male clothing, small hands and feet, or some other detectable sign of femaleness. If the same person grows a mustache, develops a lower voice, binds his breasts, or begins to bald, his body offers no evidence to contravene his social signals. When he begins to read like a man, many lesbians no longer find him attractive and some want to banish him from their social universe.[25]

Lesbians should apparently support them until they decide to leave since they 'will leave lesbian contexts on their own.'[26] Lesbian communities then should act as supportive nurseries to the rebirth of lesbians as men. It is not hard to see why lesbian feminists have difficulty offering such support. Not surprisingly, considering the enthusiasm for gay male culture in some parts of the lesbian scene, some of these FTMs want to be gay men or are as Rubin puts it 'gay male identified'. She hopes that gay men will accept gay FTMs with 'balance and good grace' but I suspect that such acceptance may be difficult. The FTMs will not have perfectly functioning penises since phalloplasty is still inadequate to provide such and penises are important to male gay eroticism.

Feminist theorists have pointed out that transsexualism is in contradiction to the pursuit of women's freedom. Janice Raymond's book, *The Transsexual Empire*, is unsurpassed in this respect.[27] It shows how the medical profession's invention and continued support for transsexualism reifies gender and undermines the feminist project of eliminating the constricting roles of masculinity and femininity which are responsible for 'gender

157

dysphoria' and all the pain and confusion of transsexualism in the first place. It is to be expected that where masculinity and femininity are fetishised and celebrated as in the new roleplaying that transsexualism will emerge because the power and limitations of roles are again being constructed and enforced.

The lesbian S/M movement in the US and in Britain for which Rubin has been an important spokeswoman uses the language of gay male culture. The lesbian proponents of S/M learnt their techniques and language in gay male clubs and practised, as many still do, on gay men. Sadomasochism has been a really prominent force on the gay male scene for several decades. Pat Califia, a founder of Samois, the first lesbian S/M group in the US decribes the difficulty she had after becoming interested in S/M in finding other lesbians to practise with. She mentions meeting an 'older dyke' who talked about 'cruising gay men's leather bars with her lover in the early sixties, looking for other women who shared their sexual interests'.[28] By the end of 1977, she explains:

> . . . the lesbians who would eventually start Samois were hanging out in the Society of Janus, a mixed group that was mostly gay men; in Cardea, which had many women members who did S/M professionally; at the catacombs, a gay male fist-fucking club which allowed women to come to their parties; and at gay men's leather bars, especially the Balcony and the Ambush.[29]

Califia has written a collection of S/M erotica. The book's title as well as its contents show Califia's enthusiasm for the male gay cult of masculinity. The title is *Macho Sluts*. In the introduction Califia defines 'machismo' as the political style of oppressed minorities because she seeks to legitimise its adoption. 'In this country, machismo is a survival mechanism by which minority men try to preserve their self-esteem and culture.'[30] In fact machismo and other forms of masculinity are mechanisms by which men maintain their power over women. But this statement contains some truth. Males who are low in the hierarchy in male supremacist culture can adopt an exaggerated masculinity as compensation since the power associated with manhood and the oppression of women, rather than that bestowed by money or birth, is all that is allowed them. But the machismo of latin culture was not invented as a response to life in the US. In the latin cultures which these men left behind, machismo was the accepted style of male dominance. Rather than being revolutionary it is simply an important component of male power over women.

It is difficult to imagine that Califia does not realise that masculinity, whatever form it takes, is not gender neutral and cannot be seen as pro-woman. Being 'macho' does not offer much to anyone in the sex class of 'woman' even if she is lesbian. But it can offer temporary advancement. Manhood is valued in heteropatriarchal culture and particularly in gay male culture, so lesbians who adopt masculine attributes can gain admiration from and influence over the women to whom male power has a positive erotic weighting and from the gay men who admire such values.

'Masculine' gay men are seen as carrying a powerful erotic charge in Califia's stories. She rejects the idea that 'porn produced for lesbian consumption has to be about women only.'[31] In The Surprise Party a lesbian is apparently arrested by three policemen who kidnap her, and perform various forms of forced sex on her, such as oral rape both with penises and guns, enemas and anal rape. The lesbian is degraded and insulted, in particular her lesbianism is insulted by the cops who make remarks like 'You're just a goddamn dyke we dragged in off the street ... Maybe you were diddling your girlfriend in a public john ... Maybe I just happen to have a thing about lesbians. Arrogant bitches. No man is good enough for 'em.'[32] These insults help the arousal of the lesbian victim. She has great admiration for masculine gay men and constructs them into heroes for lesbians. Of two of the attackers she thinks:

Were those two cops faggots? It didn't make sense. Her cunt convulsed. Leathermen were sexy enough – dark knights and princes that she loved to look at, even if women weren't supposed to touch. By comparison, cops were kings – fuck, emperors. In the hierarchy of sex objects, she guessed gay cops ranked right up there next to God. But, shit, if Don was

159

supposed to be gay . . . he could get good head anywhere . . . She knew that she hadn't the practice to be as good as the boys who went to the glory holes, fell to their knees, and stayed there for hours, taking eight inches and more down their throats until dawn. How was she going to please him enough to save herself?[33]

But she does of course manage to be a passable imitation of a gay man. One of the attackers asks, 'You must be some new kind of female pervert. Or are you just an imitation fag?'[34] The lesbian replies 'A lot of people think so.' The story goes on to indicate that this is the case. When the two gay policemen are instructed to 'fuck' their prisoner they are told:

Maybe it will help if you don't think of her as a girl. After all, she doesn't want to be a woman. She wants to be a man. She dresses like one, talks like one, walks like one. She's a queer, like you boys. Queers have sex with other queers, right?[35]

The eroticism of the story derives partly from the idea that the lesbian character is almost good enough to be a gay man.

In the story called *The Vampire*, a female S/M practitioner and vampire whips a man into submission in a gay club before finding a woman who will offer her her life's blood. The vampire sees herself as a 'leatherman' or gay male exponent of S/M. She is described as being 'known for her chivalry. It was part of a code she thought all true leathermen (regardless of gender) should obey.'[36] In *The Spoiler* a male top seeks out other tops he can conquer. Status was attached to 'taking down other tops'.[37] In gay male culture such a battle for dominance can be eroticised, most revealingly in John Rechy's work, in which the gay man who manages to induce another to be passive has scored a victory over him and the players struggle to be harder than each other.[38] It would seem from these stories that the attraction of S/M for women like Califia is that it offers a field in which they can assert their dominance not just over women but over gay men too. It offers status. A woman who can break a male gay top, by making him 'move his keys over' for her, can appear to have achieved a major personal victory in the battle to rise in the gender hierarchy. A powerful female top can appear to move into a genderless sphere where her gender is not a limitation. But the game she must play is a masculine one. She does not receive her victory as a woman or a lesbian but by abandoning her own gender in order to 'pass' as a gay man. Such a lesbian has realised that she will not gain any personal power and status in the male gay world by coming out as lesbian. That could only lose her points. A crucial aspect of male bonding, as Marilyn Frye points out, is contempt for women. Men bond through the womanhating they display in each other's presence through jokes or sexual harassment or stories of conquest. In *Macho Sluts* Califia seeks to bond with gay men through a display of woman-hating.

Her stories are full of gay male language, particularly that which reveals gay men's contempt of women. In gay male culture, especially that of drag artists, women are commonly referred to as fish on the basis that women's genitals smell fishy. Califia uses the same word to apply to women who are the clients of lesbian prostitutes in one of her stories and carries the usage one step further to describe lesbian oral sex. The heroine of this story is a lesbian S/M prostitute. Clients are called Janes.

I don't eat fish very often. But the Janes keep telling me I'm pricing myself out of business. A spanking is more expensive than a blowjob . . . [39]

Califia is aware that her practice and authorship in the field of S/M might leave her open to the accusation of womanhating. The woman who becomes involved with the S/M prostitute in the above story tells of a past relationship in which she was treated as a dog and this proves her suitability in the eyes of the heroine.

Our tail-wagging, panting little woofer spent every possible minute with her, and when she did she was always in a wooden set of stocks and had a plug up her butt. Much was made of leashes and spanking bad puppies. She slept in the aforementioned doggie-hut, and did all her drinking and eating out of little dishes on the floor. I shudder to think where she performed her baser functions. I was charmed.[40]

Califia stretches her reader's credulity by declaring in the introduction that these stories are not misogynistic but in fact a 'valentine' and an 'act of love'.[41]

It is an open secret in libertarian lesbian circles that lesbians have been learning sexual practice from gay men. Such lesbians have apparently been using gay male pornography and this might explain why the new lesbian pornography reproduces the imagery and values of gay male porn so religiously. One of those values is the importance of having a penis and being penetrated by a penis.

Lesbians looked to gay men's porn for material taboo in their own circles – sex sans romance in its endless variations. With their elaborations on technique, especially the pleasures of penetration, gay men have ironically contributed to the renaissance of vaginal sex amongst lesbians.[42]

This imitation of gay male sex has been quite conscious and determined. Cherry Smyth, a British proponent of lesbian pornography, explains that:

In the past two years more lesbians have been discussing their erotic responses to gay male pornography and incorporating gay male sexual iconography into their fantasies, sex play and cultural representations.[43]

Smyth says that this has been necessary because gay men have developed a language and explicitness about sex which lesbians lack. The phenomenon of lesbians learning sex from gay men does seem to hold in store similar problems to that of heterosexual women learning sex from straight men. It needed feminism for heterosexual women to articulate their dissatisfaction with the sex straight men did such as penis-in-vagina fucking. A new generation of lesbians will now have the task of pointing out that dildos in vaginas and anuses are not necessarily fundamental to lesbian sexuality.

Smyth tells us that the imitation of gay men has gone to some remarkable lengths. Apparently some lesbians who have chosen to reclaim roleplaying have chosen to imitate gay male roles instead of masculine/feminine ones. Gay male roles would offer greater political correctness since butch/femme could look like an imitation of heterosexuality.

> Meanwhile, dykes who had reclaimed butch-femme identifications were now shifting their sources. Unlike the butch-femme dynamic which borrows from the heterosexual model, the butch daddy dyke and lesbian boy, for example, appropriate masculine codes without denying the femaleness of their protagonists.[44]

Smyth uses the work of lesbian photographer Della Grace to illustrate the new fascination of lesbians with gay male sexuality. One of Grace's photos, called *Lesbian Cock*, 'presents two lesbians dressed in leather and biker caps, both sporting moustaches and one holding a lifelike dildo protruding from her crotch.'[45] Smyth calls this a 'delicious parody' and says it shows that lesbians envy gay male penises and sexuality. It is, she says, 'laced with an envy few feminists feel able to admit.' The values that cause the lesbian envy are 'the upfront cruising style, the eroticisation of the ass, casual sex, cottaging, penetration and the economic power and social privilege of the gay male.' Cottaging is the British name for the gay male practice of seeking sex in public lavatories. This is something else that lesbians envy gay men apparently and it does seem to be being adopted by some lesbians. Smyth tell us that lesbians have 'bemoaned the lack of cottaging.'[46] This admiration of lesbians for gay men is apparently, as we would expect, not a two-way process because 'of the relative lack of sexual and social power to which women have access.'[47]

The safe sex education which has emerged from the HIV/AIDS epidemic has provided a new avenue through which lesbians have been encouraged to experience an inferiority complex

163

about their sexual practice. Safe sex education for lesbians has been based upon a male gay model, however inappropriate this might be for lesbians, and this has contributed to making male gay sexual behaviour normative in the lesbian community. Lesbian safe sex education is based upon the idea that lesbian sex is a route of HIV transmission even though there seems little agreement about such a route of infection. Safe sex demonstrations and literature are becoming important in the culture of young lesbians. In the mid-eighties lesbians had the self-confidence to promote lesbian sex as low risk. A favourite riposte to gayhating claims that AIDS was a judgement on homosexuals was to point out that lesbians did not seem to develop it. A British lesbian in 1986 argued that the low risk nature of lesbian sex should be advertised as good publicity for lesbians and useful information for women concerned about safe sex.

I'm certainly not likely to get AIDS by having lesbian sex. It does seem to me to be important that we say loudly: LESBIAN SEX IS SAFE. For women, all women, it carries much less risk than heterosexual intercourse.[48]

This confidence has declined recently, in concert with a general decrease, I would suggest, in lesbian pride and confidence.

Lesbians have become aware that there are HIV positive lesbians in the community. AIDS then, is a lesbian issue, inasmuch as positive lesbians need special support and facilities aimed at their particular needs. But these lesbians are likely to have been infected via IV drug use, transfusions, or sex with men. AIDS organisations are saying that there is no proven incidence of woman to woman transmission of the virus, that lesbians are such a low risk group that they may be a no-risk group. The British Public Health Laboratory Service, which monitors HIV infection in Britain, has recorded no cases of HIV infection resulting from sex between women.[49] This view has been fiercely contested by some lesbian groups who are convinced that the scientific community and AIDS organisations, either by malice or lack of interest are downplaying the risk of lesbian sexual transmission. An example of the heat that can be generated in relation to this issue is the furore that erupted over the poster put out by the Terrence Higgins Trust in Britain. The poster said there is a 'very low risk in oral sex . . . so ditch those dental dams, don't bother with gloves unless it turns you on'.[50] Lesbians from ACT UP protested by defacing the poster which was being displayed at the VIII International Conference on AIDS in Amsterdam in July 1992. ACT UP calls the Trust's advice 'dangerous' and 'irresponsible'.

In *Lesbian London*, novelist and New York ACT UP activist, Sarah Schulman, states that HIV is not passed between lesbians in oral sex and attributes worries about oral sex to 'AIDS hysteria'. She also states that in the fifteen recorded cases of lesbian to lesbian transmission in the USA, 'there was a needle involved each time'.

> She explained that lesbians might need to feel under threat from AIDS because of the cult of victimisation. 'There's an enormous amount of pain and shame among lesbians. It is easy to embrace the victim role because it enhances status.'[51]

It is an interesting possibility that lesbian concern about safe sex, in a context in which there seems to be little, if any, risk, satisfies desires in lesbians which have little to do with sex. These might be the desire to maintain an outcast status, not to be excluded from the tragedies that have befallen the gay male community, a fear that lesbianism might turn out to be too easy, not sufficiently stigmatised and reviled. Lesbians who defend the view that lesbian sex is risky tend to demonstrate some confusion over what they see as an obvious connection between the existence of HIV positive lesbians and the need for safe sex. If the positive lesbians did not become infected through sex with women, and there is no evidence that any woman has been so infected, then the need for safe sex is not evident.

Lesbians from Safe Womyn, an organisation that is part of the Victorian AIDS Council in Australia, held a workshop on safe sex for lesbians in Melbourne, in January 1992. They were of the view that the lesbians that they knew of with AIDS in Australia so far had not contracted the virus from lesbian sex. They said it was not certain by any means that lesbian sex could transmit the virus, and their draft leaflet specifically exempts large areas of common lesbian sexual practice from risk. In some areas of the lesbian community it can be hard to question the riskiness of lesbian sex. One of the VAC presenters who was stressing the unlikeliness of risk was quite sternly reminded that no one really knows and that lesbian sexual transmission of HIV might not be showing up in the statistics because the wrong questions were asked or no HIV diagnosis made. There seem to be two camps on the issue. The VAC lesbians stress low risk whilst the Latex Liberation Front, closely associated in the popular lesbian mind with demonstrations of sadomasochism and the morbidifying of lesbian sex, stress the existence of risk. It seems likely that the difference is not just accidental, but political. Certainly the image of lesbianism which is being promoted both to other lesbians and to the general public, is being influenced by an assumption of the riskiness of lesbian sex. Lesbians and gay men holding a public demonstration to stress their visibility in a Melbourne shopping centre donated condoms and dental dams to what was probably a rather bewildered public. Schulman talks of 'the hype about dental dams' and says, 'There's been no debate. Their efficacy has not even been tested.'[52] But dental dams are now, in some quarters, the symbol of lesbianism. There is a new generation of lesbians for whom the use of dental dams is routine. This has changed the image of lesbian sex.

From the safe sex forum I attended it appeared that such education was more influential in teaching lesbians a new, male-gay inspired sexuality than in teaching safe sex. During the social part of the safe sex evening in which lesbians present were expected to mingle and get to know one another, a lesbian porn movie was playing on two video screens. The video was replayed later for our closer inspection. It came from the US and its purpose was ostensibly to teach lesbians safe sex. It was made by a gay men's health group according to the VAC presenter. It looked like traditional men's pornography. A group of unidentified women looking unlike the average lesbian, with long hair and negligees engaged in various sexual activities including use of double headed dildos. They giggled and looked uncomfortable. Dental dams and condoms were employed in appropriate places. One woman stripped and simulated masturbation for the group. We were told afterwards that this was the only lesbian safe sex video available and that the stripper was a prostitute who was not, herself, a lesbian. It did not seem very suitable for reaching a lesbian audience who probably had little experience with group sex or the use of other women as prostitutes.

After the movie there was a demonstration of sadomasochism. This seems to be de rigeur at these events. I naively assumed that the demonstration would be relevant to HIV transmission but this was not so. It was just a promotion for S/M and seemed fairly unsafe in its message. The top in leather chaps who performed the demonstration showed us the contents of her suitcase. She showed us leather caps, such as identify tops and bottoms. She showed us different handkerchiefs, including her own which was in camouflage print and signified military interest. Brown was for shit and yellow for urine. One of the VAC presenters asked, very sensibly, if there was a handkerchief which indicated an interest in safe sex. The top told us there was and that was check or white but it was very difficult to get hold of these. We were then shown how to strap on dildos, manacles, various forms of leather restraints and how to do bondage. This was all demonstrated on a lesbian in a short black dress and red tights who confessed to feeling uncomfortable in the 'dick'. The only reference to safe sex in an HIV context was in the form of a warning to use condoms on dildos if they were shared. Some of the practices sounded rather risky. For instance we were told to use leather rather than metal handcuffs because in the fighting which was an inevitable part of S/M play metal handcuffs would cut into the wearer's wrists and cause bleeding and injury. No warning about the transfer of body fluids was given at this point. The demonstration lasted about 45 minutes.

The powerful visual images from that evening of 'safe sex' were of group sex and prostitution, dildos, and of S/M paraphernalia. The whole evening was organised along the lines of safe sex evenings for gay men and included a video by gay men of their view of lesbian sex. Safe sex education, which for gay men might be based upon routine sexual practice, is responsible in the lesbian community for promoting a new version of lesbian sexuality based on the imitation of gay male sexual practice, the eroticising of dominance and submission and objectification and the sex industry.

When I voiced my concerns to some other lesbians present at the safe sex evening they suggested that the answer was for 'vanilla' lesbians, i.e. those not involved in dominance and submission sex, to make their own videos and organise demonstrations. Such a suggestion shows the extent to which it has already been accepted that the sex industry is 'sex'. Lesbian feminists are most unlikely to want to star in or make lesbian porn movies about vanilla sex. Vanilla sex becomes distinctly unvanilla when a women has been objectified in the process and it has been rendered fit for mass consumption. The sex that many, possibly a majority of us actually do, would become something rather different if rendered for the camera. Similarly a demonstration of two lesbians engaging in any sexual activity is indistinguishable from a standard component of the sex industry. It may be from this source that live lesbian sex acts have become a routine part of the entertainment at some lesbian clubs and even at malestream S/M clubs in Melbourne. So long as safe sex evenings depend on porn videos and performance they will not be relevant to majority lesbian sexual activity but they will help powerfully to construct a new lesbian sexuality which turns out to be based upon traditional men's (gay and straight) pornography about lesbians.

The idea that safe sex requires videos and demos, group sex and the use of prostitution is firmly established in gay male safe sex ideology. It is as yet foreign to most lesbians. One example of new safe sex forms among gay men in the USA is 'jerk-off clubs' where men gather together to masturbate in company. But these clubs existed before AIDS appeared and seem to have appealed to the voyeurism and male bonding through sex that form part of the construction of male sexuality. Dennis Altman comments:

The thought of several hundred men in an abandoned warehouse, naked except for their sneakers, and in various states of sexual excitement, may seem disgusting to some, comical to others, but many of the men who attend have found in these clubs an important source of both communal support and sexual satisfaction.[53]

It is possible to see then how gay men's safe sex practices have been based upon standard forms of pre-AIDS sexual behaviour and that when safe sex has been extended to lesbians it has unthinkingly simply replicated male forms however unsuitable.

There can be powerful contradictions between the safe sex agenda of gay men and feminist theory and practice around sexuality. This is demonstrated well in the description by an AIDS education worker in Oxford, England, of the frustrations of her work. Robin Gorna explains that feminist students found her safe sex poster pornographic.

> The consultation with the Students' Women's Committee was the most unnerving. The poster was placed on the agenda after a discussion of their latest Campaign Against Pornography (CAP) project. There was a tense silence as the women read the draft. They objected that the use of the front – and, indeed, any – photographic image was oppressive to women, and suggested that a line drawing would be less objectifying. . . . We had not anticipated this all-pervasive erotophobia, nor these 'unholy alliances'. We were hearing from women students what we had expected to hear from the 'moral right'.[54]

Feminist concerns about the construction of male sexuality and the need to reconstruct sexuality in the interests of ending male violence have been dismissed here as simply right wing moralising. Gorna accepts that safe sex education can only proceed through the medium of pornography. This is a problem with women who have not yet achieved a sufficiently objectifying sexuality and don't consume much pornography.

> The most effective erotic safer sex initiatives have been in gay communities where there is a strong tradition of enjoying sexually explicit material. The initiatives generated by, for example, Deutsche AIDS Hilfe and New York's Gay Men's Health Crisis appropriate the framework and discourse of

gay porn and integrate, naturally, safer-sex techniques and fantasies ... For men who have sex with women ... the genre of 'straight' pornography exists ... Sadly, there is a general lack of sexually explicit material directed at women.[55]

For Robin Gorna women are a problem constituency because they don't really have a sexuality. She knows that safe sex education should integrate 'with existing community values and perceived needs' but doesn't see women as having such things in relation to sex. 'Where these do not exist, we are constructing a programme without foundations,' she states.[56] Gorna has accepted that men's vision of sex, whether gay or straight, is what sex is, i.e. 'recreational, raunchy, enjoyable and diverse.' This is a long way from a feminist perspective which gives women some credit in articulating their own ideas and needs. There is an assumption that women must be retrained before they can practice safe sex. They must indeed like porn before they can receive such education. Gorna arranged for the recalcitrant students to receive retraining sessions.

> Together we planned a workshop and called it 'Women Talk Sex'. One Sunday afternoon we found ourselves in a student common room clutching a bag of sex toys and a bag of porn, and surrounded by forty eager, nervous young women.[57]

The politics of sex were not mentioned here, apparently. Important questions such as whether women want sexual intercourse, how easy it is to say no, rape, sexual abuse and the politics of pornography and the sex industry were not on the menu. Instead, it seems that women have taken over the role of the sexologists in teaching women that they are sexually deficient and that they should like the male supremacist construction of sexuality.

The issue of safe sex education for gay men has complicated the feminist campaign against pornography. Whilst pornography is held up to be the only effective vehicle of safe sex education, feminists can be accused of putting men's lives at risk by challenging pornography. Simon Watney is a British gay male theorist who is very hostile to the feminist analysis of pornography.

170

He uses the vital role of pornography in safe sex to round out his opposition. He is critical of the response of a gay man in the *New York Native* to an erotic column in that paper. This critic took an identifiably feminist position, 'Let's have a creative pornography constructed along lines other than power and the exchange of body fluids'. Watney is scathing.

> This is the authentic voice of the feminist-identified gay man, spouting forth 'on behalf' of other people perceived to be at risk, in terms which nonetheless perversely equate the possibility of HIV infection with quantitative rather than qualitative aspects of sex. This position might usefully be contrasted to a description of the video *Chance of a Lifetime*, made by New York's Gay Men's Health Crisis, and encouraging Safer Sex, as 'pornographic healing' ... As one American gay man wrote last year: 'To hate porn is to hate sex. To hate sex is to hate being human. Porn tells us that sexuality is great, and in the age of AIDS, that's a particularly important message to hear.'[58]

Lesbians need to look at the question of safe sex education critically and politically if it is not simply to function as an unnecessary conduit for the introduction of male gay sexual practice, and pornography and sadomasochism into the lesbian community. An acceptance that lesbian sex is very risky may well lead to the morbidification of lesbian sex all over again.

Lesbian sex therapists give support to the idea that lesbians are sexually deficient in comparison with gay men and provide another form of sex education to reconstruct lesbian sexuality in a male gay image. The sex therapist Margaret Nicholls considers that all lesbians are 'essentially sexually repressed.'[59] Heterosexual women are too, we are told. It is only men who are not, particularly gay men and lesbians are told that they must imitate gay male sexual practice. Nicholls asserts:

> We are at least as repressed as our straight sisters, perhaps even more. We have more sexual conflicts than do men, gay or heterosexual, lower sexual desire, and fewer ways of expressing our sexual needs. Our relationships represent the

pairing of two relatively sexually inhibited individuals; thus it is no wonder that the frequency of sex in our relationships is less than in gay male or heterosexual relationships ... Moreover, our sex is less diverse and varied than the sexual techniques of gay males and possibly even of heterosexual couples.[60]

Nicholls believes that 'our relative lack of sexuality' is a real problem. She sees gay men as much better at sex.

... gay men have more sex, both within their primary relationships and outside, than do lesbians. Their sexual forms are more diverse, more than any other type of couple, they manage to successfully incorporate nonmonogamy into their relationships. Thus in one view gay men have achieved the most advanced state of sexuality within the pair-bonding known to humankind.[61]

But gay men are not superior in everything according to Nicholls. Lesbians are better at 'closeness, sharing and intimate contact'. She enjoins lesbians and gay men to learn from each other in order to alleviate their deficiencies so that 'we can create relationships with gay men's sexiness and lesbians' connectedness.'

One specific sexual difficulty she identifies in lesbians is in their approach to non-monogamy. Lesbians tend to both be honest with their partners about other lovers and to make outside relationships into affairs rather than 'tricking'. This combination is, according to Nicholls, 'deadly' because it leads to damaging jealousy and destroys the primary relationship. Nicholls recommends that lesbians adopt the gay male practice of 'tricking' because the attempt to combine sex and love in more than one relationship is unrealistic. Nicholls writes 'Tricking, anonymous sex, fuck buddies – all concepts indulged in by gay men for years ... – all seem like lovely ideas to me ...'[62] When Nicholls offers solutions to the problem of 'lack of sexuality' amongst lesbians she suggests that lesbians must borrow them from 'heterosexual couples (through the literature on sexual enhancement within the sexology field) and from gay men.' Once again we find that lesbians are deficient. 'Lesbian sexuality,' according to Nicholls, 'needs to get more "male" in its orientation, with more emphasis on sex itself and perhaps less on romance'.[63] This, she concluded triumphantly, was already happening. In the context of such a determined campaign by a lesbian sex 'expert' to make lesbians more like gay men it is not perhaps surprising that many lesbians do not have the confidence to reject safe sex education with the same message.

Another way in which lesbians are being pulled back into cultural subordination to gay men is through 'queer' politics. The new 'queer' politics profess to be inclusive and to allow young lesbians and gay men, and black lesbians and gay men at last to organise happily under the same banner of 'queerness'. Simon Watney, British gay theorist, explains its usefulness.

> The great convenience of the term 'queer' today lies in its gender and race neutrality. This is only to say that in the USA the word 'gay' has increasingly come to mean 'white' and 'thirty-something' and 'male' and 'materialistic'. On the contrary, 'queer' asserts an identity that celebrates difference within a wider picture of sexual and social diversity.[64]

The word 'lesbian' seems to have gone into hiding here. 'Queer' is to take over from 'gay', but many lesbians had never called themselves 'gay'. Universal terms used to apply to lesbians and gay men have historically always come to mean only men. The word 'homosexual' was used by gay men and the straight world as if lesbians did not exist. If they had to be mentioned they required an adjective because gay men were the norm, so they became 'female homosexuals'. The word 'gay' suffered the same fate. 'Gay' liberation was supposed to cover both gay men and lesbians but lesbians found it necessary not only to organise separately but to develop their own word to describe their specific experience. The word 'lesbian' has a very important history. It made lesbians more than a subcategory of gay men. Lesbians had a word which allowed the development of specifically lesbian pride, culture, community, friendship, ethics. The words homosexual and gay did not start out meaning only men, but came to do so as a result of a simple material political reality, the greater social and economic power of men, the power which has allowed men to define what culture is and make women invisible. The struggle to assert the specificity of women's and lesbian experience has been long and hard and needs to be kept up daily else, our experience should tell us, women and lesbians will be incorporated, assimilated into the generic male. For British and Australian lesbians at least the word 'queer' is even less inclusive than 'homosexual' or 'gay'. From our understanding of lesbian history, the word 'queer' meant men and not women at all.

Queer politics are seen as arising from the anger and near despair felt by young gay men in particular, and some lesbians, at the way that the heterosexual world, the governments of the US and Britain, ignored the plight of gay men in relation to AIDS or actively promoted gayhating. It was this new world in which young lesbians and gay men grew up which made them abandon the politics of an older generation, label them assimilationist and espouse a radical direct action politics modelled on feminist and gay liberation tactics. Apparently, according to Watney, the new 'queers' will not have disputes about issues of gender.

> ... many of today's young 'queers' feel much more in common with one another as women and men than they do with older lesbians and gay men, who were traditionally divided along the lines of gender and by numerous political disputes, largely concerned with 'pornography'.[65]

Watney has waved a magic wand. If there are to be no disputes does this mean that the gay men will be transformed into a new fiercely pro-feminist variety, or that the lesbians should keep quiet? I suspect the latter. The new alliance depends upon keeping out those lesbians and gay men who are antipornography, because they might cause conflict. It seems then, by Watney's definition, queer politics are not inclusive, most feminists are not welcome. It is a fundamental feminist principle that objectification is the hallmark of that form of sexuality that is hostile to women's interests. It is seen as lying at the root of men's sexual violence. Watney states that sexual desire is not possible without objectification. This is an essentialist notion based upon an acceptance of the predominant social construction of male sexuality under male supremacy as being the truth about sex.

> ... lesbian and gay culture has also tended to be limited by its anxiety about the so-called 'objectification' of the body, as if sexual fantasy and desire could even exist without some degree of psychic objectification.[66]

Watney accuses 'gay culture' of being 'puritanical, and often timid about sex.'[67] Lesbians reading the gay press might not have noticed this. The sexual politics of gay liberation as well as those of lesbian feminism are now under frontal attack by sexual libertarians who espouse the new sexual 'naturalism' and see any political analysis of sexual practice as out of bounds. The sexual politics of Watney are taking us back to the sixties, when sexual practice was still seen as a politics-free zone.

'Queer' politics as defined by Watney and many of those talking in Cherry Smyth's book *Lesbians Talk: Queer Notions* is specifically hostile to what has generally been understood as lesbian feminist politics. The agenda is really quite specific and narrow and based upon a particular brand of gay male politics. But queer politics is a developing politics which is not yet, and probably never will be, rigidly defined. Many young lesbians presently involved in queer politics do see themselves as feminists and are participating with as much optimism as did lesbians in gay liberation in the early seventies. They are not those defining the terms however. A lesbian explains the inclusivity of 'queer' in *Queer Notions*. 'I love queer. Queer is a homosexual of either sex. It's more convenient than saying "gays" which has to be qualified, or "lesbians and gay men".'[68]

But qualifiers are apparently needed even in the same volume that sings the praises of the appellation 'queer'. Cherry Smyth asks in a section on art 'Where does the black or white lesbian queer artist appear in the British queer cultural renaissance?'[69] Elsewhere she uses the phrase 'mixed queer'.[70] 'Mixed queer' does not seem obviously a more felicitous term than lesbian and gay. So clearly the word queer does not perform the function of inclusivity even for its most enthusiastic aficionados. An Australian, Charles Roberts, who describes himself as an 'infected queer activist' makes it clear from his usage that for him 'queer' means male and is distinguished from 'dyke'. He talks of the word 'queer' being an example of the reclaiming of language by marginalized communities who would not tolerate persons outside those groups using the same language about them. 'I personally hope that Dykes and Queers will use this same re-appropriation of language, so that the next person who calls a Queer or a Dyke a "poofter" or a "faggot" will be the last.'[71] The question that arises then for lesbians in queer politics is whether it is worth struggling again to become included in male language or whether once more to separate.

The word 'lesbian' distinguishes women from men but is not necessarily experienced as all-inclusive by women who love women outside western culture. The Aboriginal lesbian Marie Andrews who has lectured on my courses at Melbourne University has explained that a word describing the exploits of Sapphics on a Greek island does not immediately resonate with the lives of women who love women in indigenous cultures. The word 'lesbian' creates problems for all of those who don't identify with Lesbos but a word or several words which specifically mean women and not men is clearly necessary in order for lesbians to express themselves.

'Queer' politics appeals to postmodernists who see it as representing a politics of 'difference'. Difference is very important to postmodernists who see themselves as challenging false 'universals' which appear to homogenise the experience of different genders and ethnicities. But as many critics of postmodernism have pointed out it can represent a new liberalism because of the unwillingness of postmodernist theory to wish to talk about vulgar things like oppression. If the power and subordination involved in the oppression of women and race oppression are ignored then the celebration of differences actually serves to homogenise these with sexual practices such as 'pedophilia' or 'sadomasochism' which directly oppress others or exploit the oppression of women for the purpose of sexual excitement. We then have a new liberalism indeed and one in which those who seek to talk about such problems as male power are seen as party poopers, shattering the new harmony across 'differences'. Linda Semple, a British lesbian, likes the word 'queer' for what it says about 'difference'.

> I . . . use it . . . to describe a political inclusivity – a new move towards a celebration of difference across sexualities, across genders, across sexual preference and across object choice.[72]

Semple, in accordance with postmodernist theory, adds S's as in 'sexualities'. Feminist theory tends to analyse how the construction of sexuality without an S structures the oppression of women. The S's of postmodernism which can extend to talking of 'homosexualities' in which lesbians get homogenised into gay men and 'heterosexualities', make a feminist analysis of heterosexuality as a political institution almost impossible. The concepts of postmodernism, which just happen to pop up in queer politics, exclude radical feminist theorising of sexuality, they make it unthinkable. Ironically, postmodern inclusivity turns out to exclude and to create a falsely universal white gay male politics again.

The history of mixed lesbian and gay politics has shown that lesbians are tolerated as long as they do not criticise male gay politics and accept a male gay agenda as their own. An important motive behind lesbians becoming involved in queer politics is specifically a rejection of what is seen as radical feminist politics and separatism. Cherry Smyth explains that 'loving men' is a motive for her queer politics. She explains that she was once a separatist but:

> It has been a long haul back to reclaiming the right to call my cunt, my cunt, to celebrating the pleasure in objectifying another body, to fucking women and to admitting that I also love men and need their support. That is what a queer is.[73]

Patricia Duncker in her book, *Sisters and Strangers*, is admirably clear about what is wrong with the eighties politics of 'reclaiming'.

177

One of the danger signs which indicate that someone is about to begin compromising their feminist politics, or indicating that they never had any to begin with, is the moment when they declare that they are re-claiming something: marriage, the family, love, femininity or traditional religion. Re-claiming is not the same thing as challenging, transforming, confronting; an altogether less comfortable enterprise. For feminism will always be uncomfortable, unpopular, controversial and frightening. Feminism really is the politics which touches the parts of our lives no other politics will reach.[74]

The reclamation of 'man-loving' is not a particularly challenging act under male supremacy where such man-loving is in fact compulsory, but Smyth sees it as radical. Another lesbian quoted in *Queer Notions*, Tessa Boffin, says queer means challenging 'separatism'. Smyth hopes queer politics will lead to 'ridding gay men of misogyny and creating a mutual confidence whereby lesbians no longer need to separate from men to define their own agenda'.[75] Separatism, it seems, is not to be reclaimed.

Smyth clearly has anxieties herself when she explains that despite the idea that women and men would work together in queer politics separate lesbian groups have already been set up for 'queer' lesbians to focus on women's issues such as creches which the men did not seem to be interested in. But such separation within queer organisations does not seem to be the answer. In July 1992 the London group 'Outrage' disbanded all its subgroups including the lesbian group Labia on the grounds that it was important to concentrate on the real issue: AIDS.[76] Despite the determination by lesbians such as Smyth that they are living in a brave new world in which lesbians and gay men can and should work together, all the basic problems that feminists have identified keep reappearing in blatant form. It will be interesting to see whether the lesbians who are so fiercely hostile to lesbian separatism now will find the pride to separate again as a different generation did in the early seventies. Tessa Boffin appears to have identified so closely with gay male interests that anything specifically lesbian is boring.

I get annoyed when Outrage says 'this is a lesbian action'

because queer actions should cross both sexes. The lesbian action was the most boring one they had.[77]

What we have here is not a strategic coalition politics which is carried out from a firm base in separate lesbian organisation but a fear and loathing of lesbian politics, a wish to merge into gay men and become one.

The eighties saw the politics and culture of lesbians assimilated to a large extent into that of gay men with the cheerful connivance of some lesbians who saw gay male politics as a useful antidote to lesbian feminism. This leaves lesbians as permanent underdogs. Lesbians are a paler version of gay men, according to this new politics, culturally, because they do not have camp and drag, and sexually, since they are vastly inferior to gay men in the ability to objectify, use pornography, perform toilet sex, use prostitutes. Though many lesbians are now making manful efforts to catch up they may never do so adequately because they are not men, but members of the sex class of women. Taking man, even gay man, as the measure of all things is not a sign of lesbian pride but of the woeful decline in lesbian confidence in the eighties. It is a humiliating retreat from those heady days of lesbian nation in the seventies when the idea that lesbians were inferior to gay men and should emulate them in any respect would have been laughable.

---

1. Weeks, Jeffrey (1977). *Coming Out: Homosexual Politics in Britain from the Nineteenth Century to the Present.* London: Quartet. p. 87.

2. Rowse, A. L. (1977). *Homosexuals in History.* London: Weidenfeld and Nicolson.

3. Frye, Marilyn (1983). Chapter entitled 'Lesbian Feminism and the Gay Rights Movement: Another View of Male Supremacy, Another Separatism'. In *The Politics of Reality.* New York: The Crossing Press.

4. Ibid. p. 130.

5. Humphries, Martin (1985). 'Gay Machismo.' In Metcalf, Andy and Humphries, Martin (Eds.). *The Sexuality of Men.* London: Pluto Press. p. 84.

6. For the attractions of different male gay sexual practices see: Spada, James (1979). *The Spada Report.* New York: Signet New American Library.

7. Frye, Marilyn (1983). pp. 135–136.

8. Ibid. p. 144.

9. See: Stanley, Liz (1982). 'Male Needs: The Problems and Problems of Working with Gay Men.' In Friedman, Scarlet and Sarah, Elizabeth (Eds.). *On The Problem of Men.* London: The Women's Press.

Thompson, Denise (1985). *Flaws in the Social Fabric. Homosexuals and Society in Sydney*: Sydney: George Allen and Unwin.

10. Stoltenberg, John (1990). *Refusing to be a Man.* London: Fontana, p. 40.

11. Kleinberg, Seymour (1987). 'The New Masculinity of Gay Men.' In Kaufman, Michael (Ed.). *Beyond Patriarchy.* Toronto and New York: Oxford University Press, p. 36.

12. Frye, Marilyn (1983). p. 142.

13. Ibid. p. 143.

14. Ibid. p. 145.

15. Cooper, Fiona (1989). *City Limits.* p. 11. June 8–15.

16. Ibid.

17. Frye, Marilyn (1983). pp. 137–138.

18. Sontag, Susan (1977). 'Notes on Camp.' In *Against Interpretation.* New York: Anchor Books. p. 275.

19. Kennedy, Elizabeth Lapovsky and Davis, Madeline (1992). ' "They Was No One to Mess With": The Construction of the Butch Role in the Lesbian Community of the 1940s and 1950s.' In Nestle, Joan (Ed.). *The Persistent Desire.* Boston: Alyson Publications. p. 75.

20. For a discussion of Rubin's change of mind see my book (1990). *Anticlimax.* pp. 272–275.

21. Rubin, Gayle (1992). 'Of Catamites and Kings: Reflections on Butch, Gender, and Boundaries.' In Nestle, Joan (Ed.) pp. 466–482.

22. Ibid. p. 470.

23. Ibid. p. 475.

24. See discussion of lesbians who undergo transsexual surgery in my book (1990). *Anticlimax.* pp. 184–187.

25. Rubin op. cit. p. 475.

26. Ibid. p. 476.

27. See Raymond, Janice G. (1982). *The Transsexual Empire.* London: The Women's Press. (1979). Boston: Beacon Press.

28. Califia, Pat (1982). 'A Personal History of the Lesbian S/M Community and Movement in San Francisco.' In Samois (Eds.). *Coming to Power. Writings and Graphics on Lesbian S/M.* Boston: Alyson Publications. p. 245.

29. Ibid. p. 247.

30. Califia, Pat (1988). *Macho Sluts.* Boston: Alyson. p. 20.

31. Ibid. p. 16.

32. Ibid. p. 223.

33. Ibid. p. 219.

34. Ibid. p. 224.

35. Ibid. p. 231.

36. Ibid. p. 250.

37. Ibid. p. 281.

38. See Rechy, John (1979). *The Sexual Outlaw*. London: Futura.

39. Califia, Pat (1988). p. 192.

40. Ibid. p. 205.

41. Ibid. p. 10.

42. Peg Byron quoted by Smyth, Cherry (1990). In 'The Pleasure Threshold: Looking at Lesbian Porn on Film.' *Feminist Review*. No. 34. p. 157. Spring.

43. Smyth, Cherry (1992). *Lesbians Talk: Queer Notions*. London: Scarlet Press, p. 42.

44. Ibid.

45. Ibid. p. 43.

46. Ibid. p. 29.

47. Ibid. p. 44.

48. Hart, Vada (1986). 'Lesbians and AIDS.' *Gossip*, London. No. 2. p. 91.

49. *Melbourne Star Observer* (1992). p. 8. 21 August.

50. Ibid.

51. Sarah Schulman quoted in *Lesbian London*. Issue 1. p. 1. Dec 91-Jan 92.

52. Ibid.

53. Altman, Dennis (1986). *AIDS and the New Puritanism*. London: Pluto Press. p. 158.

54. Gorna, Robin (1992). 'Delightful visions: From anti-porn to eroticizing safer sex.' In Segal, Lynne and McIntosh, Mary. *Sex Exposed. Sexuality and the Pornography Debate*. London: Virago. pp. 178–179.

55. Ibid. pp. 180–181.

56. Ibid. p. 181.

57. Ibid. p. 182.

58. Watney, Simon (1987). *Policing Desire. Pornography and the AIDS Crisis*. Minneapolis: University of Minnesota Press. pp. 75–76.

59. Nicholls, Margaret (1987b). 'Lesbian Sexuality: Issues and Developing Theory.' In Boston Lesbian Psychologies Collective (Eds.). *Lesbian Psychologies*. Illinois: University of Illinois Press. p. 100.

60. Ibid.

61. Ibid. p. 102.

62. Nicholls, Margaret (1987a). 'Doing Sex Therapy With Lesbians: Bending a Heterosexual Paradigm to Fit a Gay Lifestyle.' In Boston Lesbian Psychologies Collective. p. 257.

63. Ibid. p. 259.

64. Watney, Simon (1992). 'Queerspeak. The last word.' *Outrage*. Melbourne. p. 21. April.

65. Ibid. For further analysis of the way lesbians tend to be omitted from

'homosexual' and 'gay' studies, history and culture see: Auchmuty, Rosemary, Jeffreys, Sheila and Miller, Elaine (1992). 'Lesbian History and Gay Studies: Keeping a Feminist Perspective.' *Women's History Review*. Vol. 1. No. 1.

66. Watney, Simon (1992) 'Queerspeak. The latest word.' *Outrage*. Melbourne. pp. 18–22. April.

67. Ibid.

68. Smyth, Cherry (1992) *Lesbians Talk: Queer Notions*. London: Scarlet Press. p. 20.

69. Ibid. p. 49.

70. Ibid. p. 29.

71. Roberts, Charles (1992). 'Pricks.' *Antithesis*. Vol. 5. Nos. 1 and 2. p. 87. Melbourne.

72. Smyth, Cherry (1992). p. 21.

73. Ibid. p. 27.

74 Duncker, Patricia (1992). *Sisters and Strangers. An Introduction to Contemporary Feminist Fiction*. Oxford: Blackwell. p. 266.

75. Smyth, Cherry (1992). p. 29.

76. *Pink Paper* (1992). London. 10 July.

77 In Smyth, Cherry (1992). p. 31.

Chapter 8

A DEEPER SEPARATION

Lesbian feminist commentators have expressed feelings of grief at the events that seem to have shattered the lesbian community in the eighties. They have expressed a sense of losing community. Where once lesbian venues were a place of safety and happiness now many lesbian feminists feel that their views and values are unwelcome, that there is no longer the safety of consensus on any issue. Black lesbians, lesbians from ethnic minorities and indigenous lesbians in Australia and North America have strongly expressed their concern in the late seventies and eighties at the unacknowledged ethnocentrism, ignorance and prejudice that they have experienced in what often did not feel like community to them. They have asked whose community it was meant to be if they felt excluded.[1] But the lesbian community has never been entirely white. Lesbians have come from all ethnic and cultural backgrounds to find community with other lesbians, and to take very active parts in the lesbian feminist movement. Over and above differences of culture and ethnicity and anger over the difficulties of changing this movement so that it did not simply reflect white concerns, there has been a sharing of values. The shared values have been those of woman-loving, the need to eliminate abusive hierarchies of power whether based on sex, race or class, about the need to change the world dramatically, and not just in details, to realise the lesbian feminist vision. In the disputes over sexuality that have riven the lesbian community it has often been the voices of black and Jewish lesbians, speaking from their own bitter experience, that have been raised against the use of oppression as a source of pleasure. Audre Lorde in response to the development of lesbian sadomasochism stated, 'As a minority woman, I know dominance and submission are not bedroom issues.'[2]

It is the destruction of these shared values that has led many to feelings of loss and disorientation. Once lesbian feminists were able to take pride in their status as heretics in relation to the values of the heteropatriarchy. Now lesbian feminism is a heresy to many lesbians who seem to wish to assimilate themselves seamlessly into the values of the heteropatriarchy. The lesbian feminist iconoclasm that has developed to topple such anti-lesbian and anti-woman ideologies as biological determinism and sexology, has come to seem threatening to those lesbians who have adopted the precepts of these ideologies as the core of their being, the basis of their identity.

The disputes over sexuality that have raged within the lesbian community are but part of the disputes that have wracked areas of the whole feminist movement. Catharine MacKinnon, the American radical feminist theorist, expressed how the development of a porn-loving and pro-sadomasochist culture within the lesbian and feminist community affected her in the mid eighties. She states at the beginning of her article on *Liberalism and the Death of Feminism*, 'Once there was a women's movement'. She had been involved in the campaign for the Minneapolis Ordinance which would have given women, hurt in the production of pornography or by its use, the right to act against the producers and distributors under civil rights law. She describes the profound impact of the debate over sadomasochism as a 'breakdown in what the women's movement had meant.' She experienced grief to discover that women, including lesbians and feminists, would campaign against the ordinance in the form of the Feminist Anti Censorship Taskforce.

... women have largely rejected the politics of sadomasochism. But the residue of its defense has been extremely destructive nonetheless. In discussions of sexuality, women don't say 'women' any more, but 'speaking only for myself, I . . .' The debate over sadomasochism made 'women, we' taboo in the sexual area. It began in a moral morass and left us, politically, with an individualistic analysis of sexuality, undermining a collectivity that was never based on conformity, but on resistance.[3]

MacKinnon expresses a sense that the moorings have slipped away, the moorings that represented a bottom line commitment to women's lives and safety in feminism.

When I lived in the US for a year from 1985–86 I was at first surprised by the sense of devastation that had reached into the lesbian feminist movement. Some lesbian feminists were moving away from separatism as a result. I heard some lesbian feminist theorists and activists, for whom I had much respect, talking about how some lesbian conduct had become so anti-woman that they no longer put lesbians first, but their commitment to the class of women. They now sought to work with those of common values whether heterosexual or lesbian, and in some cases men, rather than for lesbians. I was very surprised at that time. Britain had not experienced the impact of the lesbian sex industry in the way that the US had. I was still, and remain, committed to the construction of lesbian feminist culture and value. My energies were committed to the London Lesbian History Group, the Lesbian Archive. I considered then, and still consider, that the building of lesbian community is a fundamental part of the feminist project, necessary if any women are to be free, and crucial to lesbian survival because no one will care about lesbians except ourselves. In the years that have intervened the lesbian sex industry has expanded in Britain and in Australia where I now live. As it expands it seems that lesbian feminist values are eroded everywhere.

Janice Raymond has written about this devastation in a piece whose title reflects the task which she feels has to be undertaken within the lesbian community: *Putting the Politics Back into Lesbianism*. She writes of a strong lesbian feminism movement in the past tense:

This movement was the strongest challenge to heteroreality that feminism embodied. It challenged the worldview that women exist for men and primarily in relation to them . . . This movement worked on behalf of all women . . . It criticized prostitution and pornography as sexually hip for women . . . But then something happened. Women – often other lesbians – began to define things differently.[4]

What happened, she explains, is that some lesbians began to incorporate what feminists had analysed as extrusions of abusive male supremacist sexuality into lesbian life and culture. Thus, 'Pornography came to be called erotica and enlisted in the service of lesbian speech and self-expression' and 'Violence against women came to be called lesbian sadomasochism and enlisted in the service of lesbian sex . . .'[5] It was now women including other lesbians who were endorsing these 'debasements of women's lives' instead of men. Like MacKinnon she comments on the damage this did to collectivism. Lesbian feminism, she says, 'was a movement based on the power of a "we", not on an individual woman's fantasy or self-expression.' As the abuse of women was redefined by some lesbians as fun and play the ability to say 'we' was seriously undermined.

Julia Penelope has also written about the shocks the lesbian community has suffered but strikes a more optimistic note about its survival simply because it has survived so much before, and this time around a mighty political movement has taken place which cannot easily be rolled back.

It's been a scary ten or twelve years for Lesbians, and many of us have slipped into an uneasy silence or slammed shut the doors of the closets behind us for a second or third time. We need to keep reminding each other that, *as far as we know, nothing like this has ever happened before*. As far as we know, there has never been a Lesbian Movement, and we are *global* in our connectedness.[6]

The scariness that Julia Penelope has in mind here is composed of attacks on lesbians, lesbian feminists, separatists for such faults as being 'narrow' in focus and restricting analysis to an 'insignificant' minority instead of looking at 'broader issues'.

It could be argued that not much has really changed and that disaffected lesbian feminists are exaggerating the damage that has been wrought. But two lesbian commentators have traced the movement away from lesbian feminism within the lesbian

186

community, giving some good evidence to support the view that a dramatic change in values has taken place. One is Bonnie Zimmerman who has traced this change through lesbian novels over twenty years and the other is Lillian Faderman who interviewed lesbians for her panoramic survey of lesbian history in America in the twentieth century.

What is lesbian community? Bonnie Zimmerman sees lesbian feminists as having consciously created a community as a political act. This lesbian community is different from the historical lesbian community which was a means to survive under oppression and a form of self-defence rather than a creation of 'pride, solidarity, and culture'.

Lesbian feminists (beginning with Natalie Barney's circle) have used two tactics to rehabilitate lesbian culture and community. One has been deliberate separation: rather than waiting to be thrust into a gay ghetto, many lesbian feminists take the initiative and withdraw both actually and symbolically from the dominant society into Lesbian Nation. We refuse to continue the debilitating struggle against oppression. Inside Lesbian Nation we pursue the second tactic, creating our own history, tradition, and culture. In a profound way this culture defines and sustains the community. A woman becomes a citizen of Lesbian Nation, a lesbian feminist, through the books she reads, the music she listens to, the heroes she identifies with, the language she speaks, the clothes she wears – even if at times she resents the required codes.[7]

Zimmerman's book, *The Safe Sea of Women*, is her 'own individual analysis of lesbian fiction' 1969–1989. It offers us a way of tracing the changing values of the lesbian community in this period through novels. The period witnessed a sudden and tremendous outpouring of lesbian literature. The novels surveyed show how lesbian feminists felt 'united in the warm glow of "sisterhood," sexuality and community' in the early seventies only to find this community shattered by disputes and differences in the eighties.[8] Whereas in the 1970s and early eighties the meaning of the word 'lesbian' was profoundly influenced by feminist politics and ideology, in the late eighties 'some lesbians, including a number of novelists, replaced this expansive political definition with the more specific sexual definition of lesbianism.'[9] Zimmerman distinguishes between two types of lesbian identity in lesbian fiction, the 'born-lesbians' who feel they 'always preferred women' and the 'born-again lesbians' who 'make a political choice or fall in love and then see the world anew.'[10] These models were not necessarily in opposition in the seventies she explains but in the late eighties the 'discourse of born-lesbianism' went so far as to 'substitute for the dominant feminist ideology.'[11] This change, she suggests, marks the end of the 'feminist hegemony over lesbian ideology' and may result from a need for defence against an increasingly conservative malestream culture. Looking at 1980s novels she concludes that 'the naive but invigorating optimism and idealism of our recent past' have been replaced by 'uneasiness and complacency, even a cynicism.'[12]

She suggests that the lesbian feminist community in the nineties is less 'vital' than it was with an earlier generation of idealists having 'burned out' or 'grown up' without being replaced.

Like the rest of American society, many lesbians seem primarily interested in personal and economic growth. Women who, a decade ago, might have been in the thick of the 'feminist,' 'separatist,' 'downwardly-mobile' lifestyle now dismiss such terms as anachronisms, opting instead for well-paying jobs and perhaps donor insemination. With the commercial success of lesbian culture, we can buy our books and records and our long holiday weekend at a music festival without giving a second thought to the making and sustaining of an alternative vision.[13]

She is concerned that there is less 'exclusively lesbian activism' and spaces and suggests that if the current mood of anti-separatism catches on so that it becomes 'unfashionable, indeed "politically incorrect," ' to have such then it will be 'impossible to sustain the idea of Lesbian Nation.'[14] The novels of this later period are concerned with looking inward rather than optimistically outward as in the seventies. An example is Sarah Schulman's *After Delores* which is set in 'the claustrophobic world of the narrator's own despair.'[15] Such novels look at the damage we have suffered, particularly incest, but not at how to change things. A characteristic genre of the period, the lesbian detective novel, is about the individual rather than community.

> It would appear, then, that the lesbian community, as manifested in lesbian fiction, is in retreat, both in the sense that it is pulling back from some of its most radical analyses and in the sense that it is pausing to reflect upon its situation and heal its wounds.[16]

Zimmerman says that a development evident in recent lesbian writing is an accommodation to the dominant culture in the form of the 'domestication' of the lesbian novel. This can be shown in novels that represent lesbians as precisely like heterosexuals so that 'were the sex of the protagonist's love interest changed it would make virtually no difference to the story.' She gives as examples Diana McRae's *All the Muscle You Need* and Cecil Dawkin's *Charleyhorse*. Zimmerman sees this as a worrying development in a time when lesbian and gay-hating seems to be on the rise and lesbians need novels which do more than 'soothe and pacify (or sexually titillate).'[17]

Zimmerman points out that explicit sex scenes have become compulsory in lesbian novels to such an extent that 'the stories have become an excuse for sex.'[18] The sex scenes are 'cut off from the rest of the feeling and action.' But Zimmerman does not criticise the forms of sexuality portrayed in these novels, only that they don't fit into the story. She is pleased that 'the straightjacket of political correctness is genuinely loosening.' Though Zimmerman is concerned that a sexual definition of lesbianism is replacing a political one, she does not have a political critique of sexuality. It is unfortunate that lesbian feminists such as Zimmerman have picked up the language of sexual libertarians who attack lesbian feminism for political correctness. In the US the right is using the very same words to attack many things that are precious to both lesbian libertarians and lesbian feminists alike, multiculturalism and equal opportunities, particularly as they are evidenced in fields of study that do not just look at dead white men. The right is attacking feminism as politically correct. It ill behoves feminists then to use this language to rule a political critique of sexuality out of order.

Lillian Faderman has also provided a useful overview of what has happened to lesbian feminism in her book *Odd Girls and Twilight Lovers*. I don't agree with her analysis which shares with Zimmerman's the lack of a politics of sexual practice and also accepts concepts such as the danger of political correctness but she helps our understanding of the anti-feminism of the lesbian present with her detailed description of developments within the US lesbian community. Faderman obtained much of the raw material for her book by conducting interviews with lesbians around the US. Her book turns out to represent rather well what Zimmerman sees as the 'accommodation' that has taken place amongst lesbians to the malestream society. Faderman has moved precisely in accord with the dominant trends in lesbian culture. Her first book, *Surpassing the Love of Men*, was inspired by lesbian feminism and clearly saw this as the future and the ideal form of lesbianism. In her new book she has changed her mind. Lesbian feminists are firmly relegated to 'them-ness' in this book and there is no suggestion of identification.

Faderman blames lesbian feminists themselves, particularly separatism and what she sees as extremism, for the attacks upon their values.

> The utopian world that lesbian-feminists envisioned was based largely on socialist ideals and reflected the background many of them had had in the New Left. But those ideals were filtered through lesbian-feminist doctrine, which sometimes led to extreme convictions such as the importance of separatism to attain their goals.[19]

Her complaint against lesbian feminism is that it was utopian, unrealistic, so that idealistic 'Lesbian Nation was doomed to failure because of youthful inexperience and inability to compromise unbridled enthusiasms.'[20] Later in a section entitled 'Being "Politically Correct"' she indicts lesbian feminism because it needed 'so intense an idealism and required such heroic measures that fanaticism became all but inevitable' and this fanaticism was about such things as 'nonhierarchy' which became an 'inflexible dogma'.

> Being politically correct ('p.c.') meant that one adhered to the various dogmas regarding dress; money; sexual behaviour; language usage; class, race, food, and ecology consciousness; political activity; and so forth.[21]

It is difficult at first glance to see what might be wrong with any of these things. The project of social change necessitates a certain degree of seriousness, after all, and even occasionally reiteration and development of ideas. Elsewhere she again accuses the most committed lesbian feminists of 'inflexible dogma' and says their 'failure was inevitable' 'because of their unrealistic notions' and inability to compromise.[22] The forces of reaction which led to a general attack on socialism and feminism in the eighties are not mentioned as factors in the decline of lesbian feminism's efficacy. It is blamed on some fault within lesbian feminists themselves such as idealism or in translation, the desire for sweeping social change.

One development of the eighties which she pinpoints as helping to undermine lesbian feminist idealism was the emergence of a lesbian bourgeoisie. This may have been a distinctively American and perhaps Australian phenomenon since it was not so evident in the impoverished Britain of the eighties. These bourgeois lesbians were 'women who were far less separated from the mainstream in their appearance and outlook than had been the butches and femmes of the 1950s and sixties and the lesbian-feminists of the 1970s.' She suggests that this development strengthened the most dominant and visible lesbians in the community in their 'intuition' that 'less militance was appropriate to conservative times.' They felt reinforced by the increasing number of lesbians 'whose economic status, lifestyles, and philosophy rendered them much more moderate than their lesbian-feminist predecessors.'[23] Apparently some former lesbian feminists abandoned being professional revolutionaries in the eighties and took up paying careers and 'went to work in skirts and high heels' changing into lesbian clothes when they got home.[24]

A regular component of the attacks on lesbian feminism that

have taken place in recent years is a repudiation of separatism. Faderman sees separatism as one of the reasons for the decline of lesbian feminism. On the contrary I see it as the main reason for its success. It is precisely a deeper separation, I will argue here, that is necessary if anything recognisable as lesbian feminism is to survive and put out fresh shoots in years to come. Separatism's detractors, and they are surprisingly numerous in the lesbian community which is itself based upon a serious act of separation, give the impression that separatism is outrageous and extreme instead of a basic principle of feminism. The dawning of feminist consciousness requires an act of separation. All feminists, lesbian and heterosexual, have had the courage to separate themselves intellectually if not physically, from malestream culture. All feminists will have found that they received punitive sanctions for daring that act of separation from accepted heteropatriarchal mores.

Marilyn Frye's essay on separatism is a cogent exposition of the separatist ethic. Frye explains that the theme of separation is present in everything from 'divorce to exclusive lesbian separatist communities, from shelters for battered women to witch covens, from women's studies programs to women's bars, from expansion of daycare to abortion on demand.'[25] Interestingly Frye makes a distinction between separation and what she calls 'personal solutions and bandaid projects' such as legalisation of prostitution and affirmative action. These she sees as reformist projects of assimilation. This is helpful to an understanding of the projects of the lesbian sex industry which are certainly assimilationist. Her definition of separatism throws into sharp relief the determinedly anti-separatist nature of the sort of practices I have been examining in this book.

> Feminist separation is, of course, separation of various sorts or modes from men and from institutions, relationships, roles and activities which are male-defined, male-dominated and operating for the benefit of males and the maintenance of male privilege – this separation being initiated or maintained, at will, by women.[26]

All lesbians separate from malestream culture by daring to think lesbian, and most importantly by choosing to direct their best sexual and emotional energies to women, not to men. It is for that act of separation that lesbians are punished. Lesbian sex does not hurt men. Indeed it has been employed by men in brothels and in pornography from time immemorial so that they can gain erections. It is lesbian love including sex which is separate from men that is seen as disloyal because such separation removes members of the slave class of women which forms the foundation of male power and provides a connection between women which can be the basis of resistance. It is the separateness of lesbians, which is perceived to be a failure of enthusiasm for the man and all his works, rather than the performance of naughty sexual acts, that is subversive.

There is a difference between making acts of separation without acknowledging that that is what they are and being a separatist. A separatist is a lesbian who has consciously given a political interpretation to her acts of separation. Marilyn Frye suggests that this deliberate separation is not undertaken for its own sake but 'for the sake of something else like independence, liberty, growth, invention, sisterhood, safety, health, or the practice of novel and heretical customs.'[27] A separatist she defines as a feminist who practises separation 'consciously, systematically, and probably more generally' and 'advocates thorough and "broadspectrum" separation as part of the conscious strategy of liberation.'[28]

Susan Hawthorne, co-founder of the Australian Spinifex Press, wrote a very clear description of the continuum of separatist practice in 1976. She defines separatism as 'a politically motivated strategy for empowering women and undermining patriarchy.'[29] She sees its 'manifestations' as ranging from 'Valuing dialogue with other women, e.g. in consciousness-raising groups' through to 'Living in an all-women environment and having no contacts with any men' or possibly even heterosexual women. She explains that as feminists experiment with the different degrees of separatism this enables them to 'discard the internalized and oppressive male value system.'[30] The value of the separatist position at the extreme end of her continuum lies in challenging assumptions about women's dependency on men and comments that this is a radical departure from patriarchal thinking which is 'essential if we are to claim liberation for ourselves as a real possibility.' She does not, she says, advocate complete separatism for all women but suggests that feminists 'recognize the level of separatism in which they are prepared to engage.'[31]

Attacks on separatism come from many quarters. Even the fairly modest idea of holding women-only meetings on topics such as rape can draw serious reprisals from some men. Frye suggests that this is because any act of separation from men denies them the right of access which is a crucial foundation of their power.

> When women separate (withdraw, break out, regroup, transcend, shove aside, step outside, migrate, say *no*), we are simultaneously controlling access and defining. We are doubly insubordinate, since neither of these is permitted. And access and definition are fundamental ingredients in the alchemy of power, so we are doubly, and radically, insubordinate.[32]

Criticism of separatism has come from black, ethnic minority and indigenous lesbians and white ethnic majority lesbians. Some black lesbians have suggested that separatism is the privileged practice of white middle class lesbians who did not suffer from forms of oppression which linked their fortunes to particular groups of men, that it was therefore an elitist practice which could not be defended. In fact separatism has never been a practice only of white, middle class lesbians. Some black American lesbians have explained why they chose to adopt lesbian separatism as a strategic practice, in some instances citing their background in black separatism as the ground for their choice. Anna Lee, a black American separatist explains that, 'Separating from black males is scary. It is scary because we are stepping into a void' but she chooses separatism over coalition politics.[33] Lesbians who choose to be separatists are not limited to particular class or ethnic categories but it should be recognised that the possession of money and social status do make even the decision to be a lesbian simpler. White, ethnic majority lesbians do not tend to suffer so much conflict over support for men.

Perhaps because they are aware of the treachery to the heteropatriarchal political system involved in loving women many lesbians are particularly concerned to protest their loyalty to men. But this strategy is not successful. So long as heterosexuality survives as the basic institution of male supremacy then lesbianism will be seen and treated as an act of political subversion. Even if lesbians seek to imitate the mores of the heteropatriarchy slavishly so as not to seem threatening at all, the basic act of disloyalty cannot be redeemed. Attacks on separatism in feminist literature are often veiled attacks on lesbians. For this reason it does not behove lesbians to attack separatism but to support the right to separate.

Separatists are the real 'bad' girls under male supremacy. As Frye says the separatist is often seen as a 'morally depraved man-hating bigot'. But if separatism is so unacceptable to men who wish to control women then it must actually represent a challenge to the heteropatriarchy. As Frye remarks 'if you are doing something that is so strictly forbidden by the patriarchs, you must be doing something right.'[34] Amazingly it is precisely acts of assimilation, acts by what Frye calls 'patriarchal loyalists' which are seen as daring and revolutionary by many within the lesbian community presently as we have seen. The close imitation of the roles of oppressor and oppressed, masculinity and femininity, is seen as daring, as is working with and wanting to be gay men, even by surgical intervention. The exact adoption of the precepts of the male supremacist construction of sexuality in the form of dominance and submission and objectification is seen as 'bad'. That these things are very acceptable to male supremacy, in fact, is evidenced by the existence of a whole academic industry of books about playing with gender and power which does not apparently have the patriarchs trembling in their shoes. But in the literature of women's studies the repudiation of separatism is a ritual, needed, authors feel, to be taken seriously. The slavish imitation of heterosexual forms and the slavish adoption of the ideas of what Janice Raymond describes as 'heteroreality' only seems naughty to those who are fighting feminism instead of male supremacy.

It is separation from the whole mindset of the heteropatriarchy that is necessary for the survival of any lesbian feminist challenge to male supremacy. This mindset is called 'the straight mind' by Monique Wittig. The straight mind cannot exit from its programmed adherence to the duality of opposites, masculinity and femininity, one and other, powerful and powerless. It then tells us that to think of leaving the programme as lesbian feminism has and does, is utopian, foolish, simply not possible. But it is precisely the intellectual separation that lesbian feminists perform which makes us challenging and destabilising, daring to leave the master's categories behind. Wittig writes powerfully of the effect of 'heteroreality' or the 'straight mind' on our existence as lesbians.

> The discourses which particularly oppress all of us, lesbians, women, and homosexual men, are those which take for granted that what founds society, any society, is heterosexuality... These discourses of heterosexuality oppress us in the sense that they prevent us from speaking unless we speak in their terms... But their most ferocious action is the unrelenting tyranny that they exert upon our physical and mental selves... we forget the material (physical) violence produced by the abstract and 'scientific' discourses of the mass media.[35]

Wittig indicts in particular as an example of the straight mind in operation, the discourse of psychoanalysis and the work of exponents such as Lacan. She also attacks the 'pornographic discourse' which is 'one of the strategies of violence which are exercised upon us: it humiliates, it degrades, it is a crime against our "humanity".'[36] She condemns those exponents of the 'straight mind' who act as the apologists of pornography, the 'experts in semiotics' who say that feminists confuse 'the discourses with the reality'. These exponents include many lesbian theorists and many male gay ones who are unable to effect a clear intellectual separation or do not see any need for it, as we saw in the chapter on postmodernism.

Julia Penelope speaks of the importance of developing a specifically 'lesbian perspective'. Penelope explains that the basis of a lesbian perspective lies in lesbians separating themselves out from the categories of 'women' or 'gays' in which they are usually hidden or lost.

> Our invisibility, even to ourselves, is at least partially due to the fact that our identity is subsumed by two groups: women and gays ... Instead of creating free space for ourselves, we allow men to oppress us invisibly in both categories, as 'women' or as 'gays', without even the token dignity of being named 'Lesbians'.[37]

The 'lesbian perspective' is not 'natural' or even easily acquired she explains.

> (It) isn't something we acquire as soon as we step out of our closets. It's as much a process of unlearning as it is learning. It's something we have to work at, nurture, encourage, and develop. The Lesbian Perspective is furious self-creation.[38]

Penelope's idea of how specifically 'Lesbian perceptions' can be recognised is problematic. She says that the 'Lesbian process of self-definition' begins with 'the recognition and certainty that our perceptions are fundamentally accurate, regardless of what male societies say.'[39] Unfortunately it is this assumption that lesbians should be able to trust any of their perceptions that has led to much of the current confusion around sexuality that abounds presently in the lesbian community. I would rather suggest a harder task which is the comparison of our feelings, our experience and our perceptions with the ideas of the straight mind in consciousness raising and with other lesbians. This needs to be rigorous and to employ what Janice Raymond calls 'discernment'.

The idea that lesbian feminists should be visionaries working towards a vision of a world in which women are not oppressed and indeed all oppressive hierarchies have become unthinkable was widespread in the seventies. Lesbians were not afraid to have visions. We plotted deep into the night in circles of lesbians fiercely ignited by our new friendships, and that most glorious of possible human relationships, friendship formed out of and directed towards our passion to transform the world. Admittedly those rooms were smoke-filled and we were still in many respects unreconstructed. In the eighties vision became unfashionable. As Janice Raymond expresses this:

> For better or for worse, feminists have grown more 'mature' in their aspirations, to the extent that maturity is often equated with a rejection of vision and with a hard-nosed realism that forecloses a sense of the feminist future, even before its possibilities appear.[40]

The lesbian theorists who inspired much of the visionary thinking of lesbians such as Mary Daly have received a harsh press in much lesbian academic writing in the last decade. The continuation of lesbian vision is vital to our project of creating change. Fundamental to it is separation from the ideas of the heteropatriarchy, the thinking of what Mary Daly calls the sado-society. This does not mean ignorance of those ideas. We need to analyse them carefully, as lesbian scholars continue to do, so that we understand their elements, and their influence. And, as Raymond explains, we cannot afford to forget the actual condition of women. Vision not firmly rooted in the material reality of the lives of women and lesbians would be escapism.

> Too little 'materialism' about the man-made world encourages an enfeebled, empty, and escapist vision which can overlook the blatancy of woman-hating, thereby conditioning women not to react, oftentimes even to the most extreme and urgent states of female atrocities.[41]

Raymond suggests that we need to live as insider outsiders, both within and aware of the man-made world and able to envision and work for a world beyond it. The bleak and terrible vision of a lesbian future presented to us by the lesbian sex industry for instance is actually simply an acceptance and adjustment to the heteropatriarchal reality. Change is ruled out by the deliberate incorporation into lesbian lives of all the values and brutal practices of the masters.

The lesbian philosopher, Sarah Lucia Hoagland, is a lesbian visionary, committed to the creation of lesbian value and lesbian meaning. She wrote her book, *Lesbian Ethics*, in order to understand what was undermining the lesbian movement. She is optimistic about the lesbian future.

It is possible for us to engage in moral revolution and change the value we affirm by the choices we make. It is possible for lesbians to spin a revolution, for us to weave a transformation of consciousness.[42]

She explains that lesbian organisations collapsed for various reasons including 'outright violence, severe economic limits, legal threats, f.b.i. penetration and disruption, and all manner of other male sabotage' as well as the 'values of the fathers' that we still carried within us such as 'classism, racism, ageism, antisemitism, sizeism, ablebodyism, and imperialism, as well as sexism and heterosexism.' Besides these factors she identifies two others, taking survival skills learned in the heteropatriarchy into our relations with each other and relying on traditional ethics. She sees traditional ethics as arising from 'heterosexualism'. Heterosexualism is her word for what might be called by other lesbian theorists 'heterosexuality as an institution'. It is a way of life that 'normalizes the dominance of one person and the subordination of another'. Traditional Anglo-European ethics is the ethics of dominance and submission.

The relationship between women and men is considered in anglo-european thought to be the foundation of civilization. I agree. And it normalizes that which is integral to anglo-european civilization to such an extent that we cease to perceive dominance and subordination in any of their benevolent capacities as wrong or harmful: the 'loving' relationship between men and women, the 'protective' relationship between imperialists and the colonized, the 'peace-keeping' relationship between democracy (u.s. capitalism) and threats to democracy.[43]

She believes that heterosexualism has to be undermined if this whole system of ethics which sees ethical virtues as 'master/slave virtues' is to be dismantled. Her task in the book is that of 'exploring ways to work the dominance and submission of heterosexualism out of lesbian choices.' When she thinks about ethics, she explains, she thinks of 'choice under oppression' and 'lesbian moral agency'.[44]

It is in the area of sexuality that lesbian perception and lesbian ethics need most urgently to be developed because it is disputes over sexuality which are creating terrible damage within the lesbian community presently. Perhaps because there is acceptance by so many lesbians that they 'are' their sexuality, because they 'are' a sexual deviation, that sex, on the male supremacist model has been seen as so sacred. Judith Barrington, the poet and editor of *The Intimate Wilderness*, a collection of lesbian writings on sexuality which are not erotica, suggests that lesbian defensiveness in the face of lesbian-hating has influenced lesbian sexuality and prevented, as yet, much discussion of a vision beyond this. One theme of her volume, she says, is:

> ... the degree to which lesbian sexuality involves a need to be defensive or reactive in the face of homophobia. When writing about our lives, many of us continue to describe the encoded interactions of a group whose sex lives are 'dangerous'. There is a pervasive sense of forbidden sexuality, of a love life on the defensive against a hostile world. Although the new language we are now creating may, in time, play a part in creating new sexual possibilities, our sex lives now are still under siege.[45]

Clinging to and expanding the patriarchal model has been defended because it is what turns lesbians on, because it is the only sexuality that some of those trained by male abuse feel able to engage in, because it is what men have and lesbians must have equal opportunities, because it is profitable. Let us leave that model behind for a moment and look at what some lesbian feminists have offered to the understanding of sexuality.

Sarah Hoagland, like other lesbian philosophers such as Mary Daly and Julia Penelope, stresses the importance of being aware of language and how it shapes the way we think and act. She points out that the very word 'sex' is fraught with difficulty for lesbians because it comes from 'the latin *sexus*, akin to *secus*, derivative of *secare*, "to cut, divide," as in section, and itself suggests fragmenting or severing.'[46] Marilyn Frye remarks that ' "sex" is an inappropriate term for what lesbians do' and 'whatever it is that lesbians do ... we apparently do damned little of it.'[47] In examining the puzzling phenomenon that lesbians are said to do very little 'sex' she takes apart the idea that male supremacist notions of what sex is can be applied to lesbians. She quotes a survey that shows that 'only about one-third of lesbians in relationships of two years or longer "had sex" once a month or less, while among heterosexual married couples only fifteen percent had sex once a month or less.'[48] She turns such statistics on their heads by interrogating what would constitute 'how many times' for lesbians. She points out that the idea of being able to count times depends upon a male model in which a 'time' for a man consists of erection to ejaculation whereas a 'time' for any woman involved might be something very different.

She speculates on what lesbians, responding to such questionnaires, might call 'times' and in the process throws some light on how very different lesbian experience of sexuality is from the male model.

> Some might have counted a two or three cycle evening as one 'time' they 'had sex'; some might have counted it as two or three 'times'. Some may have counted as 'times' only the times both partners had orgasms; some may have counted as 'times' occasions on which at least one had an orgasm ... perhaps some counted as a 'time' every episode in which both touched the other's vulva more than fleetingly and not for something like a health examination.[49]

She suggests that lesbians did once know that they did not simply 'have sex' because that was a concept based on a male model but that in the eighties that knowledge slipped away so that lesbians were prepared to worry about how much 'sex' they were 'having'. She asserts that lesbians cannot use a 'male-dominant-female-subordinate-copulation-whose-completion and-purpose-is-the-male's-ejaculation' model to speak of our sexuality.

> Our lives, the character of our embodiment, *cannot* be mapped back onto that semantic center. When we try to synthesize and articulate it by the rules of that mapping, we

end up trying to mold our loving and our passionate carnal intercourse into explosive 8-minute events. That is not the timing and the ontology of the lesbian body.[50]

Frye suggests that lesbians need to develop their own language for the very many forms of 'doing it' that they engage in.

Audre Lorde's famous article entitled *Uses of the Erotic: The Erotic as Power*, written as far back as 1978, takes the explosion of heteropatriarchal concepts of sexuality rather further, to encompass areas of lesbian experience which are far outside malestream, traditional concepts of the sexual. Lorde defines the erotic as 'an assertion of the lifeforce of women; of that creative energy empowered, the knowledge and use of which we are now reclaiming in our language, our history, our dancing, our loving, our work, our lives'.[51] She explains that oppressive forces must 'corrupt or distort' this to control the oppressed. Thus 'we are taught to separate the erotic demand from most vital areas of our lives other than sex.'[52] She distinguishes explicitly between the erotic and pornographic, seeing the latter as 'a direct denial of the power of the erotic, for it represents the suppression of true feeling.'[53] The functions of the erotic for her, she explains, are in the 'sharing of you, whether physical, emotional, psychic, or intellectual,' with another which can be the basis for their understanding one another and in '(the) underlining of my capacity for joy.'

In the way my body stretches to music and opens into response, hearkening to its deepest rhythms, so every level upon which I sense also opens to the erotically satisfying experience, whether it is dancing, building a bookcase, writing a poem, examining an idea.[54]

She points out that as a Black lesbian feminist she recognises that 'this erotic charge is not easily shared by women who continue to operate under an exclusively european-american male tradition.'[55] What is most significant about Lorde's contribution is that she does not allow what is commonly understood as the 'sexual' to be separated out from the rest of life but would like to incorporate it as but one aspect of the erotic. It scarcely

202

needs saying that such a concept is very far removed from the philosophy underlying the new lesbian sex industry.

It is not surprising that when Lorde was asked to address the issue of sadomasochism for the 1982 collection, *Against Sadomasochism*, she did not mince her words.

> Sadomasochism is an institutionalized celebration of dominant/subordinate relationships. And, it *prepares* us either to accept subordination or to enforce dominance. *Even in play*, to affirm that the exertion of power over powerlessness is erotic, is empowering, is to set the emotional and social stage for the continuation of that relationship, politically, socially and economically. Sadomasochism feeds the belief that domination is inevitable.[56]

Lorde expresses particularly well the interweaving of the way we express ourselves sexually with the whole of the rest of our lives as lesbians. She does not believe that sadomasochism stops in the bedroom. She believes that 'life statements' are made as 'the nature and effect of my erotic relationships percolate throughout my life and my being' and concludes her thoughts on S/M by asking, 'As a deep lode of our erotic lives and knowledge, how does our sexuality enrich us and empower our actions?'[57]

For lesbians who do believe that what they do sexually is connected with the whole of their lives and their politics the question is how to go forward. There are lesbians who have chosen to eschew sexual practice altogether on the grounds that dominance and submission are too deeply ingrained in how we feel about sex to be altered. One American group which includes both lesbians and heterosexual women takes this view and suggests three ways forward, 'Radical celibacy together with deconstructive lesbianism and sex resistance (in heterosexuality) are the only practical choices for women oppressed under male supremacy.'[58] They see 'deconstructive lesbianism' as a 'transitional political choice'.

> It attempts to unweave the pattern of dominance and submission which has been incarnated as sexuality in each of us.

203

At its most basic level, deconstructive lesbianism means being who we are as lesbians, but without sex.[59]

In my book, *Anticlimax*, I suggested a different tactic, the deliberate construction of 'homosexual desire'. I defined 'homosexual desire' as eroticised sameness of power whether expressed within lesbian, gay or heterosexual relationships and 'heterosexual desire' as the eroticised difference, or inequality of power which arises from the sexual system of the heteropatriarchy. It may well be true that a lesbian reared under male power can never entirely know what a sexuality constructed in a context of equality might resemble. But I think that the struggle to transform sexuality and pursue homosexual desire by emphasising the areas of our sexual experience we feel comfortable with and limiting those which seem to be in conflict with our vision of a lesbian sexual future is worthwhile. A lesbian sexual future which is in concert with our project of changing the world is one in which our sexual lives are incorporated into our love and respect for ourselves and other women.

The question of lesbian friendship is central to the building of lesbian community and realising a lesbian vision. Where once in the seventies lesbian feminists saw womanloving as the very basis of our politics, the precise workings of this love for women were not defined. The events and upheavals of the eighties were damaging to lesbian friendships. As it became more difficult to organise politically and lesbians retreated into the safety of their homes or intimate networks, friendship and love for women had to be rethought. Janice Raymond has carried through the task of rethinking female friendships in her book, *A Passion for Friends*, motivated by her belief in the fundamental importance of 'gynaffection' to the feminist struggle and a concern for the fracturing of lesbian friendships that took place during the political disputes of the 80s. On the broadest level she defines friendship for women as that which motivates feminist struggle. She explains that 'Working for women is a profound act of friendship for women. It makes friendship political.'[60] She seeks to understand why female friendship in operation has proved so much more difficult than feminist optimism would have suggested. What she calls one of the most 'horrendous obstacles' is the very serious condition of oppression in which women live, which she describes as 'violation, surbordination and atrocity'.

> And one of the most devastating consequences of this state is to make women not lovable to their own selves and to other women. When a woman sees a sister dehumanized and brutalized throughout history, throughout her own life, in almost every culture; when a woman sees the endless variations of this abuse and brutality, and how few women really survive; when a woman sees this graphically depicted all around her, female friendship is erased from memory, and women are not affected by other women. The state of pornography, incest, and surrogacy (among others) reinforces the absence of women to each other. Violence against women is not only central to women's oppression. It is central to the lack of female friendship.[61]

This leads us back to questions raised by the earlier content of *The Lesbian Heresy*. To understand what is happening to many lesbians in the present, both the way they are treating themselves and each other, it is necessary to have a very present sense of the profound impact of our oppression as women and as lesbians upon our lives. There is a tendency for some lesbians to want to believe that they are free and equal citizens in a capitalist consumer paradise, burdened with choices and preferences. But lesbians are not free and oppression does not necessarily ennoble. Lesbians suffer always the double burdens of the oppression of women and of lesbians, and often those of class and of race oppression. Many lesbians are driven from their families of origin by sexual abuse, or are abused in care. They have lived on the street or in prostitution, they suffer from addiction to alcohol and other drugs. Lesbians who are not suffering from such poisonous gifts of the heteropatriarchy nonetheless often experience lack of self love and a bitter lack of forgiveness for their bodies. It may be unfashionable to talk of oppression and its effects on us all but the failure to do so makes it difficult to speak of what love and respect for ourselves and other women might look like and how it might be and is effected in our practice, in sex, in friendship, and in political action. It should be very clear that the use of another woman as a prostitute, or the abuse of another woman in sadomasochism is not an act of love or kindness but to many this is not clear.

Lesbian feminists who make judgements about the damage that lesbians are doing to themselves and each other in the name of sex are accused of dividing the lesbian community, of presenting barriers to lesbian friendship. But it is not an act of friendship to remain silent about the abuse of women, whether it is women or men inflicting that abuse. 'What kind of unity', Janice Raymond asks, 'can be built on an unwillingness to make judgements about what is pornography, about sadomasochism, about incest?'[62] The desire to retain safety in the lesbian community by not applying the same standards of what is good for women to the actions of lesbians as we do to the actions of men has resulted in a lesbian community that does not feel very safe to many lesbians.

In conclusion, I would like to suggest the need for a deeper separation. This deeper separation should be an intellectual, and ethical one. The creation of separate spaces is not enough if we do not continue to put energy into the creation of a lesbian perspective and lesbian ethnics which allow the development of specifically lesbian community, lesbian friendship and lesbian sexuality. Before readers affected by postmodernism start to assume that such use of the word 'lesbian' bespeaks essentialism it should be said that when lesbian feminists speak of 'lesbian' anything, they are generally speaking of something that has to be consciously created by lesbians as a political act, not any natural 'essence'. Attacks by postmodernist lesbians and gays on lesbian feminist theorising using male authorities such as Foucault and Derrida to back them up, should perhaps be understood as either wilful misunderstanding or deliberate attempts to constrain the construction of an alternative lesbian vision.

Lesbian philosophers and the philosopher in every lesbian are working with great energy to construct this different view. It does and will continue to require separate lesbian organising, or at least a separate lesbian base, separate lesbian spaces, centres, archives, galleries, workshops, presses. The tension within the lesbian community presently derives from the conflict between separation and assimilation. Those who wish to create lesbian value are ranged against those who wish to disappear invisibly into the culture of gay men. Though assimilation might appear at times to be winning we should not forget that thousands of specifically lesbian projects still exist and form the core and strength of the lesbian community. As the political tide turns, as it seems likely to do in the nineties to a context in which social change seems possible again, and a new generation of lesbians tire of much of the bleak fare offered to them as lesbian culture, then it is from our separate spaces that the new growth will spring. This new growth will ensure that instead of lesbians having to clothe themselves in the worn out dominant/submissive clichés of the heteropatriarchy to fit in, Lesbianism will continue to be a heresy until the world has been changed to suit a lesbian feminist vision.

---

1. See for example the lesbian contributors to *This Bridge Called My Back. Writings by Radical Women of Color*. Moraga, Cherrie and Anzaldua, Gloria (Eds.) (1981). Watertown, Massachusetts: Persephone Press.

2. Lorde, Audre (1982). 'Interview by Susan Leigh Star.' In Linden, Robin Ruth *et al* (Eds.). *Against Sadomasochism. A Radical Feminist Analysis*. Palo Alto, California: Frog in the Well. p. 70.

3. Catharine A. MacKinnon (1990). 'Liberalism and the Death of Feminism'. In Leidholdt, Dorchen and Raymond, Janice G. (Eds.). *The Sexual Liberals and the Attack of Feminism*. London: Pergamon (now TCP). p. 9.

4. Raymond, Janice G. (1991). 'Putting the Politics Back into Lesbianism'. *Journal of Australian Lesbian Feminist Studies*. Vol. 1. No. 2. p. 13.

5. Ibid. p. 14.

6. Penelope, Julia (1990). 'The Lesbian Perspective.' In Allen, Jeffner (Ed.). *Lesbian Philosophies and Cultures*. New York: State University New York Press. p. 100.

7. Zimmerman, Bonnie (1990). *The Safe Sea of Women. Lesbian Fiction 1969–1989*. Boston: Beacon Press. p. 159.

8. Ibid. p. xiii.

9. Ibid. p. 12.

10. Ibid. p. 52.

11. Ibid. p. 57.

12. Ibid. p. 208.

13. Ibid.

14. Ibid. p. 209.

15. Ibid. p. 212.

16. Ibid. p. 222.

17. Ibid. p. 227.

18. Ibid. p. 224.

19. Faderman, Lillian (1991). *Odd Girls and Twilight Lovers. A History of Lesbian Life in Twentieth Century America*. New York: Columbia University Press. p. 218.

20. Ibid. p. 220.

21. Ibid. p. 230.

22. Ibid. p. 235 and p. 244.

23. Ibid. p. 273.

24. Ibid. p. 276.

25. Frye, Marilyn (1983). *The Politics of Reality: Essays in Feminist Theory*. New York: The Crossing Press. p. 96.

26. Ibid.

27. Ibid. p. 97.

28. Ibid. p. 98.

29. Hawthorne, Susan (1991a). 'In Defence of Separatism.' In Gunew, Sneja (Ed.). *A Reader in Feminist Knowledge*. London and New York: Routledge. p. 312.

30. Ibid. p. 314.

31. Ibid. p. 315.

32. Frye, Marilyn (1983). p. 107.

33. Lee, Anna (1990). 'For the Love of Separatism.' In Allen, Jeffner (Ed.). *Lesbian Philosophies and Cultures*. New York: SUNY. p. 153.

34. Frye, Marilyn (1983). p. 98.

35. Wittig, Monique (1992). *The Straight Mind and Other Essays*: Boston: Beacon Press. pp. 24–25.

36. Ibid. p. 26.

37. Penelope, Julia (1990). p. 103.

38. Ibid. p. 106.

39. Ibid. p. 105.

40. Raymond, Janice G (1986). *A Passion for Friends*. Boston: Beacon Press. p. 205.

41. Ibid. p. 208.

42. Hoagland, Sarah Lucia (1989). *Lesbian Ethics. Toward New Value*. California: Institute of Lesbian Studies. p. 1.

43. Ibid. pp. 7–8.

44. Ibid. p. 12.

45. Barrington, Judith (Ed.) (1991). *An Intimate Wilderness. Lesbian Writers on Sexuality*. Portland, Oregon: The Eighth Mountain Press. p.v.

46. Hoagland, Sarah Lucia (1991). 'Desire and Political Perception.' In Barrington, Judith (Ed.) (1991). *An Intimate Wilderness*. p. 166.

47. Frye, Marilyn (1990). 'Lesbian "Sex".' In Allen, Jeffner (Ed.) (1990). *Lesbian Philosophies and Cultures*. p. 305.

48. Ibid. p. 306.

49. Ibid. pp. 307–308

50. Ibid. p. 313.

51. Lorde, Audre (1984). 'Uses of the Erotic: The Erotic as Power.' In *Sister Outsider. Essays and Speeches*. Freedom, California: The Crossing Press, p. 55.

52. Ibid.

53. Ibid. p. 54.

54. Ibid. pp. 56–57.

55. Ibid. p. 59.

56. Lorde, Audre (1982), p. 68.

57. Ibid. p. 71.

58. A Southern Women's Writing Collective (1990). 'Sex Resistance in Heterosexual Arangements.' In Leidholdt and Raymond (Eds.) (1990). *The Sexual Liberals and the Attack on Feminism*. New York: Pergamon, p. 146.

59. Ibid. p. 145.

60. Raymond, Janice G. (1990). 'Not a Sentimental Journey: Women's Friendships.' In Leidholdt and Raymond (Eds.)(1990), p. 225.

61. Ibid.

62. Ibid. p. 224.

APPENDIX

This paper was written in 1984 when I was in the group Lesbians Against Sadomasochism in London. Lesbian feminists in Britain were aware of the development of lesbian sadomasochism in the US but no group was set up around this issue until the new London Lesbian and Gay Centre agreed that sadomasochists should be allowed to meet there. The events of this time are described in the chapter 'A Pale Version of the Male' in this volume. The paper was originally written for group consumption and was in fact given out to other interested lesbians in xeroxed form. It should not be regarded as a definitive statement of the group's politics, but an individual view. In 1986 it was published in *Lesbian Ethics* in the US.

SADOMASOCHISM: THE EROTIC CULT OF FASCISM

I became aware of the links between sadomasochism and fascism in 1981 when I visited Amsterdam from my home in London to attend the women's festival. An important, if not the main, theme of the festival was sadomasochism. Women at the Amsterdam festival demonstrated S/M scenarios, e.g. a male-to-constructed female transsexual whipping a woman, both dressed in fetishistic 'feminine' clothing and black leather. Quite a number of women at the festival were dressed in black leather and some were on collars and leads being led around by other women. The promotional workshops for S/M argue from the basis of personal freedom for sexual minorities. The promoters argued that S/M was basically a private affair, though S/M practitioners had to 'come out' because they were oppressed by prejudice and discrimination against their preferred sexual practice.

In the same week as the festival took place the first fascist member of parliament was elected in Amsterdam since the war. There were street fights that weekend in which fascists celebrated by beating up members of Amsterdam's immigrant population, and a telephone tree had to be operated to get anti-fascists to different parts of the town to resist the racist violence. The Amsterdam feminists who told me of the violence and the election triumph did not see any connection between the increase in fascism and the promotion of S/M as a sexual practice. They accepted that S/M was simply a personal matter. I was not convinced. A main Amsterdam police station was in the same street as the building, the Melkweg, in which the festival took place. Outside the festival building there was a massive wall poster of a full length naked woman with her hands tied behind her. The slave woman appeared opposite the police station. She did not to me represent a symbol of defiance. It seemed likely that S/M, the police, a burgeoning fascist threat, the teenage boys who threw stones at myself and my lover for holding hands a street away from the festival, had a great deal in common. What was the common thread?

BERLIN IN THE THIRTIES

There is a historical example of the connection between S/M and fascism which we ignore at our peril. Before the nazi takeover in Germany in 1933 S/M was a flourishing and growing sexual practice, particularly among gay men. Christopher Isherwood, a gay British novelist who lived in Berlin at that time, has left a written record of the flirtation with S/M which was taking place, not just among gays, but also amongst unemployed and alienated German youth. In a 1962 book, *Down There on a Visit*, Isherwood mused on the connections between S/M and the growth of fascism in his description of a German youth, Waldemar.

I'm sure that Waldemar instinctively feels a relation between the 'cruel' ladies in boots who used to ply their trade outside the Kaufhaus des Westens and the young thugs in Nazi uniforms who are out there nowadays pushing the Jews around. When one of the booted ladies recognised a promising customer, she used to grab him, haul him into a cab and whisk him off to be whipped. Don't the S.A. boys do exactly the same thing with *their* customers – except that the whipping is in fatal earnest? Wasn't one a kind of psychological dress rehearsal for the other?[1]

Martin Sherman uses S/M as an important underlying theme in his powerful play, *Bent*. The play opens with the main character, Max, having picked up and taken home with him, presumably for a threesome with his lover, a young man in leather who is into S/M. It is the morning after and Gestapo officers arrive in pursuit of the young German and slit his throat. The date is 1934. Max and his lover are then on the run. After his lover is killed, Max ends up in a concentration camp. In the most moving scene in the play Max and a fellow prisoner, who is in the camp because he signed a petition for the repeal of Germany's anti-homosexuality statute, make love to each other just by speaking, whilst moving rocks under heavy guard. Max is unable to make love without pain and includes painful nipple biting in the spoken fantasy. Horst, the lover, complains and links the S/M with the fascism which has imprisoned them.

Horst:	. . . You try to hurt me. You make me warm, and then you hurt me. I hurt enough. I don't want to feel more pain. Why can't you be gentle.
Max:	I am.
Horst:	No, you're not. You're like them. You're like the guards. You're like the Gestapo. We stopped being gentle. I watched it, when we were on the outside. People made pain and called it love. I don't want to be like that. You don't make love to hurt.[2]

The play links Max's sadomasochism with his inability to accept his homosexuality and actually love other men. At the end of the play, though Horst is killed, Max achieves some kind of moral and personal triumph by demonstrating that he loves Horst, deliberately donning the pink triangle of the homosexual and walking into the electrified fence.

The tragedy of S/M practice in 1930s Berlin was that the scenarios that gay men were enacting, complete with nazi uniforms, for their sexual enjoyment were only an anticipation of the greater violence which was to befall them from fascist thugs when they were interned in concentration camps. The experience of male gays in these camps is graphically described in Heinz Heger's *The Men with the Pink Triangles*. One example of the torture and death of a male gay prisoner is interesting for the way in which it illumines S/M practice.

The first 'game' that the SS sergeant and his men played was to tickle their victim with goose feathers, on the soles of his feet, between his legs, in the armpits, and on other parts of his naked body. At first the prisoner forced himself to keep silent, while his eyes twitched in fear and torment from one SS man to the other. Then he could not restrain himself and finally broke out in a high-pitched laughter that very soon turned into a cry of pain, while the tears ran down his face, and his body twisted against his chains. . . .

But the depraved SS men were set on having a lot more fun with this poor creature. The bunker capo had to bring two metal bowls, one filled with cold water and the other with hot. 'Now we're going to boil your eggs for you, you filthy queer, you'll soon feel warm enough,' the bunker officer said gleefully, raising the bowl with hot water between the victim's thighs so that his balls hung down into it.

'He's a bum-fucker, isn't he, let him have what he wants,' growled one of the SS men, taking up a broom that stood in the corner and shoving the handle deep into the anus . . . [3]

The man was eventually killed by being hit on the head with a wooden stool.

The descriptions that follow are from a chapter in a lesbian S/M primer on how to do S/M safely.

> Fisting or fist-fucking means moving the whole hand around inside or in and out of someone's vagina or rectum. The fister starts out putting one or two fingers inside her partner, working her way up one finger at a time, with a couple of minutes stimulating movement between each increase, until she has her whole hand inside, at which time the fingers often curl up to fit the space, forming a 'fist'. At this point, the fistee's usual inclination is to ask, 'Can't you put any more in?'
>
> The first thing you need before you do any fisting is short, smooth fingernails. Your fingernails should be trimmed right down to the quick and then filed with an emery board or elkhorn file both side to side and back-of-hand side to palm side. It's also important to use a nice, heavy lubricant that won't all end up in a puddle in five minutes, shortening is good. The top should cover her hand fairly thickly with the shortening and not push it past the point where it fits fairly easily ... [etc].
>
> The way to drip wax from a candle safely is to let a drop or two fall at a time, rather than letting melted wax accumulate around the base of the wick and spilling it onto your partner's skin all at once ... [etc.][4]

I have included the two practices above because they come closest to replicating the torture methods used in the real-life concentration camp example. (Other instructions include how to cut a woman's breasts with razors and how to pierce her labia.) They make it clear that S/M practice comes from nowhere more mysterious than the history of our very real oppression. S/M scenarios re-enact the torture of gays by fascists as well as the torture of blacks by whites, Jews by nazis, women by men, slaves by slave-owners. Such S/M practice could be seen as a ritual enactment, like a talisman. Since it seems unlikely that gay S/M practitioners actually desire to be tortured in a way that is entirely out of their control, it seems likely that such a practice plays the role of garlic in warding off the devil, or simply an anxious anticipation of the worst that could happen to try to get used to it.

FASCIST AMBIENCE

S/M proponents are usually quite upfront about their use of fascist and nazi symbolism, costumes, e.g. black leather SS caps, swastikas, black leather SS lookalike uniforms and greatcoats. Pat Califia, the main US S/M theorist, explains it thus:

> An SM scene can be played out using the personae of guard and prisoner, cop and suspect, Nazi and Jew, white and black, straight man and queer, parent and child, priest and penitent, teacher and student, whore and client, etc. However, no symbol has a single meaning. Its meaning is derived from the context in which it is used. Not everyone who wears a swastika is a Nazi, not everyone who has a pair of handcuffs on his belt is a cop, and not everyone who wears a nun's habit is a Catholic. SM is more a parody of the hidden sexual nature of fascism than it is a worship of or acquiescence to it. How many real Nazis, cops, priests or teachers would be involved in a kinky sexual scene?[5]

The answer to Califia's naive question is, of course, quite a few. At least one member of the London lesbian S/M support group has been seen wearing SS cap and swastikas at social events. She was challenged on the grounds that these symbols were offensive to a lot of women and replied with the threat of violence if any further criticism was made.

In early 1984 gay skinheads attended the mixed gay disco at the Bell at Kings Cross. One made an abrupt siegheil salute directly and deliberately into the face of a black gay man on the floor and three followed a disabled black gay man into the toilets and threatened him. A white gay man pulled the plug on the stereo to get the incident discussed and action taken. He was expelled and barred from the disco. This was a disco which was supposedly part of the alternative, political or at least non-commercial gay scene. The skinheads were regular attenders. The national organiser of the Young National Front also turned

215

up at the Bell and was turned out when he took off his jacket and revealed swastikas. The collective at the Bell and some other disco collectives had to institute a dress code, i.e. no swastikas or 'Hitler's European Tour' T-shirts, but the black leather was accepted.

But, the S/M proponents would say, we only wear nazi insignia for fun and would not wish to be associated with violent behaviour. That may be so, but how are other gays to know the difference? The fear will be real whether the swastikas are worn for 'fun' or to persecute. Where swastikas are concerned, one woman's fun is another woman's terror. Fascists get exactly the same 'fun' out of wearing swastikas that S/M proponents do, power from other women's fear and distress. One serious danger that will result from tolerance of nazi insignia in the gay scene, under the guise of 'fun', sexual practice, or fashion, is the paralysis of our will or ability to act in the face of actual fascist violence. It is as important now to challenge and reject the sporting of nazi emblems as it was in Germany in the twenties and thirties as fascism took hold. Doubtless anti-fascists then who challenged the swastikas were met with the same threats that S/M proponents are already making when their pleasure is questioned. Was nazism the fashion then? Is that how it took hold in artistic and avant garde circles?

THE SADISM OF GERMAN FASCISM

One of the terms of abuse hurled at London feminists who were holding a meeting to challenge the promotion of S/M was 'fascists'. The lesbian feminists were accused of being 'just like the National Front' for having dared to call such a meeting. This line of attack, which fits in with current attempts by socialist sexual libertarians to label feminists right-wing, is made on the basis of an assumption that fascist politics would be opposed to S/M. Quite the reverse is true in fact, and this accusation is a good example of what Mary Daly calls 'patriarchal reversal'.[6]

Dorchen Leidholdt, of the New York group Women Against Pornography, in an illuminating article, *Where Pornography Meets Fascism*, explains the extent to which erotic sadomasochism was a mainstay of fascist ideology and practice.

Hitler adopted the whip as his personal symbol, for example, and when excited he would often thrash his own legs with it. He took great pleasure in quoting Nietszche's maxim. 'Thou goest to women? Do not forget thy whip!' Perhaps most revealing about Hitler's sexual response to women was the delight he took in watching scantily clad women risk their lives. In *The Psychopathic God*, Waite notes, 'He was particularly fond of watching pretty women in a circus on the high trapeze and tight ropes . . . He was not particularly impressed with wild animal acts unless pretty women were involved. Then he watched avidly, his face flushed, and his breath came quickly in little whistling sounds as his lips worked avidly.' Hitler's sadism toward women probably had something to do with his bad track record in romantic relationships: of the six women he was romantically involved with during his life five committed or attempted suicide.

Sadomasochism also characterized Hitler's interaction with his immediate subordinates. 'Every time I face him' rhapsodised Hermann Goering, 'my heart falls into my trousers' – as well as his relationship to the German people as a whole. Eric Fromm has pointed out that Hitler's sadomasochistic orientation played into the sadomasochistic bent of the German masses, their desire to be dominated by a powerful leader while dominating others. And Hitler was only too conscious of the tenor of both the times and the people he ruled. In an address to German military cadets in 1942 he declared, 'Why babble about brutality and be indignant about torture? The masses want that. They need something that will give them a thrill of terror?'[7]

Leidholdt seems to be suggesting that the German people had a particular bent for sadomasochism. All the evidence would suggest that the whole of male supremacy is imbued with the same bent. But her remarks force us to consider the extent to which the appeal of fascism and the appeal of racism itself are fuelled by eroticism. She goes on to point out that Jacobo Timerman, an Argentinian Jew tortured by rightists, described Argentinian anti-semitism as having an erotic and sadistic character: 'Hatred of the jew was visceral, explosive, a supernatural bolt, a gut excitement, the sense of one's entire being abandoned to hatred.'[8]

By some mysterious process all that pertains to sex in this society has been separated off from politics, even by those who would consider themselves socialist and radicals. In order to make sexual practice a private enclave of individual delight, sexuality has been seen as somehow removed from the effects of sexism, racism, any oppression in the world outside the bedroom, and considered to have no effect upon or relevance to that world. In fact sex plays a crucial part in fuelling and regulating the oppression of women and racist oppression. There is nothing pure about sex nor anything which might claim for it a special exemption from political criticism.

The promoters of S/M call their feminist opponents fascists in order to forestall us, to shut us up, to make it difficult for us to point out the links between S/M and fascism. They must know that they are in an exposed position and they desperately scream 'fascist' lest we should level such an accusation at them.

Are S/M proponents fascists? Probably they are not members of fascist organisations and do not care for any aspects of fascism apart from the erotic one. I would say that most are not fascists, even though experiencing pleasure from the terrorising of other lesbians by wearing fascist regalia comes pretty close, but promoters of fascist values. The eroticising of dominance and submission, the glamourising of violence and of the oppression of gays, Jews and women, is the stuff of fascism.

THE EROTIC ROOTS OF FASCISM

What is the main appeal of fascism? The political system of fascism offers capitalists a way of maintaining their profits with no threat of working class resistance. The violence and racism of fascism offer to the disillusioned and unemployed, the young and alienated, a scapegoat for their troubles and a substitute form of 'fulfillment' and excitement. It offers them rallies, a feeling of power (bullying), nationalistic pride and a spurious self-respect based on the idea that if they are white, male and gentile, they are at least superior to other racial groups and to women. There are doubtless many other mechanisms operating

218

as fascism and its values take hold. These include the excitement of eroticism. The erotic roots of fascism have not received much attention, perhaps because they require too threatening an appraisal of our own sexuality.

To understand the erotic roots of fascism it is necessary to have a rather different and more complex analysis of fascism than the simplistic version generally touted by the male left. It is wrong to assume that fascism is an evil force that exists somewhere fully fledged in the outside world, is easily recognisable and will suddenly arrive, obvious, calling itself fascism and in a form that is easily challenged. This was, I think, the mistaken concept behind much anti-fascist work in the middle seventies. The Anti-Nazi League confronted, very successfully, the upfront fascist organisations. Whilst these parties are slumbering currently as the tory government in Britain does much of their work for them, political people of the left are able to regard the wearing of swastikas by people who are not members of those organisations as unimportant. But fascism does not fall fully formed from the skies in the form of fascist organisations. Fascist parties require widespread support, or at least tolerance to be successful. Party members are not born fascists and are sometimes men and women who have been socialists. Oswald Mosley is the most famous British example of this phenomenon. The young men Isherwood describes as being in the nazi party one day and the communist party the next, drawn by the lure of opportunities for violence and feelings of personal power, are another.

There was a time in the late sixties and early seventies, when left radicals talked of the psychological and emotional roots or fascism in everyone living in male supremacist society. Wilhelm Reich was read avidly. Papers were written about the formation of the authoritarian personality within the patriarchal family and the need to create a completely new way of living which would reduce the attraction of the fuehrer type figure. The analysis was partial because there was not much consideration of women's oppression beyond the simple belief that eliminating the nuclear family would solve women's problems. But there was an understanding that fascism's emotional roots are built into our personalities from the type of family structures we

219

are born into and the kinds of authority we are subjected to throughout childhood and growing up. This was a crucially important understanding and the fruits of it exist today in new attitudes towards childrearing and political organisation within feminism and some parts of the left and gay movement. This understanding of the importance of personal politics, on the basis of which the women's liberation movement was formed, seems now to be increasingly unpopular. I feel convinced, but it may be wishful thinking, that the significance of wearing swastikas would have been clear in 1971 in a way which it is not today.

The erotic roots of fascism lie in the way in which sexuality under male supremacy is structured in individuals. Because western male supremacy encourages us to experience sexuality as an immensely powerful and nigh uncontrollable force, the erotic aspect of fascism has great significance. We do not learn to express ourselves sexually in a world of equal, loving relationships. Women and men are born into the heterosexual system of male dominance and female submission. This holds true whether or not we are able to escape sufficiently to love women. Childhood sexuality is constructed through interaction with aggressive boys pulling girls' knickers down and through sexual abuse and exploitation by adult men. The models we are offered of female sexuality are of passivity and submission. We are taught to respond sexually to aggressive male overtures. Many lesbians have difficulty learning the correct female response to submissive sexual docility to men, but nevertheless we do not easily emerge unscathed from the construction of female sexuality around sadomasochism. Where we live under oppression and where there is virtually no escape for us, at least until we reach an advanced age, toward egalitarian relationships in which we take sexual initiatives, we have little alternative but to take pleasure from our oppression. The most common response is to eroticise our powerlessness in masochism. For some women who see this as too 'effeminate' the role of humiliating women can be eroticised in sadism – the models for this in a woman-hating culture are everywhere.

Lesbians and gay men suffer particular pressures which can lead to the possession of a sexuality constructed around sadoma-

220

sochism. As a result of heterosexism and anti-lesbianism, we have often grown up hating ourselves and particularly our sexuality. It is hard for us to build for ourselves a sexuality that is positive, egalitarian and free from S/M overtones. Some lesbians and gay men know no other sexuality than that of sadomasochistic fantasies which influence their practice, though they may studiously avoid acting out S/M ritual. Any challenge to sadomasochism is felt by some such lesbians and gay men as a serious threat. They see themselves as having no sexual practice at all if they have to abandon that which is based on eroticising oppression. But there lies, in our very understanding that sexuality is something constructed and not given, a message of hope. We can reconstruct. There is every ground for optimism. Some lesbians and gay men are very little affected by S/M, and are able to practise a different kind of sexuality. Even those of us who do know the extent of S/M influence in our lives usually have experienced moments of unusual sexual intensity and pleasure which have not involved fantasised dominance and submission to any degree. In all of us are the seeds of change. We can seek to maximise positive sexuality instead of maximising the negative sexuality of S/M.

The triggers to a sexual response built around masochism are the symbols of power and authority. Particularly powerful symbols are those which represent abusive, cruel and arbitrary power and authority, the whip is a more powerful symbol than the prefect's badge. The trappings and rituals of fascism are perfect symbols for the purpose. Uniforms, marches, swastikas, portraits of Hitler, authoritarian speechmaking are erotic triggers. The sadists in the National Front are stimulated by repeated viewing of videos of German nazi marches and parades. All the paraphernalia of fascism is calculated to draw a powerful erotic response from those whose sexuality has been formed under male supremacy and modelled on sadomasochism. That is most of us.

It is the capacity to be attracted to nazism that numbs the response of outrage that many people might otherwise feel toward it. The construction of S/M sexuality is a mighty clever ploy for the oppressor. Our resistance is undermined in our very guts if our response to the torture of others or to the trappings of militarism is erotic rather than politically indignant. It is very hard to fight what turns you on. This is a problem which feminists fighting porn have already recognised and understood. It feels humiliating and paralysing to be turned on by the very degradation of women that you wish to challenge. The only way to fight is to turn that pain into anger. We are not to blame for the way our sexuality is constructed, though we have total responsibility for how we choose to act on it. We have the right to be furious and to direct our pain into attacking the porn merchants, the porn apologists (and they include, unfortunately, S/M dykes), the porn buyers and consumers. It's hard but we have to understand that the images and messages – of women being objects, tortured, used and abused – that influence our own sexual response are meant to paralyse us. We cannot afford to be weakened by these images but must share our feelings and build our rage.

As with sexism, the trappings of fascism and even its practice can be turn ons not just for the oppressor but for his victims. Edmund White, US gay novelist, interviewed a couple of gay men who were into wearing police uniforms in his book *States of Desire: Travels in Gay America*. He explained that there was a bar staffed with gay men in police uniforms in which the customers included gay men dressed as cops and real life policemen. This tragic and degrading flirtation with oppression had alarming implications. One cop lookalike, when arrested later outside the bar, spent his time entranced by the policeman's boots. Another who was arrested and beaten up could speak of nothing but his infatuation for his tormentor.[9]

S/M promoters constantly stress that S/M is 'only fantasy' and bears no relation to reality. This is a comforting illusion. What is ritual today can be reality tomorrow. The promotion of S/M and its imagery will ensure that it will be more and more difficult in the future for some lesbians and gay men, perhaps for all those who use the gay social scene, which is flooded with S/M imagery, to be purely angry and in no sense erotically aroused by the imagery of real life, practising fascists, policemen, and thugs. I think it is important that we are able to distinguish fascist threats accurately and fight them clearly. I do not want to think that, when tanks and marching boots and swastikas pass by in a real fascist coup, the gay population will be experiencing a thud of erotic desire which immobilises us.

IS SADOMASOCHISM RACIST?

US and British S/M promoters are righteously indignant about the suggestion that there might be anything racist about their politics. Thus, Pat Califia, doyenne of Californian lesbian sado-masochism, a prominent 'top' or sadist, dismissed criticisms of racism made when the S/M group Samois was told they could not rent space in the San Francisco women's building. 'We were expected to defend ourselves against accusations that we were racist . . .' she complained indignantly.[10] She does not of course do so, or mention anywhere the substance of the allegations or the ways in which she saw them to be false. Such an arrogant belief by white women that they are above and beyond the possibility of racist behaviour or attitudes would, hopefully, in any other sphere but that of sexuality, be seen as a form as racism.

S/M proponents should be aware of the offence given to all gays of colour by the insignia of a political ideology which means death or hideous persecution to all non-aryans. The Gay Black Group made their view very plain in response to the appearance of nazi regalia at mixed gay events.

We are becoming increasingly aware of people wearing fascist and nazi insignia at various lesbian/gay venues, proudly dis-playing the regalia of the British Movement and the National Front. Reports are growing of attacks on gay men and women by such types. It is no longer acceptable to us for people wearing such offensive clothing to be excused by saying it is just 'fashion'. We find it offensive and disturbing that racism remains unchallenged, taken for granted or otherwise con-doned by the entire lesbian/gay community. We are stunned at the ignorance as regards the numerous attacks and abuse and hostility to gay people shown by groups of fascists. We feel that a concerted effort needs to be begun to identify and eradicate the seeds of racism and fascism inherent in the lesbian/gay community . . .

The Gay Black Group has experienced violence at the hands of fascists both due to racism and because of our sexuality.[11]

The US black feminist, Alice Walker, in a moving and, one might have thought, unanswerable article, did explain the way in which she saw S/M practice as being racist. Walker writes as a teacher who had spent a term with women students, black and white, trying to 'come to terms, in imagination and feeling' with what it meant to be a slave or a master or mistress. 'Black and white and mixed women wrote of captivity, of rape, of forced breeding to restock the master's slave pens. They write of attempts to escape, of the sale of their children, of dreams of Africa, of efforts at suicide.'[12] Then she writes of the effect of watching a TV show in which two Samois women took part as mistress and slave. Though the article is written in a fictional style and was originally published in a book of short stories, the S/M TV program was not fiction but really took place as she describes.

Imagine our surprise, therefore, when many of us watched a television special on sadomasochism that aired that night before our class ended, and the only interracial couple in it, lesbians, presented themselves as mistress and slave. The white woman, who did all the talking, was mistress (wearing a ring in the shape of a key that she said fit the lock on the chain around the black woman's neck), and the black woman, who stood smiling and silent, was – the white woman said – her slave . . .

All I had been teaching was subverted by that one image, and I was incensed to think of the hard struggle of my students to rid themselves of stereotypes, to combat prejudice, to put themselves into enslaved women's skin, and then to see their struggle mocked, and the actual enslaved condition of literally millions of our mothers trivialized because two ignorant women insisted on their right to act out publicly a 'fantasy' that still strikes terror in black women's hearts. And embarrassment and disgust, at least in the hearts of most of the white women in my class.

One white student, apparently with close ties to our local

lesbian S and M group, said she could see nothing wrong with what we'd seen on TV. (Incidentally there were several white men on this program who owned white women as 'slaves', and even claimed to hold legal papers to this effect. Indeed, one man paraded his slave around town with a horse's bit between her teeth and 'lent' her out to other sado-masochists to be whipped.) It is all fantasy, she said. No harm done. Slavery, real slavery is over after all.

But it isn't over ... and Kathleen Barry's book on female sexual slavery and Linda Lovelace's book on being such a slave are not the only indicators that this is true.[13]

Pat Califia chose to reply to Alice Walker's article in two entirely dismissive sentences in her contribution to the Samois book, *Coming to Power*. '... In an attempt to prove that S/M is racist, Walker describes those women [those playing mistress and slave on the TV program] as a white woman top and a black woman bottom [masochist]. In fact, the top in this couple is a Latina lesbian.'[14] This is the level of seriousness with which the Samois group, on which the British S/M dykes support group appears to be modelled, takes the subject of racism.

The British S/M dykes support group supported by the English Collective of Prostitutes (ECP) and Wages Due Lesbians (two of the subgroups within the umbrella organisation Wages for Housework, a strongly anti-feminist campaign which tries to muscle in whenever it sees women's issues that could be used to damage the women's liberation movement) came to a meeting of some London lesbian feminists who wanted to plan a campaign to challenge the spread of S/M politics. A woman from ECP gave a reason, culled from standard S/M apologist literature, for why S/M could be very useful in relationships. She explained that in relationships between black and white women S/M rituals could be acted out which would even out the power differences or at least help to understand them. This woman, who was white, did not say who was to act as top and who to act as bottom in such relationships. In the US example above the bottom was a black woman. But just supposing this was not always the case, do we really see the acting out of racist rituals, even if in some cases the power relationship were not white top and black bottom, as helping to eliminate racism? In men's pornographic literature the black woman is represented either as submissive slave victim or as dominatrix. S/M rituals can only reinforce one or both of these stereotypes. S/M does not offer any chance to break out of them.

CAN SADOMASOCHISM BE SAVED?

Pat Califia explains, in *Coming to Power*, that some members of the Samois group found that some of their principles were in opposition to S/M practice, and that this led to problems in the group. She does not say what those principles were and she is not sympathetic to them, but we could make a guess that they concerned such things as the wearing of swastikas and even rituals in which black women were slaves. It does not seem that British S/M women are as yet troubled by their consciences, since at least one has been seen out and about in swastikas. But would it be possible for S/M practitioners to 'clean-up' their act and cut out obvious racist symbolism as the result of criticism? (So far their response to criticism has been to call the critics fascist and racists and to tell them the S/Mers will not allow them to have any public meetings without S/M dykes in costume and preventing discussion.)

S/M ritual is about eroticising dominance and submission and involves the acting out of oppression. The scenarios of nazi and Jew or slave and mistress could possibly be left off the agenda by those with tender consciences. This would leave plenty of scope for scenarios and costumes representing sexist oppression, using images of prostitution, sexual harrassment or simply fetishised gender stereotyping with one figure dressed as a tough biker and one effeminised in corsets and frills. Is this a solution?

Quite apart from the fact that the imagery would remain appallingly sexist and heterosexist, any eroticising of power, any glorifying of oppression can only strengthen the vales which maintain all forms of oppression. Racist oppression depends as much on the ideas that might is right, that violence is a reasonable way to treat those deemed to be inferior, and that inequalities of power are desirable and inevitable, as does sexism. The practice of S/M reinforces these values. It does not allow any space for the existence of an alternative to these values. If we are committed to the achievement of a society in which no group in the population is subject to violence, discrimination and exploitation, then we must build a sexual practice which reflects the sort of society we want to create. Otherwise what we are saying is that sex and the emotions that go with it really are quite unconnected with the rest of our lives and of no political significance. Such a practice would be mutual, caring and egalitarian. This is, of course, anathema to S/M proponents. Such practice is called *bambi* by male gay S/M apologists like Jeffrey Weeks and *vanilla* by Samois lesbians.[15] Both terms are designed to show contempt and put people off. Egalitarian sexual practice is represented as lacking in intensity, monotonous, suitable only for sissies.

S/M proponents are aware that they are open to political criticism and so some of them have developed an ingenious defence. A few years ago a member of the then recently defunct gay group, Gay Left, gave a promotional talk on S/M, with slides, to a gay workshop. He showed slides of men in nazi uniforms pissing into gutters and forcing handcuffed men to lick it up on their knees. Intrigued, I asked him what all this had to do with socialism. At first he replied that it had nothing to do with socialism really, it was just sexual practice. Later he provided a form of justification which some US ex-political S/Mers have felt obliged to develop. This is that S/M practice helps those involved to understand the power differences which exist in the world and to work more effectively to end them. (See also the argument described above given by the ECP and British S/M dykes support group.) A US S/M apologist expressed his defence quite succinctly:

> Maybe one of the most effective ways to fight political power and even render it unnecessary is to understand the impulses to power and submission in oneself and integrate them, rather than trying to extend them in political systems. Involvement in S/M tends to take away a person's 'need' to oppress and be oppressed, manipulate and be manipulated socially and politically – another reason why political power-trippers tend

227

to oppose it so strongly. S/M can be part of an outright rebellion against social, structuralised oppression, which is part of the reason anarchists and libertarians are overrepresented among S/M people.[16]

To this man oppression seems to be something which people 'need' and invite on themselves. That's a logical analysis from the perspective of S/M, which sees violence and abuse as something which people can 'need' and choose. It is an entirely individualistic analysis in which actual real life oppression plays no part. It is a self-indulgent, spurious argument. How would S/M practice help us to dismantle the military-industrial complex, confront a group of fascist thugs, or help a lesbian mother get custody of her children?

To fight structural oppression we require self-respect and some idea that an alternative exists to the cycles of dominance and submission. We can only be guided by the notion that oppressive power structures do not 'need' to exist for human happiness, sexual or otherwise.

SADOMASOCHISM AS POLITICS

S/M promoters are attracting support from liberals on the basis of their claim to individual freedom, the personal right to pursue their chosen sexual practice. But the argument of personal freedom is not necessarily progressive. It is the mainstay of Thatcherite economic and social policy. Such an argument must depend on the proviso that the behaviour in question does no harm to anyone other than the practitioner herself. (Some would argue that there should be limits on the right of any human being to do physical harm to themselves or require any human being to do physical harm to them. What would our responsibility be if confronted by a brutal anal fistfucking scenario in a context of drugs and alcohol when we knew that the practice could lead to dreadful injury or death? Would we intervene, get off on it, or walk by?) The promotion of S/M does do harm to more than the practitioners and it is promotion of far more than a sexual practice; it is not a hobby but a politics and a way of life.

The wearing of S/M clothing at social events, on marches,

etc., in the form of black leather costumes, handcuffs, studs, creates an atmosphere of threat and anxiety for all lesbians present. Lesbians often seek out women-only company to escape men's harassment and intimidation on the street, in adverts and porn. We are used to 'masculine', aggressive males using S/M clothing routinely to intimidate, e.g. Hell's Angels. We should not have to suffer fear with other lesbians or be cut off from communication because we cannot cope with intimidating clothing. There are many lesbians in London right now whose social life is restricted by the prevalence of S/M clothing whether in the guise of fashion or as an extension of S/M practice. These lesbians are not sissies. We have the right not to be afraid and the right to violence-free environments.

The wearing of nazi and fascist regalia, e.g., swastikas, black leather SS caps, black leather SS greatcoats, causes grave offence and distress to all those lesbians who are conscious of what German fascism meant in terms of violence and death for Jews, gypsies, lesbians, the physically and mentally different, indeed all but white, gentile, heterosexual, able-bodied males.

An acceptance of S/M clothing, particularly nazi regalia, makes the lesbian community less able to withstand the very real burgeoning of fascist values and practice in British society right now. We do not need a blurring of distinctions. We must see and challenge clearly any attempt to make racist and fascist values or behaviour acceptable. Some wearers of fascist regalia are harassing and attacking gays, particularly black gays, right now. They are harder to expose and reject when fascist regalia and 'masculine', aggressive values have become commonplace on the gay social scene.

The eroticising of power and oppression in the sexuality of cruelty that is S/M trains us to be turned on by the trappings of fascism. The erotic appeal of fascism, structured into our sexuality as we learn our sexual responses under male supremacy, is enhanced by the politics of S/M. Only the building of an egalitarian sexual practice can fit into anti-fascist politics.

S/M is not a sexual practice which drops from the skies but a response to and echoing of the increasing hold of fascist values and practice in the world outside the gay ghetto. As in Germany in the early 1930s, racist attacks are now on the increase.

Increasingly militarism infects western society. Porn and adverts become more and more violent and sadistic toward women. We have a tory government which is dedicated to restricting personal freedom in the name of increasing it. There is an atmosphere of increasing social tension and fear as government policies polarise differences between poor and rich, black and white, women and men. In this context S/M can be seen to be, not an adventurous and radical new departure, but a way in which lesbians can translate directly into their relationships with each other the hatred and contempt of women and particularly of lesbians which fascist values represent. Perhaps it is a misguided form of self defence, i.e. if lesbians cause each other fear and pain right now it won't be so distressing when we receive such abuse from others in the future.

S/M promoters contend that their sexual practice in no way affects their relationships with other and the rest of the world outside the bedroom, except in making them feel stronger. In the torture training schools in Greece under the military dictatorship and under other extreme right wing regimes, trainee torturers were trained by being tortured. It could be that 'bottom' or M lesbians, who are the vast majority, do have their sensibilities blunted by the torture they choose to undergo. In order to create a sufficient number of Ss, some Ms have to progress into dishing out what they have previously received.

S/M practice does spill out from the bedroom into other areas of lesbian relationships. The following extract is from a *Coming to Power* article in which Susan Farr explains how she and her lover use physical punishment to overcome jealousy at each other's non-monogamy.

If I give Rae a whipping after she has had sex with someone else, it also expresses directly how angry and jealous I feel. It is an exertion of power over, no question about it. It gives me an outlet for the 'negative' and very natural feelings that exist regardless of my commitment to the principle of non-monogamy. The punishment also functions to relieve the guilt of the person having the affair, another 'negative' and natural feeling that exists regardless of sincere beliefs that the upsets of occasional non-monogamy are preferable to the suffocation of unrelieved monogamy . . . This discussion of punishment rituals used as a response to non-monogamy is one example of how physical aggression can function to keep a relationship clean.[17]

S/Mers would have it that there is a difference between what is described here and a straightforward battering relationship. The distinction, based on the false premise that we can consent to abuse (remember the old chestnut of how battered wives really love it) can easily become blurred so that the battering becomes very damaging for one or both partners. Marissa Jonel, an S/M survivor, describes such a situation in *Against Sadomasochism*.[18] Such 'consensual' battering cannot help our struggle as women and as lesbians to assert women's right to live free from violence, our right not to be seen as appropriate targets of violence. S/M is much more than a sexual practice. It is a lifestyle and approach to the world which glorifies and legitimates violence. Battering relationships reduce the potential of the participants and of us all to find alternative ways to handle conflict. Lesbian-battering, through which lesbians take out their internalised anti-lesbianism and self-hatred on each other, is a serious problem for the lesbian community to deal with, not a game.

It is important to understand that it is a politics of sadomasochism that is being promoted, not simply a sexual practice. The tactics of S/Mers make that clear. S/M promoters, in their guise as an oppressed minority, carried an S/M banner on the Lesbian Strength march in June 1984. This meant that many lesbians who knew about the banner never attended the march and many others felt unable to join the march on the day. The S/M promoters were well aware that they were thus dividing lesbians and excluding many lesbians from the march, but the right of the three S/M dykes to do such damage to lesbian unity and politics was upheld by the stewards and all objections overruled. S/M promoters deliberately incite such confrontations and the splintering of political unity this brings about. In the US Samois first destroyed the unity of Gay Pride marches, then sought to split the San Francisco women's centre collective by booking space, then took to intimidating and harassing feminist bookstores which would not display their promotional literature prominently. The British S/M dykes group has sought to book space at the central London women's centre, A Woman's Place. The same tactics were used on the Lesbian and Gay Centre. Despite the opposition of the vast majority of lesbian feminists who were members of the centre, the S/Mers were allowed space in June 1985.

Such a co-ordinated campaign to spread confusion and disunity and fear out of all proportion to their numbers resembles nothing so much as fascist tactics. Relying on the support of liberalism they create confrontations to drive wedges into the political opposition and weaken our capacity to confront fascist values and practice in any form. (One example of fascists using this tactic is the recent move by the National Front to demand help from the National Council for Civil Liberties. This was calculated to split the NCCL and did cause considerable trouble). What is happening is far more than the attempt of an 'oppressed' minority to gain the right to act out their sexual practice. S/M is politics with definite tactics, which include intimidation by women wearing black leather uniforms. Seldom has an 'oppressed' group been so oppressive and potentially destructive.

The implications of S/M politics are too alarming to ignore. Not just feminist politics, but anti-racist, anti-fascist and anti-capitalist politics depend upon an understanding that the oppressed do not seek, need or want their oppression. The great myth that holds the ideology of western democracy together is that of consent. In western democratic thought all groups within the population consent to the system of government. There is consensus. This is not really so. Only those white males with wealth are in any position to exercise true consent to a political system which routinely degrades, exploits and controls everyone else. S/M uses this politically manipulative notion of consent to justify S/M. The notion that anyone deliberately sets out to seek abuse and degradation can be extrapolated very easily to justify politically oppressive systems, i.e., the basic fascist value that the masses 'need' a strong ruler. The basic political tenet of S/M is thus in contradiction to our struggle for a political system based upon the right of every human being to dignity, equality, self-respect and self-government.

The sexuality of cruelty that is S/M is neither innate or inevitable. Though many of us have experienced fantasies and practice which incorporate S/M values of dominance and submission, we also have experience of positive sexuality with egalitarian values. It is this positive sexuality that we need to promote and extend. Our capacity to love one another with dignity and self-respect, not just with intensity of sensation and pleasure, has been damaged by our experience of oppression. But this capacity is not destroyed. We can fight back against all the pressures that encourage us to love the boot that will kick us into submission. We can decide not to conduct a romance with our oppressors. We can have a sexuality which is integrated not into our oppression but into our politics of resistance.

1. Isherwood, Christopher (1962). *Down There on a Visit*. London: Methuen, pp. 73–74.

2. Sherman, Martin (1980). *Bent*. Derbyshire, UK: Amber Lane Press, p. 67.

3. Heger, Heinz (1980). *The Men with the Pink Triangles*, trans. David Fernback. London: Gay Men's Press, pp. 82–83.

4. Bellwether, Janet (1982). 'Love Means Never Having to Say Oops: A Lesbian Guide to S/M Safety.' In Samois (Ed.) (1982). *Coming to Power: Writings and Graphics on Lesbian S/M*. Second edition. Boston: Alyson, pp. 70–71 and 74.

5. Califia, Pat (1981). 'Feminism and Sadomasochism.' *Heresies*. Sex Issue 12, p. 32.

6. See various passages in Daly, Mary. *Gyn/Ecology* (1978). Boston: Beacon Press; and *Beyond God the Father: Toward a Philosophy of Women's Liberation* (1973). Boston: Beacon Press.

7 Leidholdt, Dorchen (1983). 'Where Pornography Meets Fascism.' *WIN*, March 15, (1983), p. 18. Quotations cited by Liedholdt are in Robert G. L. Waite, *The Psychopathic God*. New York: Basic Books, pp. 153, 375, 380.

8. Timerman, Jacobo (1981). *Prisoner without a Name, Cell without a Number*. New York: Knopf, p. 66.

9. White, Edmund (1983). *States of Desire: Travels in Gay America*. New York: Dutton. If anything, the use of real-life torment as a sexual turn-on has increased since White's observations. Recently a staff person at the Glad Day bookstore in Boston told me that Daniel P. Mannix's *History of Torture* (1983) New York: Dell, is the store's best seller.

10. Califia, Pat 'A Personal View of the History of the Lesbian SM Community

and Movement in San Francisco,' in Samois (Ed.) (1982). *Coming to Power*, p. 274.

11. Gay Black Group (1984). 'Letter to the Editor,' *Capital Gay*. London. February 14.

12. Walker, Alice (1982). 'A Letter of the Times, or Should This Sadomasochism Be Saved?' In Linden, Robin Ruth *et al* (Eds.) *Against Sadomasochism: A Radical Feminist Analysis*. Palo Alto, California: Frog in the Well Press, pp. 206–207. Reprinted from Alice Walker (1981). *You Can't Keep a Good Woman Down: Stories by Alice Walker* New York: Harcourt Brace, pp. 118–123.

13. Walker, Alice (1982). 'A Letter of the Times', p. 207.

14. Califia, Pat (1982). 'A Personal View', p. 268.

15. See Jeffrey Weeks' contribution to *Gay News* (1982). No 243. Tenth Anniversary Issue. *Vanilla* occurs frequently in lesbian S/M literature, 1982.

16. Young, Ian (1978). Remarks in 'Forum on Sadomasochism', in Jay, Karla and Young, Allen (Eds.). *Lavender Culture*. New York: Harcourt Brace, p. 104.

17. Farr, Susan (1982). 'The Art of Discipline: Creating Erotic Dramas of Play and Power.' In Samois (Ed.). *Coming to Power*, p. 186.

18. Jonel, Marissa (1982). 'Letter from a Former Masochist.' In Linden, Pagano, Russell & Star (Eds.). *Against Sadomasochism*, pp. 16–22.

REFERENCES

Auchmuty, Rosemary (1989). 'You're a Dyke, Angela! Elsie J. Oxenham and the Rise and Fall of the Schoolgirl Story.' In Lesbian History Group (Eds.). *Not a Passing Phase*. London: The Women's Press.

Auchmuty, Rosemary, Jeffreys, Sheila and Miller, Elaine (1992). 'Lesbian History and Gay Studies: Keeping a Feminist Perspective.' *Women's History Review* Vol 1, No. 1.

Alderson, Lyn and Wistrich, Harriet (1988). 'Clause 29: Radical Feminist Perspectives.' *Trouble and Strife*. No. 13. Spring.

Allen, Jeffner (ed.) (1990). *Lesbian Philosophies and Cultures*. New York: State University New York Press.

Altman, Dennis (1986). *AIDS and the New Puritanism*. London: Pluto.

Altman, Dennis *et al* (Eds.) (1989). *Which Homosexuality?* London: Gay Men's Press.

Austin, Paula (1992). 'Femme-inism'. In Joan Nestle (Ed.). *The Persistent Desire*. Boston: Alyson.

Bad Attitude (1985). Winter.

Bannon, Ann, (1970). *Women of the Shadows*. London: Sphere. (1986). Tallahassee, Florida: Naiad. First published 1959.

Barrington, Judith (Ed.) (1991). *An Intimate Wilderness. Lesbian Writers on Sexuality*. Portland, Oregon: The Eighth Mountain Press.

Bearchell, Chris (1983). 'Why I am a Gay Liberationist: Thoughts on Sex, Freedom, the Family and the State'. *Resources for Feminist Research*. Vol. 12. No. 1.

Bell, A. P. and Weinberg, M. (1978). *Homosexualities: A Study*

235

in Diversity among Men and Women. New York: Simon and Schuster.

Bellwether, Janet (1982). 'Love Means Never Having to Say Oops: A Lesbian Guide to S/M Safety.' In Samois (Ed.). *Coming to Power*. Boston: Alyson.

Bodacious Bitch (1986). 'Letter from a Mistress to her Pet.' *On Our Backs*. Summer.

Boston Lesbian Psychologies Collective (Eds.) (1987). *Lesbian Psychologies*. Illinois: University of Illinois Press.

Bright, Susie (1986). *On Our Backs*. Winter.

Brittain, Vera (1968). *Radclyffe Hall. A Case of Obscenity*. London: Femina Books Ltd.

Brittain, Vera (1980). *Testament of Friendship*. London: Virago. First published 1940.

Brodribb, Somer (1992). *Nothing Mat(t)ers: A Feminist Critique of Postmodernism*. Melbourne: Spinifex Press.

Brother/Sister (1992). 27 November. Melbourne.

Brown, Jan (1992). 'Sex, Lies, and Penetration: A Butch Finally "Fesses Up".' In Joan Nestle (Ed.). *The Persistent Desire*. Boston: Alyson.

Brown, Rita Mae (1973). *Rubyfruit Jungle*. Plainfield, Vermont: Daughters Inc.

Brownmiller, Susan, (1975). *Against Our Will: Men, Women and Rape*. London: Secker and Warburg. (1981). New York: Bantam. (1986). London: Penguin.

Butler, Judith (1990). *Gender Trouble. Feminism and the Subversion of Indentity*. London and New York: Routledge.

Califia, Pat (1981). 'Feminism and Sadomasochism.' *Heresies* 12. Sex Issue.

Califia, Pat (1982). 'A Personal View.' In Samois (Eds.). *Coming to Power*. Boston: Alyson.

Califia, Pat (1988). *Sapphistry: The Book of Lesbian Sexuality*. Tallahassee: Florida: Naiad.

Califia, Pat (1989). *Macho Sluts*. Boston: Alyson.

Califia, Pat (1992a). 'A House Divided. Violence in the S/M Community.' *Wicked Women*. Vol. 2. No. 4. pp. 24–26.

Califia, Pat (1992b). 'The Femme Poem.' In Nestle, Joan (Ed.). *The Persistent Desire. A Femme-Butch Reader*. Boston: Alyson.

Campaign (1992). No. 199. October. Australia.

Chester, Gail P. and Dickey, Julienne. (Eds.) (1988). *Feminism and Censorship*. London: Prism.

Carpenter, Edward (1921). *The Intermediate Sex*. London: George Allen and Unwin. First published 1908.

Cartledge, Sue and Ryan, Joanna (Eds.) (1983). *Sex and Love*. London: The Women's Press.

Cole, Ellen and Rothblum, Esther (Eds.) (1988). *Women and Sex Therapy: Closing the Circle of Knowledge*. New York: Harrington Park Press.

Cooper, Fiona (1989). *City Limits*. London. June 8–15.

Cott, N. F. and Pleck, E. H. (Eds.) (1979). *A Heritage of Her Own*. New York: Simon and Schuster.

Coveney, Lal *et al* (Eds.) (1984). *The Sexuality Papers*. London: Hutchinson.

Creet, Julia (1991). 'Daughter of the Movement: The Psychodynamics of Lesbian S/M Fantasy.' *Differences: A Journal of Feminist Cultural Studies. Queer Theory Issue*. Summer.

Daly, Mary (1973). *Beyond God the Father: Toward a Philosophy of Women's Liberation*. Boston: Beacon Press.

Daly, Mary (1978). *Gyn/Ecology: The Metaethics of Radical Feminism*. Boston: Beacon Press. (1979). London: The Women's Press.

Davis, Madeline (1992). 'Epilogue, Nine Years Later.' In Joan Nestle (Ed.). *The Persistent Desire. A Femme-Butch Reader*. Boston: Alyson.

Dollimore, Jonathan (1991). *Sexual Dissidence: Augustine to Wilde, Freud to Foucault*. Oxford: Clarendon Press.

Duberman, Martin Bauml, Vicinus, Martha and Chauncey, George (Eds.) (1991). *Hidden From History. Reclaiming the Gay and Lesbian Past*. London: Penguin. (1990). New York: Plume.

Duffy, Maureen (1967). *The Microcosm*. London: Panther. (1989). London: Virago. (1990). New York: Penguin. First published 1966.

Duncker, Patricia (1992). *Sisters and Strangers. An Introduction to Contemporary Feminist Fiction*. Oxford: Blackwell.

Dworkin, Andrea (1981). *Pornography: Men Possessing*

Women. New York: Perigee. (1981). London: The Women's Press. (1991) New York: Plume.

Dyer, Richard (1991). 'Believing in Fairies: The Author and the Homosexual'. In Fuss, Diana (Ed.). *Inside/Out*. London.

Ehrenreich, Barbara *et al*. (1987). *Re-making Love: The Feminization of Sex*. London: Fontana/Collins. (1986) New York: Doubleday.

Ellis, Henry Havelock (1913). *Studies in the Psychology of Sex Vol. 2. Sexual Inversion*. Philadelphia: F. A. Davis. First published 1903.

Faderman, Lillian (1984). *Surpassing the Love of Men*. London: Junction Books. (1985). London: The Women's Press. (1981) New York: Quill.

Faderman, Lillian (1991). *Odd Girls and Twilight Lovers. A History of Lesbian Life in Twentieth-Century America*. New York: Columbia University Press. (1992) London: Penguin.

Faludi, Susan (1991). *Backlash*. San Francisco: Crown. (1992). London: Chatto & Windus.

Farr, Susan (1982). 'The Art of Discipline: Creating Erotic Dramas of Play and Power.' In Samois (Ed.) *Coming to Power*. Boston: Alyson.

Fish (1992). 'We're Not Knitting Doilies.' *Wicked Women*. Vol 2. No. 4. Sydney.

Fitzroy, A. T. (1988). *Despised and Rejected*. London: Gay Men's Press. First published 1918.

Foucault, Michel (1978). *The History of Sexuality Volume I*. London: Allen Lane.

Franeta, Sonja (1992). 'Bridge Poem.' In Nestle, Joan (Ed.) *The Persistent Desire*. Boston: Alyson.

Friedman, Scarlet and Sarah, Elizabeth (Eds.) (1982). *On the Problem of Man*. London: The Women's Press.

Frye, Marilyn (1983). *The Politics of Reality: Essays in Feminist Theory*. New York: The Crossing Press.

Frye, Marilyn (1990). 'Lesbian "Sex".' In Allen, Jeffner (Ed.). *Lesbian Philosophies and Cultures*. New York: State University New York Press.

Fuss, Diana (1990). *Essentially Speaking. Feminism, Nature and Difference*. London and New York: Routledge.

Fuss, Diana (1991). *Inside/Out. Lesbian Theories, Gay Theories*. London and New York: Routledge.

Gay Black Group (1984). 'Letter to the Editor'. *Capital Gay*, London. February 14.

Gorna, Robin (1992). 'Delightful Visions. From Anti-porn to Eroticizing Safer Sex.' In Segal, Lynne and McIntosh, Mary. *Sex Exposed*. London: Virago.

Gunew, Sneja (Ed.) (1991). *A Reader in Feminist Knowledge*. London and New York: Routledge.

Hall, Mary *et al* (1992). 'In Conversation.' *Feminism and Psychology*. Vol.2. No. 1.

Hall, Radclyffe (1982). *The Well of Loneliness*. London: Virago. (1990). New York: Doubleday.

Hamadock, Susan (1988). 'Lesbian Sexuality in the Framework of Psychotherapy.' In Cole, Ellen and Rothblum, Esther (Eds.). *Women and Sex Therapy*. New York: Harrington Park Press.

Hart, Vada (1986). 'Lesbians and AIDS.' *Gossip*. No. 2.

Hawthorne, Susan (1991a). 'In Defence of Separatism.' In Gunew, Sneja (Ed.) *A Reader in Feminist Knowledge*. London and New York: Routledge.

Hawthorne, Susan (1991b). 'What Do Lesbians Want? Towards a Feminist Sexual Ethics.' *Journal of Australian Lesbian Feminist Studies*. Vol. 1. No. 2.

Hayman, Amanda (1989). 'The Flame.' *In Sheba Collective (Eds.) Serious Pleasure*. London: Sheba.

Hegeler, Inge and Stan (1963). *An ABZ of Love*. London: New English Library.

Heger, Heinz (1980). *The Men with the Pink Triangles*. London: Gay Men's Press.

Hoagland, Sarah Lucia (1989). *Lesbian Ethics. Toward New Value*. Palo Alto, California: Institute of Lesbian Studies.

Hoagland, Sarah Lucia (1991). 'Desire and Political Perception.' In Barrington, Judith (Ed.). *An Intimate Wilderness*. Portland, Oregon: The Eight Mountain Press.

Holdsworth, Angela (1988). *Out of the Doll's House*. London: BBC Publications.

hooks, bell (1992). *Black Looks: Race and Representation*. Boston: South End Press.

Humphries, Martin (1985). 'Gay Machismo.' In Metcalf, Andy

and Humphries, Martin (Eds.). *The Sexuality of Men*. London: Pluto Press.

Isherwood, Christopher (1962). *Down There on a Visit*. London: Methuen.

Istar, Arlene (1992). 'Femme-Dyke.' In Joan Nestle (Ed.). *The Persistent Desire*. Boston: Alyson.

Jay, Karla (1986). 'The Lesbian Bar as Metaphor.' *Resources for Feminist Research*. Vol. 12. No. 1.

Jay, Karla and Glasgow, Joanne (Eds.) (1990). *Lesbian Texts and Contexts. Radical Revisions*. New York: New York University Press.

Jay, Karla and Young, Allen (ed.) (1978). *Lavender Culture*. New York: Harcourt Brace Jovanovitch.

Jeffreys, Sheila (1985). *The Spinster and Her Enemies. Feminism and Sexuality 1880–1930*. London: Pandora Press.

Jeffreys, Sheila (1989). 'Butch and Femme Now and Then.' In Lesbian History Group (Eds.) *Not a Passing Phase*. London: The Women's Press.

Jeffreys, Sheila (1990). *Anticlimax: A Feminist Perspective on the Sexual Revolution*. London: The Women's Press. (1991) New York: New York University Press.

Jo, Bev, Strega, Linda and Ruston (1990). *Dykes-Loving-Dykes*. Oakland, California: Battleaxe.

Jonel, Marissa (1982). 'Letter from a Former Masochist.' In Linden, Robin *et al* (Eds.). *Against Sadomasochism*. Palo Alto, California. Frog in the Well Press.

Juicy Lucy (1982). 'If I Ask You to Tie Me Up, Will You Still Want to Love Me.' *In Samois (Eds.). Coming to Power*. Boston: Alyson.

Kaufman, Michael (Ed.) (1987). *Beyond Patriarchy*. Toronto and New York: Oxford University Press.

Kennedy, Elizabeth Lapovsky and Davis, Madeline (1992). ' "They Was No One to Mess With": The Construction of the Butch Role in the Lesbian Community of the 1940s and 1950s.' In Nestle, Joan (Ed.). *The Persistent Desire*. Boston: Alyson.

Kessler, Jo Marie (1988). 'When the Diagnosis is Vaginismus: Fighting Misconceptions.' In Cole, Ellen and Rothblum,

Esther (Eds.). *Women and Sex Therapy*, New York: Harrington Park Press.

Kitzinger, Celia (1987). *The Social Construction of Lesbianism*. London: Sage Publications.

Kitzinger, Celia and Perkins, Rachel (1993). *Changing Our Minds: Lesbianism, Feminism and Psychology*. London: Onlywomen Press.

Kleinberg, Seymour (1987). 'The New Masculinity of Gay Men and Beyond.' In Kaufman, Michael (Ed.) *Beyond Patriarchy. Essays by Men on Pleasure, Power and Change*. Toronto/New York: Oxford University Press.

Koertge, Noretta (1986). 'Butch Images 1956–86.' In *Lesbian Ethics* Vol. 2. No. 2.

Lee, Anna (1990). 'For the Love of Separatism.' In Allen, Jeffner (Ed.). *Lesbian Philosophies and Cultures*. New York: State University Press. New York.

Leidholdt, Dorchen (1983). 'Where Pornography Meets Fascism.' *WIN* March 15.

Leidholdt, Dorchen and Raymond, Janice G. (Eds.) (1990). *The Sexual Liberals and the Attack on Feminism*. New York: Pergamon (now TCP).

Lederer, Laura (Ed.) (1980). *Take Back the Night*. New York: Quill.

Lesbian History Group (Eds.) (1989). *Not a Passing Phase. Reclaiming Lesbians in History 1840–1985*. London: The Women's Press.

Linden, Robin Ruth, Pagano, Darlene, Russell, Diana E. H., Leigh Star, Susan (Eds.). (1982). *Against Sadomasochism. A Radical Feminist Analysis*. Palo Alto, California: Frog in the Well Press.

Lorde, Audre, (1982). 'Interview by Susan Leigh Star.' In Linden, Robin *et al* (Eds.). *Against Sadomasochism*. Palo Alto, California: Frog in the Well Press.

Lorde, Audre (1984). 'Uses of the Erotic: The Erotic as Power.' In *Sister Outsider. Essays and Speeches by Audre Lorde*. Freedom, California: The Crossing Press.

Loulan, JoAnn (1984). *Lesbian Sex*. San Francisco: Spinsters.

Loulan, JoAnn (1990). *The Lesbian Erotic Dance*. San Francisco: Spinsters.

241

McIntosh, Mary (1968). 'The Homosexual Role.' *Social Problems* 16.

MacCowan, Lyndall (1992). 'Re-collecting History, Renaming Lives: Femme Stigma and the Feminist Seventies and Eighties.' In Nestle, Joan (Ed.). *The Persistent Desire*. Boston: Alyson.

MacKinnon, Catharine A. (1984). 'Not a Moral Issue.' *Yale Law and Policy Review*. Vol II No. 2.

MacKinnon, Catharine A. (1987). *Feminism Unmodified*. Boston: Harvard University Press.

MacKinnon, Catharine A. (1989). *Toward a Feminist Theory of the State*. Boston: Harvard University Press.

MacKinnon, Catharine A. (1990). 'Liberalism and the Death of Feminism.' In Leidholdt, Dorchen and Raymond, Janice G. (Eds.). *The Sexual Liberals and the Attack on Feminism*. New York: Pergamon (now TCP).

McLeod, Eileen (1982). *Women Working: Prostitution Now*. London: Croom Helm.

Mannix, Daniel P. (1983). *The History of Torture*, New York: Dell.

Meese, Elizabeth (1990). 'Theorizing Lesbian: Writing – A Love Letter.' In Jay, Karla and Glasgow, Joanne (Eds.). *Lesbian Texts and Contexts: Radical Revisions*. New York: New York University Press.

Melbourne Star Observer (1992). 21 August.

Mercer, Kobena (1992). 'Just Looking for Trouble: Robert Mapplethorpe and Fantasies of Race.' In Segal, Lynne and McIntosh, Mary (Eds.) *Sex Exposed, Sexuality and the Pornography Debate*. London: Virago.

Metcalf, Andy and Humphries, Martin (Eds.) (1985). *The Sexuality of Men*. London: Pluto Press.

Miller, Isabel (1973). *Patience and Sarah*. Greenwich, Connecticut: Fawcett Publications. (1979). London: The Women's Press. (1985). Santa Barbara, California: Crest.

Moraga, Cherrie and Anzaldua, Gloria (1981). *This Bridge Called My Back. Writings by Radical Women of Color*. Watertown, Massachusetts: Persephone Press.

Mushroom, Merrill (1983). 'Confessions of a Butch Dyke.' *Common Lives, Lesbian Lives*. No. 9.

Nestle, Joan (1987). *A Restricted Country*. Ithaca, New York: Firebrand Books. (1988). London: Sheba.

Nestle, Joan (Ed.) (1992a). *The Persistent Desire. A Femme-Butch Reader*. Boston: Alyson.

Nestle, Joan (1992b). 'My Woman Poppa.' In Nestle, Joan. (Ed.) *The Persistent Desire*. Boston: Alyson.

Newton, Esther (1991). 'The Mythic Mannish Lesbian: Radclyffe Hall and the New Woman.' In Duberman, Martin *et al* (Eds.). *Hidden from History*. London: Penguin.

Nicholls, Margaret (1987a). 'Doing Sex Therapy with Lesbians: Bending a Heterosexual Paradigm to Fit a Gay Life-Style.' In Boston Lesbian Psychologies Collective (Eds.). *Lesbian Psychologies*. Illinois: University of Illinois Press.

Nicholls, Margaret (1987b). 'Lesbian Sexuality: Issues and Developing Theory.' In Boston Lesbian Psychologies Collective (Eds.). *Lesbian Psychologies*. Illinois: University of Illinois Press.

On Our Backs (1986). Fall.

On Our Backs (1986). Summer.

O'Sullivan, Sue (1990). 'An Interview with Cindy Patton. Mapping: Lesbianism, AIDS and Sexuality.' *Feminist Review*. No. 34. Spring.

Pateman, Carol (1988). *The Sexual Contract*. Cambridge: Polity Press. Palo Alto, California: Stanford University Press.

Pateman, Carol (1989). *The Disorder of Women*. Cambridge: Polity Press.

Penelope, Julia (1984). 'Whose Past Are We Reclaiming?' *Common Lives, Lesbian Lives*. No. 13.

Penelope, Julia (1987). 'The Illusion of Control: Sadomasochism and the Sexual Metaphors of Childhood.' *Lesbian Ethics*. Vol. 2. No. 3.

Penelope, Julia (1990). 'The Lesbian Perspective.' In Allen, Jeffner (ed.). *Lesbian Philosophies and Cultures*. New York: State University New York.

Pink Paper (1992). 10 July.

Plummer, Kenneth (Ed.) (1981). *The Making of the Modern Homosexual*. London: Hutchinson.

Raymond, Janice G. (1979). *The Transsexual Empire*. Boston: Beacon Press. (1982). London: The Women's Press.

Raymond, Janice G. (1986). *A Passion for Friends. Toward a Philosophy of Female Friendship*. Boston: Beacon Press. London: The Women's Press.

Raymond, Janice G. (1989). 'Putting the Politics Back into Lesbianism.' *Women's Studies International Forum*. Vol. 12. No. 2. (1991). *Journal of Australian Lesbian Studies*. Vol. 1. No. 2. December.

Raymond, Janice G. (1990). 'Not a Sentimental Journey: Women's Friendships.' In Leidholdt, Dorchen and Raymond, Janice G. (Eds.). *The Sexual Liberals and the Attack on Feminism*. Oxford and New York: Pergamon (now TCP).

Rechy, John (1979). *The Sexual Outlaw*. London: Futura.

Rich, Adrienne (1984). 'Compulsory Heterosexuality and Lesbian Existence.' In Snitow, Ann *et al* (Eds.). *Desire: The Politics of Sexuality*. London: Virago. (1983). New York: Monthly Review Press. Published as *Powers of Desire*.

Roberts, Charles (1992). 'Interview' and 'Pricks.' *Antithesis*. Vol. 5. Nos. 1 & 2.

Rowse, A. L. (1977). *Homosexuals in History*. London: Weidenfeld and Nicolson.

Rubin, Gayle (1982). 'A Personal History of the Lesbian S/M Community and Movement in San Francisco.' In Samois (Eds.). *Coming to Power. Writings and Graphics on Lesbian S/M*. Boston: Alyson Publications. 2nd Edition.

Rubin, Gayle (1992). 'Of Catamites and Kings: Reflections on Butch, Gender, and Boundaries.' In Nestle, Joan (Ed.) *The Persistent Desire*. Boston: Alyson.

Ruehl, Sonja (1983) 'Sexual Theory and Practice: Another Double Standard.' In Cartledge, Sue and Ryan, Joanna (Eds.) *Sex and Love*. London: The Women's Press.

Saalfield, Catherine and Navarro, Ray (1991). 'Shocking Pink Praxis: Race and Gender on the ACT UP Frontlines.' In Fuss, Diana (Ed.). *Inside/Out. Lesbian Theories, Gay Theories*. London and New York: Routledge.

Sahli, Nancy (1979). 'Smashing. Women's Relationships Before the Fall.' *Chrysalis*. No. 8.

Samois (eds.) (1982). *Coming to Power*. Boston: Alyson.

Scarlet Woman (1992). 'Roll Me Over and Make Me a Rose.' In Nestle, Joan (Ed.). *The Persistent Desire*. Boston: Alyson.

Schulman, Sarah (1990). *After Delores*. London: Sheba. (1989). New York: N.A.L./Dutton.

Segal, Lynne and McIntosh, Mary (1992). *Sex Exposed. Sexuality and the Pornography Debate*. London: Virago.

Sheba Collective (1989). *Serious Pleasure. Lesbian Erotic Stories and Poetry*. London: Sheba Feminist Publishers.

Sherman, Martin (1980). *Bent*. New York: Avon. Derbyshire. UK: Amber Lane Press.

Smith, Barbara (1988). 'Sappho was a Right-Off Woman.' In Chester, Gail and Dickey, Julienne (Eds.). *Feminism and Censorship*. London: Prism.

Smith-Rosenberg, Carroll (1991). 'Discourses of Subjectivity: The New Woman 1870–1936.' In Duberman, Martin *et al* (Eds.). *Hidden From History. Reclaiming the Gay and Lesbian Past*. London: Penguin.

Smith-Rosenberg, Carroll (1979). 'The Female World of Love and Ritual: Relations Between Women in Nineteenth-Century America.' In Cott, N. F. and Pleck, E. H. (Eds.). *A Heritage of Her Own*. New York: Touchstone Books, Simon and Schuster.

Smyth, Cherry (1990). 'The Pleasure Threshold: Looking at Lesbian Pornography on Film.' *Feminist Review*. No. 34. Spring.

Smyth, Cherry (1992). *Lesbians Talk: Queer Notions*. London: Scarlet Press.

Snitow, Ann *et al* (1983). *The Politics of Sexuality*. New York: Monthly Review Press.

Sojourner (1988). March.

Sojourner (1988). May.

Sojourner (1988). June.

Sontag, Susan (1977). *Against Interpretation*. New York: Anchor Books.

A Southern Women's Writing Collective (1990). 'Sex Resistance in Heterosexual Arrangements.' In Leidholdt, Dorchen and Raymond, Janice G. (Eds.). *The Sexual Liberals and the Attack on Feminism*.

Spada, James (1979). *The Spada Report*. New York: Signet New American Library.

Stack, Carolyn (1985). 'Lesbian Sexual Problems.' *Bad Attitude*. Spring.

245

Stanley, Liz (1982). 'Male Needs: The Problems and Problems of Working with Gay Men.' In Friedman, Scarlet and Sarah, Elizabeth (Eds.). *On the Problems of Men*.

Steinem, Gloria (1980). 'Erotica and Pornography: A Clear and Present Difference.' In Lederer, Laura (Ed.). *Take Back the Night*. New York: Quill.

Stolenberg, John (1990). *Refusing to Be a Man*. London: Fontana. (1989). New York: Breitenbush Books.

Susan M. (1986). 'The Phoenix Chair.' *On Our Backs*. Summer.

The Weekly Law Report (1992). 27 March.

Thompson, Denise (1985). *Flaws in the Social Fabric*. Sydney: George Allen and Unwin.

Thompson, Denise (1991). *Reading Between the Lines. A Lesbian Feminist Critique of Feminist Accounts of Sexuality*. Sydney: Gorgon's Head Press.

Timerman, Jacobo (1981). *Prisoner Without a Name, Cell Without a Number*. New York: Knopf.

Tripp, C. A. (1975). *The Homosexual Matrix*. New York: McGraw Hill.

Tyler, Carol-Anne (1991). 'Boys Will Be Girls: The Politics of Gay Drag.' In Fuss, Diana. (Ed.). *Inside/Out*. London and New York: Routledge.

Waite, Robert G. L. (1977). *The Psychopathic God*. New York: Basic Books.

Walker, Alice (1981). *You Can't Keep a Good Woman Down: Stories By Alice Walker*. New York: Harcourt Brace.

Walker, Alice (1982). 'A Letter of the Times, or Should this Sadomasochism be Saved?' In Linden, Robin *et al* (Eds.). *Against Sadomasochism*. Palo Alto, California: Frog in the Well Press.

Walters, Aubrey (1980). *Come Together: Collected Writings from Gay Liberation in the UK*. London: Gay Men's Press.

Watney, Simon (1987). *Policing Desire. Pornography, AIDS and the Media*. Minneapolis: University of Minnesota Press.

Watney, Simon (1992) 'Queerspeak. The Latest Word.' *Outrage*. Melbourne. April.

Weedon, Chris (1987). *Feminist Practice and Poststructuralist Theory*. Oxford: Basil Blackwell.

Weeks, Jeffrey (1977). *Coming Out. Homosexual Politics in*

Britain from the Nineteenth Century to the Present. London: Quartet.

Weeks, Jeffrey (1982). *Gay News*. No. 243.

Weeks, Jeffrey (1985) *Sexuality and Its Discontents. Meanings, Myths and Modern Sexualities*. London: Routledge Kegan Paul.

Whitbread, Helena (Ed.). (1988). *I Know My Own Heart. The Diaries of Anne Lister 1791–1840*. London: Virago.

Whitbread, Helena (Ed.) (1992). *No Priest But Love. The Diaries of Anne Lister 1824–1826*. Otley, W. Yorks: Smith Settle.

White, Edmund (1983). *States of Desire: Travels in Gay America*. New York: Dutton.

Wicked Women (1992). Vol. 2. No. 4. Sydney.

Wieder, Judy (1992). 'Are We Born To Be Gay?' *Campaign Australia*. No. 199. October.

Wieringa, Saskia (1989). 'An Anthropological Critique of Constructionism: Berdaches and Butches.' In Altman, Dennis *et al* (Eds.). *Which Homosexuality?* London: Gay Men's Press.

Wilde, Oscar (1975). *The Complete Works of Oscar Wilde*. London: Collins.

Wittig, Monique (1992). *The Straight Mind and Other Essays*. Boston: Beacon Press.

Wolf, Naomi (1991). *The Beauty Myth*. London: Vintage. (1991). New York: Anchor/Doubleday.

Young, Ian (1978). 'Forum on Sadomasochism.' In Jay, Karla and Yong, Allen (Eds.). *Lavender Culture*. New York: Harcourt Brace Jovanovitch.

Zimmerman, Bonnie (1990). *The Safe Sea of Women. Lesbian Fiction. 1969–89*. Boston: Beacon Press.

INDEX

A

abuse, sexual *see* sexual abuse
ACT UP 135, 165
advertising 42–3, 151
age, and queer politics 174, 175
AIDS: and gay-hating 138, 143, 174; lesbians and 163–9; as real issue 178; and sexology 17
alcohol 124; *see also* bars
Alderson, Lyn 94
Allison, Dorothy 30
Altman, Dennis 94, 168–9
Amsterdam 210–11
Andrews, Marie 176
androgyny 85–6, 100
anti-feminism x, 150–1; lesbian sex industry and 42–4; outlawry and 130; roleplaying and 84–5; sex therapy and 70–1; sexology and 20–1
anti-lesbianism x; opposition to separatism as 197; sex therapy and 68–9; sexology and 7–8
Anti-Nazi League (UK) 221
anti-pornography campaigns *see* pornography, campaigning against

anti-semitism 220
Anzaldua, Gloria 207
appearance 70–1; gay men and 145–6; *see also* clothing; femininity
archetypes 80–1, 83, 94
assertiveness, and stereotypes of lesbians 4–5
assimilation 195, 197–8, 200, 206–7
attraction xi–ii; appearance and 70–1; *see also* desire
Auchmuty, Rosemary 18, 182
Austin, Paula 79, 81
Australian National University 117

B

backlash x
Bad Attitude 33, 38, 62, 65
Bannon, Ann 127–8, 129
Barney, Natalie 187
Barrington, Judith 200
Barry, Kathleen 225
bars 122–30
battered women's shelters 41
battering: in lesbian relationships

39–40, 63–4, 231;
sadomasochism and 231
Bearchell, Chris 132–3
belief 36, 198
Bell, A. P. 56
Bellwether, Janet 233
binary oppositions 99, 101, 137
biological determination *see under* determinism
bisexuals/bisexuality 68, 150
Bodacious Bitch 56
Boffin, Tessa 178
Bolen, Jean Shinoda 95
bondage 167
Bordo, Susan 106
brains, studying 75–6
Bright, Susie 56
Bristol Crisis Service for Women 41
Britain *see* UK
Brittain, Vera 10–11
Brodribb, Somer 118
Brother/Sister 45
Brown, Jan 89, 90–1
Brown, Rita Mae 141
Brownmiller, Susan 54
Bunch, Charlotte 98
burn-out 188–9
Burroughs, William 132
butch/femme identities 13–16;
essentialism and 73, 84–9,
93–4; gender roles and 87–9;
political definitions 93–4; sex
therapists and 64–5; theory of
denial of 65, 86; woman-
hating and 79
butch gay men *see* masculinity,
gay
Butler, Judith 97, 98–9, 102–3,
105, 111; on gender and drag
98–9, 102–3, 104–5, 115
Byron, Peg 181

C

Califia, Pat 65, 67, 133, 158–62,
225–6; on fantasies 67–8;
fiction/poems 89, 159–62; on
morality 50, 226; on
pornography 30; on racism
223, 225; and
sadomasochism 50–1, 67,
158–62, 215, 225–6
California 155, 157
camp 153, 154, 155–7; and
oppression 158; and
resistance 157
Campaign Against Pornography 191
Carpenter, Edward 4–5
celibacy 203
censorship, feminist critique and
59–61
Chesser, Eustace 27
child sexual abuse *see* sexual
abuse
childcare 150, 178
children 150, 220
choice 222; sadomasochism and
48–9; *see also* consent;
lesbianism, possibility
class ix, 191; and butch/femme
identities 13; and separatism
199; *see also* sex class
clothing 70, 77, 92–4, 107,
153–4, 215–16; *see also* drag
clubs: jerk-off 168; sadomasochist 44–5, 168
coalition politics 143–4, 177–9;
lesbian feminists and 186
condoms 167, 169
conferences 74, 116–7
congenitality *see under*
determinism

consciousness, raising x, xiii, 14, 15

consent 24–5, 46–51; fascism and 232; feminism and 50, 62; nonconsensuality, consensual 50–1; political criticism and 46; sadomasochism and 39, 46–51, 232, 233; violence and 51

conservative politics see right-wing politics

Cooper, Fiona 152–3

Corinne, Tee 29–30

cottaging 163

counterculture 123, 125; see also outlawry

Coveney, Lal 54

creches 178

crisis lines 41

cultural studies 98

D

Daly, Mary 98, 198, 200, 216

Davis, Madeline 88, 154–5

Dawkin, Cecil 189

decadence xvi, 123, 125, 126–7; gender and 126, 129–31; prostitution and 129–31

demonstrations 135, 167, 231

denial 65, 88

dental dams 135, 164, 165, 167

Derrida, Jacques 97, 98–9, 101, 114, 137, 206

desire: construction 23–4; consent and 50; heterosexual 23, 27, 43, 53–4; fascism and 222, 229–30; pornography and 29, 31; prostitution and 130; roleplaying and 88–9; sadomasochism and 222; sex therapy and 54, 61–4, 71;

homosexual 24, 206; see also sex, egalitarian; objectification and xiv, 192–6; see also attraction

determinism: biological 73, 76, 82, 94; congenitality theories 5–13, 82; psychological/ psychoanalytic 5, 13, 82; and roleplaying 82–4; see also essentialism

difference, postmodernism and 116, 118, 179

dilators 69

dildos 33–4, 35, 89, 162, 163, 167; double headed 167; sex therapy and 69

Divine 153

Dollimore, Jonathan 15–16, 136–8

drag 97, 102–3, 151–3; and oppression 154; women and 15, 102–3, 153, 154

Duffy, Maureen 126–7

Duncker, Patricia 177–8

Dworkin, Andrea 29

Dyer, Richard 108, 109–10

Dysphoria, gender 13, 158

E

ECP see English Collective of Prostitutes

Ehrenreich, Barbara 53

Ellis, Havelock 3, 4, 5, 71

emotion 68

English Collective of Prostitutes 225, 227

erotic, inclusiveness 202–4

erotica 29–31, 33–4, 42; feminist/alternative 30–1, 33–4

eroticised subordination *see* desire, heterosexual

erotophobia *see* repression

essentialism xiv–xv, 74–8, 82, 101–2; feminism and 111; gay men and 74, 108–9, 109–11; lesbian feminism and 206; of objectification 178–9; over butch/femme identities 14–15; postmodernism and 101–2, 108–9, 111; and security 110; *see also* determinism

ethics *see* morality

F

Faderman, Lillian 6–8, 64, 114, 187, 189–91; on sexology xiii, 2–3, 6

Faludi, Susan ix

family, fascism and 220

fancying *see* attraction

fantasies 67–8, 90, 221, 222, 233

Farr, Susan 230–1

fascism xvii, 210–34; appeal of 218–22, 227–8; lesbian feminists accused of 216, 217–18; recognising 218

feelings 68; sexual 28, 221

femininity 77, 93; choice and 104–5; lesbians and 95, 102–3, 105

feminism/lesbian feminism ix, xii–xiv, 24–5, 114, 197–9, 206–7; and androgyny 88–9; and consent 50, 63; devastation 183–7; and diversity x, 183; and essentialism 75–7, 82; and femininity 110; gay male politics xviii, 150; and gender

88, 100–2, 103–4, 138; legislation and 75; and lesbian community/culture x–xi, xiii, 143, 183–7; lesbianandgay theory and 97, 98, 108–11; nineteenth-century 7; opposition to from lesbians 17, 183–7, 193–9; and outlawry 121, 133, 134, 137, 138–9; postmodernism and 97, 99–103, 179–81; and queer politics 139; and reclaiming 181; and roleplaying 86, 89, 90–2; and safe sex education 165–7; separation and 195, 200, 202; and separatism 186, 195; and sex 9, 54–6, 59–60, 67, 72, 200–3; and sex industry 45; sex therapists and 60; and sexology ix, 1, 13; and social constructionism xv, 13–14, 16, 73, 101, 107, 114; and stereotypes of lesbians 5–6, 12; and theories of lesbianism 74, 76–7; and transsexuals 160

Feminist Anti Censorship Taskforce 184

film 98, 128, 129

Fitzroy, A. T. xvi

Foucault, Michel 97, 98, 99, 136, 206; and lesbians 12, 113–4; theory of sexuality 15, 109, 112–3, 137

Franeta, Sonja 91

friendship 197, 204–5; men's 16–17; as political 205; romantic/passionate 2, 6–11, 16–17

frigidity 63–4

Fromm, Erich 217

Frye, Marilyn: on lesbian feminism 146, 148, 190–1, 197–8; on lesbian sex 200–1; on men 144, 146, 148–9, 153, 161; on separatism 195, 197–8
fundamentalism 94
funding 149–50
Fuss, Diana 97, 98, 112–14

G

Gay Black Group (London) 116, 223–4
gay identities see under identity/identities
Gay Left 227–8
gay liberation movement xiii, 73, 144, 176; diversion/betrayal of 107, 150
gay male culture xvi–xviii, 142; lesbians and 143, 158–62
gay male politics/theory xiv, 73, 107; and essentialism 73, 111–12, 115–17; and lesbian feminism xviii, 150; and sex 148; see also lesbianandgay theory
gay masculinity 107, 144–6
gay men: and deviance 17; law and 24, 50–1; lesbians wishing to be xviii, 143, 155, 162, 191; and personal politics xv; profeminist 149, 173; as role models for lesbians 130–1, 137, 143, 150–4, 158, 159–60, 195; politically 137, 143, 182; sex therapy 70, 176–7; sexology 17–18; see also homosexuality/homosexuals
Gay Pride marches (USA) 231

gay space 150–2
gender: biological determinism 75, 76; decadence and 127, 131–2; and drag 97, 102; feminist analysis 88, 100–1, 102–3, 138; lesbianandgay theory and 97–8; outlawry and see under outlawry; playing with 102, 103, 104–7; sex and 88, 160; sexology and 5–6, 9, 13; see also binary oppositions; roleplaying; transsexuals
genitals, female, representation of 30
Germany 211–14, 217–19, 221, 230
Gide, Andre 136
Goering, Hermann 217
Gomez, Jewelle 83
Goma, Robin 169–70
Grace, Della 106, 163

H

Hall, Marny 61
Hall, Radclyffe 4, 9–10, 12; The Well of Loneliness 4, 9–11, 12, 15–16, 124–5
Hamadock, Susan 60
Hamilton, Cicely 52
handcuffs 167
Hart, Vada 181
Hawthorne, Susan 55, 193–4
Hayman, Amanda 56
Hegeler, Inge and Stan 55
Heger, Heinz 213–14
heterofeminism xiv
heteroreality 88, 195–6
heterosexual desire see desire, heterosexual
heterosexual women 130, 146;

feminists 147; and gender 88;
pornography for 47; and
roleplaying 80
heterosexualism 199
heterosexuality 9; and male
supremacy 24, 88;
postmodernism and 100;
pressure and 9–10, 24;
resistance to 121
Hite Report 34
Hitler, Adolf 217, 221
HIV *see* AIDS
Hoagland, Sarah Lucia 98, 198,
200
Holdsworth, Angela 94
Holtby, Winifred 10
homoeroticism, male, as
compulsory 146
homosexual desire *see* desire,
homosexual
homosexual rights movement:
and essentialism 76;
sexology and 2–3, 5–6; *see
also* gay liberation movement
homosexuality/homosexuals:
lesbian identity and 118;
meaning male homosexuality
142, 174, 175; of oppressors/
of oppressed 145–9; as
possibility for all 73–4, 113;
theories of 1–18, 73–8; *see
also* lesbianandgay theory;
sexology; *see also* gay men;
lesbianism/lesbians
hooks, bell 106
humour 78–9, 154
Humphries, Martin 119, 179

I

identity/identities: butch/femme
see butch/femme identities;
dominant 114–15; gay/
homosexual 1–3, 110–14;
language and 178–9, 180–2;
lesbian 73–4, 110–17, 178–9,
199; ethnicity and 108, 182;
western/urban culture and
108, 182; politics of 16;
radical uncertainty 107–8,
109–10, 119
imperialism 133–4
incest survivors 36, 42–3; *see also*
sexual abuse
independence, and stereotypes of
lesbians 5–6, 12
individualism: feminism and 188;
right-wing politics and 228,
229
inequality: eroticisation of *see*
desire, heterosexual;
pornography and 35
Irigaray, Luce 105
Isherwood, Christopher 211–12,
219
Istar, Arlene 88

J

Jakarta 85–6
Jay, Karla 120, 123–4
Jeffreys, Sheila 35, 77–8, 94, 96,
182; *Anticlimax* 54, 55,
58–9, 182, 201; *The Spinster
and Her Enemies* 19, 35, 54,
55, 57
jerk-off clubs 168
Jo, Bev 77, 91–2
Johnston, Jill 87
Jonel, Marissa 231
judgement 22–3, 45, 50, 59–60,
204
Juicy Lucy 57

K

Kamikaze Hearts 128, 129–30
Kennedy, Elizabeth Lapovsky
    154–5
Kerouac, Jack 132
Kessler, Jo Marie 72
Kinsey Institute 34
kissing, prostitutes and 44
Kitzinger, Celia 56, 61
Kleinberg, Seymour 120, 147–8
Koertge, Noretta 95
Krafft-Ebing, Richard von 1

L

Lacan, Jacques 97, 98–9, 105,
    107, 196
language: and identity 176–7,
    178–9; and oppression
    99–100; queer *see* queer
    politics; of reclaiming 180;
    reverse affirmation 15, 16,
    139; romanticising
    oppression xviii; and sex
    199–200; of therapy 35;
    woman-hating 173
LASM *see* Lesbians Against
    Sadomasochism
Latex Liberation Front 166
Lawrence, D. H. 57
Lee, Anna 194
legal action 51–2, 53
legislation x, 75, 144
Leidholdt, Dorchen xviii, 54,
    216–17
Lesbian Archive (London) 185
lesbian community/culture x–xiii,
    122–8, 144, 183–4; divisions/
    collapse xii, 17, 183–6, 200;
    feminists and ix–x, xii, 144,
    183–7; gay male culture and

xvii–xviii; history ix–x, 144,
    186–8; necessity 185, 207–9;
    separatism and 190
lesbian feminism *see* feminism/
    lesbian feminism
Lesbian History Group (London)
    8, 185
lesbian perspective 200
Lesbian Strength marches
    (London) 231
lesbianandgay theory 22, 97–9,
    110–12, 118; and identity
    108–10, 113
lesbianism/lesbians: alliances
    with gay men 144–6; black x,
    183, 200; and sadomasochism
    220–3; and separatism 195;
    bourgeois 191; and class of
    women xiv–xvi, 11, 16, 50,
    81; deconstructive 205;
    definitions 1, 5–16, 18, 188,
    190; differences with gay men
    144–60; ethnic minority x,
    183; explanations, whether
    required ix, 13, 73–5; and gay
    men as role models *see under*
    gay men; identities *see under*
    identity/identities; indigenous
    x, 109, 179, 180; Jewish 183;
    naming *see* identity/identities,
    lesbian; as norm 1; political
    78, 112; portrayal in novels
    see novels, lesbian; possibility
    for all women ix, xv, 13, 73–4,
    78–9, 113; radical potential
    ix, 147–8; as role model for
    gay men 176; safety 164–8;
    self-hatred and xviii; self-love
    and ix; and sex 53; sexology
    and 1–7, 9, 10–13, 16, 17;
    visibility 90–4; wish to be gay
    men *see under* gay men;

working class x; *see also* feminism/lesbian feminism

Lesbians Against Sadomasochism (London) xviii, 50, 210

LeVay, Simon 75–6

liberalism: postmodernism and 119; sexual 21, 23, 24, 48, 60–2, 129, 131

lifestyle lesbians 121

Lima 85–6

Linden, Robin Ruth 56

Lister, Ann 2

London, A Woman's Place 230

London Lesbian and Gay Centre 150–2, 210, 230

looks-ism 70–2

Lorde, Audre 98, 184, 202–3

Loulan, JoAnn 59–60, 61; and essentialism xiv–xv; and fantasies 67; and feminism 60–2, 67, 69, 70–1, 82–4, 85; and roleplaying 52, 64–5, 69, 70–1, 82–4, 85, 88, 93–4

Lovelace, Linda 225

M

M., Susan 56

MacCowan, Lyndall 81–2, 85–6, 88–9

machismo 165

McIntosh, Mary 2

MacKinnon, Catherine 24–5, 31, 51, 184–5, 186

McLeod, Eileen 44

McRae, Diana 189

Madonna 105–6, 118

magazines 40–1, 45, 49, 68, 150

male bonding 148, 158; and male sexuality 172

male homosexuality *see* gay men; homosexuality/homosexuals

male power 160; and right of access 148, 150, 194; sexual intercourse and 25–7

male sexuality 67, 170; *see also* gay men; penis

male supremacy 84; fascism and 220; gay men and 150; gender and 100–2; heterosexuality and 24; lesbianism/lesbians and 55, 56, 147–8, 190–1; male homosexuality and 148; sexual revolutions and 20; sexual violence and 22, 24

man-loving 145–7, 180

Mannix, Daniel 233

Mapplethorpe, Robert 116–17, 118

marriage: consent and 48–52; rape in 23, 91

masculinity: feminism and 14; gay 104, 145–6; lesbians and 14–15, 154–5, 160–2

masochism: sexology and 29; *see also* sadomasochism

media 133; *see also* publications

medical models *see* determinism; essentialism; sexology

Meese, Elizabeth 110

Melbourne 44–5, 133, 170, 172

Melbourne, University of 23, 176

men: profeminist 14, 149, 172; *see also* male bonding; male sexuality; man-loving

menopause 65

Mercer, Kobena 116–17

Miller, Elaine 182

Miller, Isabel 141

Mills and Boon 79

mimicry 103, 104, 114, 160

Minneapolis Ordinance, campaign for 185

money xiv, 149–51; *see also* sex industry
monogamy xiv, 178–80, 230
Moraga, Cherrie 183
morality 21–3, 25, 43, 50, 207; heterosexualism and 200; law and 52; lesbian 200; sadomasochism and 53, 224; sex therapy and 60–3
Mosley, Oswald 219
mothers 151, 228
Mushroom, Merrill 87–8

N

naming 110; *see also* identity/ identities
National Council for Civil Liberties (UK) 231–3
National Front (UK) 215–16, 224, 230–2
Navarro, Ray 132
nazism *see* fascism
necrophilia 26
needs 66; sexual 66–7
Nestle, Joan 34, 77–8, 79, 81, 83, 89
newsletters 150
Newton, Esther xiii, 9–10, 11–14, 17
Nicholls, Margaret 60–1, 62–4, 68–9, 70–1, 93, 171–2
nonmonogamy xiv, 177–9
nostalgie de la boue xvi, 126, 130
novels, lesbian 127–9, 187–9; *see also* Hall, Radclyffe, *The Well of Loneliness*

O

objectification: desire and xiii, 180–2; male sexuality and 68; of men 48; pornography and 30, 32, 67; power and 48; prostitution and 48; safe sex education and 171, 173; sex industry and 20; sex therapy and 68–9; sexual violence and 38; videos and 172
On Our Backs 32, 33, 47
Operation Spanner 48–50
oppression xiv, 205–7; consent and 50; eroticised *see* desire, heterosexual; fantasies and 92; lesbianandgay theory and 97–8; morality and 23; outlawry and 125–7; postmodernism and 98–100, 101, 178; prostitution and 49; romanticising xvi, 16; sadomasochism and 223–7; sex and 53–6, 72; sex industry and 39; sexualities and 128; similarities between lesbians' and gay men's 143–5
orgasm 28, 68
O'Sullivan, Sue 37–8
outlawry xvi, 10, 121–40; AIDS and 170–2; gender and 125, 130–1, 133, 138; postmodernism and 138–41; prostitution and 130; sadomasochism and 121, 122, 134–8
Outrage (London) 178

P

Pankhurst, Christabel 52
parody see mimicry
passing 89, 93–6, 107
passionate friendship see under friendship
Pateman, Carol 44
Patton, Cindy 37–8, 118
pedophiles, and gay space 150
Penelope, Julia 39–40, 78, 98, 186, 196–7
penetration 91, 159; as requirement 68–70; see also dildos; penis
penis: assumption of universal access 148, 150; dildos and 38, 40; envy of 159; gay men and 157; lesbians and 161; as requirement 32, 34; worship of 32
perceptions, trusting 36, 200
Perkins, Rachel 24, 61
phone lines, sex 31, 41
photography 27–8, 115, 170
Playgirl 47
police 220; discriminatory prosecutions 50–2; lesbians and 50, 55
political correctness, opposition to 62, 190
political lesbianism 101, 115
politics: cultural studies and 98; mixed gay and lesbian 144–6, 146, 180–2; personal xiv, 24, 218; liberalism and 20; see also feminism/lesbian feminism
pornography 27–32; campaigning against 27–8, 185; and safe sex education 174, 175; defenders of x; erotica and 30, 31, 42, 204; feminist analysis of 31; for heterosexual women 43; lesbian 27–8, 29, 35, 168; examples 31, 33, 34, 156–8; objectification and 29, 31, 68; postmodernism and 117; and racism 117, 121; and sadomasochism 29, 35, 184; safe sex education and 136, 172–4; user's roles 29; women used in making 42, 173
postmodernism xv–xvi, 97–102, 199–200; and anti-lesbianism 207; and difference 116, 118; feminism and 97, 99–102, 180; lesbianandgay theory and 22, 97–100; and oppression 98–101, 102, 179; and outlawry 136–8; and pornography 117; and queer politics 178–80
poststructuralism xvi, 117; and outlawry 137–8; see also postmodernism
power 48, 145; eroticisation of see desire, heterosexual; sex and 52; see also male power; male supremacy; oppression
Power, Bet 47
privacy 24–5, 60, 216
prostitution 48–9; decadence and 131–3; lesbian 31, 47–8; and safe sex education 163
psychology/psychoanalysis 3, 13, 200; postmodernism and 103
publications see magazines; publishers
publishers 31, 35, 129

Q

queer politics 1, 138–9, 176–82;
    postmodernism and 198–202

R

racism 105, 183, 211, 216, 230;
    pornography and 117, 119;
    sadomasochism and 216,
    220–4
Radicalesbians 32
rape: lesbian 91–2, 128; marital
    26, 91
Raymond, Janice 98, 185–6, 188,
    193, 197–8, 204–6; on
    androgyny 86, 100; on
    friendship 197–8; on
    heteroreality 86, 195; on
    transsexuals 157–8; with
    Dorchen Leidholdt xviii, 54
Rechy, John 131–2, 160
reclaiming 180
reformism 191
Reich, Wilhelm 219
repression/erotophobia 62, 70,
    176, 179–81; see also denial
reversal, patriarchal 215
reverse discourse 15, 17, 138
revolutions, sexual 20–2, 55, 58
Rich, Adrienne 78, 87, 114
Rich, Ruby 122
right-wing politics x, 189, 190,
    230, 231; poststructuralism
    and xvi
Riviere, Joan 105
Roberts, Charles 176
roleplaying 16, 74–94; in
    different cultures 80–1; and
    essentialism 78–9; gay male
    roles, lesbians and 159;
    postmodernism and 103–4;

role swapping 90; and
    sadomasochism 89–91; sex
    therapists and 63–4; sexology
    and 86; see also butch/femme
    identities
romantic friendship see under
    friendship
romanticising: of oppression xvi,
    16; of prostitution 131; see
    also outlawry
Rowse, A. L. 142–3
Rubin, Gayle 118, 133–4, 136,
    155–7
Ruehl, Sonja 18
Ruston 77, 91–2

S

Saalfield, Catharine 132
sadomasochism xvii; abuse and
    38, 50, 90–3; clubs 43, 173;
    consent and 38, 42–50, 230,
    232; and constructed
    sexuality 218; dildos and 31;
    fascism and 210–33;
    feminists and 183–5; gay male
    culture and 155–7; and gay
    space 149, 210, 232;
    heterosexual 27, 49, 52–3,
    154; justifications 222–4, 225;
    and life 200–1; morality and
    54, 228; and oppression
    228–31; and outlawry 121,
    122, 132–4; political criticism
    and 46; as politics 230–2;
    pornography and 30, 35–6,
    185; prosecutions for 53–4;
    racism and 216, 220–4;
    roleplaying and 89–94; safe
    sex education and 172–3,
    175; self-hatred and 219–20;
    self-injury and 46; sex therapy

and 61–3, 66; support for 28; violence and 40–2, 54, 93–4

safe sex education 179–85; child sexual abuse and 38; pornography and 136

Safe Womyn 165–6

Sahli, Nancy 18

Samois 39, 158–9, 223, 224–7, 231–2

San Francisco women's centre 220, 232

Sax, Marjan 47

Scarlet Woman 89–90

Schulman, Sarah 122, 127–8, 170–1, 188–9

self-hatred ix, xvii; oppression and 205–7; and sadomasochism 220–2; sex industry and 37

self-injury 38, 43, 225

self-love ix, xvii

semen 145–6

Semple, Linda 177

separation 144, 186–8, 191–3; necessity 194, 196, 203–4; political 144; and queer politics 180–2

separatism xvii, 182, 190–2; class and 193; continuum of 192; ethnicity and 193; feminism and 186, 191; lesbian xv; lesbianandgay theory and 98; opposition to 193–5; attacks as anti-lesbianism 193; from lesbians 191, 193; and outlawry 136, 139–40; queer politics and 180, 182; repudiating 180, 185, 191–3

sex 173–4, 223–4; consensual see consent; and definitions of lesbianism 5, 7, 9–10, 53; dualism over 24–5; egalitarian 223–4; see also desire, homosexual; emotion and 69; frequency 68, 71, 77, 146–7; gay male 146–8; gender and 90; as good 24–5; imitation heterosexual/male 37, 91–3, 168, 199; safe sex and 162–7; lesbian 20, 21, 172–3; feminism and 203–7; as harmless 191; as resistance 191–3; safety 160–2; and life 204–8; morality and 21–5; need for 68; and oppression 56, 72; political function 25–6; politics/political criticism and 23–8, 43, 47, 60–2, 216, 223–5; and power 54; prescriptions for 175; see also sex advice; sex therapy; pressure and 9–10; quantifying 68, 71, 77, 146–7, 204–5; safe see safe sex; surveys/statistics on 36, 41; see also sexual intercourse; sexuality

sex advice 25, 26, 31; safe sex education and 175–6; see also sex therapy

sex class xiii–xv, 16, 18; lesbianism/lesbians and xiii–xv, 11, 16, 47, 80

sex industry 20; abuse and 47, 55; decadence and 125, 131–4; lesbian 20–1, 27, 31–5, 45–7, 52; as assimilationist 191, 201; and eroticised subordination 57; objectification and 68; as users 42–7; and self-hatred 37; women used in 43, 52, 54; see also pornography; prostitution; sex therapy

sex panic *see* repression
sex therapy 25, 58–72;
    objectification and 68–71;
    problems brought to 61, 63;
    and sadomasochism 61–3,
    67; training in 58–9, 60; and
    view of gay men as superior
    to lesbians 178–80
sex toys 31–3; *see also* dildos
sexology 1, 2–7, 14–16; as
    barrier xv; feminism and ix, 1,
    13; gay men and 16–17; and
    heterosexual desire 61; and
    lesbianism *see under*
    lesbianism; and pressure
    25–7; queer politics and 139;
    resisting constituencies 67–9;
    sex therapy and 60, 62, 63,
    70; and sexual need 65; and
    social control 15
sexual abuse 36, 37–41, 149;
    prostitution and 44–5;
    responsibility for 54;
    sadomasochism and 54, 92;
    sex industry and 37, 41
sexual activity *see* sex
Sexual Attitude Reassessment 60
sexual difference 1, 2; *see also*
    determinism; essentialism;
    sexology; sexualities
sexual feelings 25, 29, 224
sexual harassment 35, 44
sexual intercourse: political
    function 27–9, 49–56;
    pressure and 9–10, 20
sexual practice *see* sex
sexual revolutions *see*
    revolutions, sexual
sexual violence *see* violence,
    sexual
sexualities 118, 180
sexuality 68; construction 24,

28–9, 35, 43, 114, 130, 218,
    220; egalitarian 232; fascism
    and 217–18, 226–7; need for
    healing 41; reconstructing
    192, 224, 233; *see also* desire;
    lesbianism/lesbians; male
    sexuality; sex; sexualities
Sheba Press 31
SHELIX 41
Sherman, Martin 212–13
slavery 222–3; lesbians and 139;
    prostitution and 44;
    roleplaying and 94; women
    and 192
S/M *see* sadomasochism
SM Dykes Support Group
    (London) 214, 223, 225, 229
Smith, Barbara 30
Smith-Rosenberg, Carroll xiii, 2,
    3, 6, 7–9
Smyth, Cherry 105–6, 162–3,
    175, 177–8
social construction 73; and
    roleplaying 84; *see also* under
    feminism
social control 24, 25; sexology
    and 15; sexual violence and
    24, 25
Sojourner 40, 51
soldiers 68
Sontag, Susan 154
Spada, James 179
Spanner, Operation 48–50
Stack, Carolyn 62, 65–6, 67–8
Stanley, Liz 147
Steinem, Gloria 29, 40
Stekel, Wilhelm 26–7
stereotypes 5–6, 9, 103
Stoltenberg, John 147
Strega, Linda 77, 91–2, 93
strippers 35

subject positions 114; *see also* identity/identities

subordination, eroticised *see* desire, heterosexual

suicide 38

surgery, transsexual 153, 154–5

surrender 26, 27

survivors *see* incest survivors

Sydney 45

T

talkliness 35, 42

Terrence Higgins Trust 165

therapy 25; *see also* sex therapy

Thompson, Denise 119, 147

Timerman, Jacobo 217–18

torture 38, 213–15, 231; response to 224, 225

transsexuals xviii, 150; female-to-male 154, 155–6, 199; male-to-female 154

tricking 67, 172–3

Tyler, Carol-Anne 105

U

UK: law on male homosexuality 24; Local Government Act 1988 (Section 28) x, 74, 144; prosecutions for sadomasochism in 48–50

uncertainty, radical 110–1, 113–15, 118

V

VAC *see* Victorian AIDS Council

vaginismus 69

Vance, Carol 118

vibrators 35

Victorian AIDS Council 162–5

videos 35; as evidence for prosecutions 52; in safe sex education 162–5

violence: privacy and 25; sadomasochism and 40–2, 54, 92–3; sexual 21, 22, 23; objectification and 35; roleplaying and 91–4

voyeurism 175

vulva, representation of 30

W

Wages for Housework/Wages Due Lesbians 225

Waite, Robert 216–17

Walker, Alice 224–5

war 66

Watney, Simon 170–1, 173, 174–5

Weedon, Chris 102

Weeks, Jeffrey 2–3, 24, 118, 138–9, 142, 227–8

Weinberg, M. 55

Whitbread, Helena 18

White, Edmund 222, 233

Wicked Women 39, 44, 53, 55

Wieringa, Saskia 84

Wilde, Oscar xv, 121–3, 126–7, 131, 136

Wistrich, Harriet 94

Wittig, Monique xiii, 24, 52–3, 78, 87, 140, 196

Wolf, Naomi ix, 77

woman-hating: drag and 152–3; lesbian pornography and 36–7; male-bonding and 168

261

woman-loving: friendship and 203–5; as resistance 182–4

Woman Against Violence Against Women 30

women *see* heterosexual women; lesbianism/lesbians; sex class

women-only space 144, 225; in mixed gay centres 149; sadomasochism and 231–2

Women's Aid *see* battered women's shelters

Women's Liberation Movement 219; *see also* feminism

women's studies 115, 199

Y

Young, Ian 47–8, 50, 234

Z

Zimmerman, Bonnie 187–9